LANGUAGE TEACHING AND LINGUISTICS:
SURVEYS

LANGUAGE TEACHING AND LINGUISTICS: SURVEYS

Centre for Information on Language Teaching and Research
and
English Teaching Information Centre of the British Council

Edited by Valerie Kinsella

CAMBRIDGE UNIVERSITY PRESS
CAMBRIDGE
LONDON · NEW YORK · MELBOURNE

Published by the Syndics of the Cambridge University Press
The Pitt Building, Trumpington Street, Cambridge CB2 1RP
Bentley House, 200 Euston Road, London NW1 2DB
32 East 57th Street, New York, NY 10022, USA
296 Beaconsfield Parade, Middle Park, Melbourne 3206, Australia

First published 1978
Reprinted 1979

Printed in Great Britain at the
University Press, Cambridge

Library of Congress cataloguing in publication data

Main entry under title:

Language teaching and linguistics.

English or French.

'Articles which originally appeared in the journal,
Language teaching and linguistics abstracts.'

CONTENTS: Burstall, C. Factors affecting foreign-language learning. – Coulthard,
M. Discourse analysis in English. – Le Page, R. B. Sociolinguistics and the problem of
'competence'. [etc.]
1. Languages, Modern – Study and teaching – Addresses, essays, lectures. 2. Linguistics
– Addresses, essays, lectures. I. Kinsella, Valerie. II. Centre for Information on Language
Teaching and Research.   III. English Teaching Information Centre, London.   IV.
Language teaching & linguistics.
PB35.L34   407   77-88871
ISBN 0 521 21926 4

CONTENTS

PREFACE

This collection includes eleven articles which originally appeared in the journal *Language Teaching and Linguistics: Abstracts*, published by Cambridge University Press. All were specially commissioned for that journal. Writers were asked to provide general surveys of recent research in fields in which they were known to be expert, supported by extensive bibliographical references.

It was intended that the surveys would provide not only a critical review of recent work of help to other specialists working in the same disciplines, but would also offer an authoritative guide to those who wished to begin serious studies on these subjects.

Collectively they are of considerable value in providing an overview of work in a number of subjects and disciplines (although by no means all) which now contribute to the field of applied linguistics and language teaching. It is hoped that language teachers will find them particularly useful in bringing themselves up to date with recent research.

The articles appear in their original form apart from minor corrections to the text and references, where necessary. Authors have been able to add short postscripts covering work since the date of original publication shown for each article.

It is hoped that further collections of such articles covering other subjects will be published in future.

FACTORS AFFECTING FOREIGN-LANGUAGE LEARNING: A CONSIDERATION OF SOME RECENT RESEARCH FINDINGS

Clare Burstall

National Foundation for Educational Research in England and Wales

There have been few carefully designed long-term studies of the factors affecting the acquisition of a foreign language during childhood and adolescence. Anecdote abounds, but reliable evidence is hard to find. Reviewing the previous five years' research into foreign-language learning in 1966, Carroll commented on the 'dearth of studies' in this area and concluded: '...we have as yet no respectable longitudinal studies of persons who have learned a foreign language in the primary school and continued its study through adolescent and adult years' (Carroll, 1966). Earlier, Stern (1963) had pointed to the lack of evidence regarding the social and emotional factors thought to be involved in foreign-language learning during the early school years. Up to that time, studies of foreign-language learning had tended to concentrate on the measurement of language proficiency, neglecting the possible influence of motivational factors (e.g. Agard & Dunkel, 1948; Vollmer & Griffiths, 1962; Dunkel & Pillet, 1962). Stern considered that there was a particularly urgent need for research into those factors which might lead to the childhood development of positive or negative attitudes towards foreign peoples and their culture, with potentially beneficial or detrimental effects on the acquisition of the language in question.

Unfortunately, much of the research undertaken in this area in recent years has been limited in scope or deficient in control procedures. A number of excellent small-scale studies have been carried out, but their findings are subject to inevitable constraints. For example, the most recent report on the St Lambert project (Lambert, Tucker & d'Anglejan, 1973), in which the attitudes and attainments of English-speaking Canadian children, taught mainly through the medium of French since kindergarten, are compared with those of monolingual French-speaking and English-speaking controls, reveals that the experimental sample has dwindled to 30 children in Grade 4 and 20 children in Grade 5. Similarly, the investigation of children's attitudes towards foreign peoples, carried out within the University of Illinois Foreign Language Instruction Project (Riestra & Johnson, 1964), is based on an experimental sample of 63 children. It goes without saying that findings based on such limited samples must

1

be interpreted with extreme caution. In this connection, it is interesting to note that Gardner and Lambert, in a recent review of their research programme (Gardner & Lambert, 1972), advocate a 'shift' to large-scale longitudinal studies, in which information about intellectual abilities, as well as attitudes, values and other motivational factors, would be gathered from children and parents before the beginning of a foreign-language programme, as well as during its course or upon its completion. Gardner and Lambert consider this change in approach to be necessary in order to 'disentangle attitudes and proficiency so that one can follow more clearly the causal sequence'.

The purpose of the present paper is to move towards a disentanglement of the kind envisaged by Gardner and Lambert. The available research evidence will be examined and findings which have a bearing, whether direct or indirect, on the factors affecting foreign-language learning will be discussed. The first part of the paper will be devoted to an examination of the influence of motivational factors on foreign-language learning and will consider 'integrative' versus 'instrumental' motivation, the effect of contact with the foreign culture, the influence of socio-economic factors, sex differences in foreign-language learning, achievement in the small school, teacher–pupil interaction and, finally, the effect on the pupil of different methods of presenting foreign-language material. The second part of the paper will consider the evidence for the existence of an 'optimum age' for foreign-language learning.

1. Motivation for foreign-language learning

(i) *'Integrative' versus 'instrumental' motivation*

It has been argued, notably by Gardner and Lambert and their associates, that the successful acquisition of a foreign language depends, in the main, on specific motivational factors. Gardner and Lambert have on a number of occasions advanced the view that the key to success in foreign-language learning lies in the adoption of an 'integrative' orientation towards the foreign culture, as characterised by the student's willingness to share certain of the attributes of members of the other 'linguistic community' and to regard himself as a potential member of that community. According to this view, foreign-language learning is less likely to meet with success if the student's underlying motivation is 'instrumental' rather than 'integrative' – if, that is, he places a utilitarian value on the achievement of proficiency in the foreign language, without seeking active contact with the speakers of that language nor further knowledge of their culture (Gardner & Lambert, 1959; Lambert, Gardner, Olton & Tunstall, 1961; Gardner, 1966).

This hypothesis was examined in the course of the NFER evaluation of the teaching of French in primary schools (1974), but the findings of the evaluation lent only partial support to the view put forward by Gardner and Lambert: although pupils' attitudes and achievement proved to be closely associated, the motivational characteristics of individual pupils appeared to be neither exclusively integrative nor wholly instrumental. On the one hand, the majority of pupils taking part in the experiment, whether they liked learning French or not, tended to share an integrative motivation, evincing a strong desire for contact with French people and agreeing that they were primarily learning French in order to be able to communicate with other speakers of the language. On the other hand, there was also ample evidence of instrumental motivation in the emphasis placed by the experimental pupils on the 'pay-off' value of learning French, in terms of enhanced employment opportunities (Burstall, 1970, 1974). It is interesting to note in this connection that Gardner and his associates have recently begun to depart somewhat from their original view that success in foreign-language learning is crucially dependent upon the adoption of an integrative orientation towards the foreign culture. It is now suggested that an integrative orientation may not inevitably lead to superior achievement in foreign-language learning, if the cultural context is one in which the acquisition of the foreign language has obvious practical value. Reporting their study of foreign-language learning in the Philippines, Gardner and Santos (1970) conclude: 'In this cultural context where the second language has unequivocal instrumental value, students who are instrumentally oriented and who receive support from their parents for this orientation are more successful in acquiring the second language than students not evidencing this supported type of orientation.' These findings are consistent with those reported during the course of the NFER evaluation, which indicated an association between parents' support for foreign-language learning and their evaluation of its relevance to their children's employment prospects.

It was notable, for example, throughout the period of the NFER study, that the attitudes of the girls towards foreign-language learning were consistently more favourable than those of the boys. For instance, significantly more girls than boys agreed that they would like to speak many languages, go to France and meet French people, and continue their study of French in future years. Significantly more girls than boys also thought that all children should start to learn French in the primary school and that French would be useful to them in their future life. In addition, the girls were more confident than the boys of their parents' support and encouragement. The boys' attitudes towards foreign-language learning tended to be comparatively unfavourable. Significantly more boys than girls felt that learning French was a waste of time and that there were more important subjects on which they should be concentrating their effort. Unlike the girls, the boys did not believe that a knowledge of French would be useful to them after they had left school. Evidence from other studies suggests that the more positive attitudes expressed by the girls represent, in the main, a response to social and cultural pressures. Robinson (1971) has suggested that

3

being 'good at language' may be seen as admirable for girls, but unmanly for boys. The view that foreign-language learning is a more suitable accomplishment for girls than for boys is undoubtedly still current in our society, reinforced by the fact that a knowledge of foreign languages has a direct and obvious application to the future employment possibilities open to girls, but is less clearly relevant to those available to boys. Adolescent pupils of both sexes have been reported as viewing the enhancement of vocational success as the primary function of education and, in consequence, to place a high value on school subjects, such as Mathematics and English, which have an obvious relevance to their future employment prospects. Girls and their parents are also reported as accepting the vocational value of foreign-language learning, but boys and their parents are reported as not doing so (Schools Council, 1968; Summer & Warburton, 1972).

(ii) *Contact with the foreign culture*

It has been suggested that pupils will develop positive attitudes towards foreign peoples simply as a result of receiving foreign-language instruction. Riestra and Johnson, for example, investigated the attitudes of fifth-grade pupils towards Spanish-speaking peoples and found that the attitudes of the experimental pupils, who were studying Spanish, were significantly more positive than those of the control pupils, who had no knowledge of Spanish. The authors interpreted their findings as evidence that 'teaching a foreign language to elementary-school children...is a potent force in creating more positive attitudes towards the peoples represented by that language' (Riestra & Johnson, 1964). The findings of the NFER evaluation cited above would appear to indicate, however, that the mere process of foreign-language learning is not in itself sufficient to promote positive attitudes towards the foreign culture, although actual contact with the representatives of that culture may be an important factor both in the development of positive attitudes and in the achievement of linguistic competence. For example, it was found repeatedly that pupils who had been to France differed significantly in attitude and achievement from those who had not had this opportunity: those who had been to France expressed more positive attitudes towards France and the French, as well as towards learning French, than did those who had not been to France; the former also reached a significantly higher level of achievement in both spoken and written French (Burstall, 1974). Carroll, in his survey of the foreign-language attainments of American college and university students majoring in modern languages, also found that students who had been abroad were superior in foreign-language skills to those who had not been abroad: the longer the period abroad, the more marked the differences in level of achievement. Summing up his findings, Carroll wrote: '...it is tempting to conclude that going abroad is an important causative variable influencing language competence, and such a conclusion accords with common experience...Nevertheless, until more information is available from studies based on pre-test and post-test comparisons of groups who are and who are not sent abroad, it is impossible to state with certainty – at least on the basis of the present data – just what the effect of travel and study abroad may be' (Carroll, 1967).

The longitudinal nature of the NFER study permitted such comparisons to be carried out: the early attitudes and achievement of pupils who later went to France were compared with those of pupils who did not subsequently visit France. The outcomes indicated that those who later visited France had already reached a level of achievement superior to that of the rest of the experimental sample before their visit to France; they were also more favourably inclined towards learning French. As might have been anticipated, the pupils who were later to visit France also proved to be disproportionately representative of the higher socio-economic strata. It seems probable, therefore, that the enhanced achievement and more positive attitudes of those who went to France derived at least in part from their more favoured socio-economic status. It is, however, interesting to note that one of the areas in which the two groups of pupils differed most significantly was in their attitudes towards spoken French. Significantly more of those who had been to France than of those who had not done so expressed a preference for the spoken aspects of learning French and indicated that they would like to be able to speak several languages. Those who had not been to France tended to express a great deal of anxiety about speaking in French, complained that they were unable to understand spoken French and indicated that they would prefer to limit their studies to the acquisition of a reading knowledge of the language. Taylor and her associates (Taylor, Catford, Guiora & Lane, 1971) investigated the factors involved in acquiring spoken fluency in a foreign language (in this instance, Japanese) and concluded that 'empathic capacity' accounted for more than half the variance in performance. Empathic capacity was held to include the ability to understand other people's feelings, to appreciate the details of their behaviour and to respond appropriately. It is possible that this is a capacity which develops more rapidly when pupils are brought into direct contact with a foreign culture than when they are attempting to learn a foreign language in a monocultural setting.

(iii) *Socio-economic factors*

Evidence has recently been put forward which suggests that there are social class differences in the rate at which children acquire mastery of the syntactic rule system of their mother tongue (Dewart, 1972) and that there are corresponding differences in language production, working-class 'message systems' being more stereotyped and therefore more readily predictable than middle-class ones

5

(Poole, 1972). The possible effect of social class differences on the development of foreign-language skills has hitherto received scant attention. However, during the NFER evaluation, it rapidly became apparent that the pattern of results emerging from the enquiry pointed to a linear relation between the pupil's social class, his attitude towards learning French and his level of achievement in French. On each occasion of testing, the pupils in the experimental sample differed significantly in attitude and achievement according to their socio-economic status: positive attitudes towards learning French and high scores on the French achievement tests were consistently associated with high socio-economic status, negative attitudes and low scores with low socio-economic status (Burstall, 1968, 1970, 1974). This trend was evident during the primary stage of the experiment, but became even more prominent when the pupils in the experimental sample transferred to the different types of secondary school: higher levels of achievement and more positive attitudes towards foreign-language learning and foreign culture were found to be most characteristic of the grammar school and the comprehensive school pupils, while lower levels of achievement and more ethnocentric attitudes were found to be most characteristic of the bilateral school and the secondary modern school pupils, a finding which adds support to the existing evidence that children with parents in higher-status occupations tend to receive more parental support when they approach new learning experiences than do those with parents in lower-status occupations (Douglas, 1964; Central Advisory Council for Education, 1967; Robinson, 1971).

A similar association between socio-economic status and achievement in school subjects has been reported by a number of research workers (Douglas, 1964; Morris, 1966; Goodacre, 1968; Barker-Lunn, 1970), but it was thought possible that the influence of socio-economic factors might be less potent in the context of the French experiment, since all pupils were to begin their study of the language from a standpoint of equal ignorance. In the event, however, this was to underestimate the powerful influence of motivational factors on achievement: children with a previous history of failure in school tend to develop low aspirations and a negative view of their learning potential, reinforced by the perception that others have equally low expectations of their success. Such children in no way approach a new learning situation on a footing of equality with children whose previous record of achievement has led to high aspirations and a confident expectation of further success.

(iv) *Sex differences*

Studies which have investigated children's verbal skills in the mother tongue have commonly found significant differences in achievement in favour of girls, prominent during the early years of schooling but tending to diminish with the approach of puberty (Douglas, 1964; Wisenthal, 1965; Morris, 1966; Barker-Lunn, 1970). In the field of foreign-language learning, however, there are few studies which have supplied data on sex differences in achievement: this has often been because the samples used have been too small to split by sex. Carroll (1963 *b*) did report that girls showed a slight but significant superiority to boys in foreign-language aptitude, but had no comparable data on sex differences in achievement. Johnson and his associates, in their study of the teaching of Spanish at the elementary level, reported that the girls in their sample reached a higher level of achievement in Spanish than did the boys (Johnson, Flores, Ellison & Riestra, 1963). Nisbet and Welsh (1973) investigated achievement in French during the first two years of secondary school and found also that the level of achievement of the girls was consistently higher than that of the boys. Brega and Newell (1967), however, found no sex differences in achievement in French when they studied a group of late-adolescent students. Similarly, Carroll (1967) found no sex differences in the foreign-language attainments of male and female college and university students.

The findings of the NFER evaluation are in harmony with those of Johnson and his associates and of Nisbet and Welsh, but at variance with those of Brega and Newell and of Carroll. Sex differences in achievement favouring the girls were evident on the first occasion of testing and persisted throughout the period of the experiment, showing no sign of diminution when the pupils entered the adolescent period. At the age of 13, the girls in the experimental sample were still scoring significantly higher than the boys on all tests measuring achievement in French, just as they had done during the primary stage of the experiment. From the age of 13 onwards, the low-achieving boys in the sample tended to 'drop' French to a significantly greater extent than the low-achieving girls did, with the result that the sample of girls still learning French at the age of 16 represented a considerably wider range of ability than the corresponding sample of boys. However, in spite of this disparity, the girls still continued at the age of 16 to score significantly higher than the boys on each of the French tests. If the composition of the original experimental sample had been maintained until the end of the secondary stage of the experiment, there can be little doubt that sex differences in achievement in French favouring the girls would have been even more prominent.

It is, of course, important to bear in mind that the studies carried out by Brega and Newell and by Carroll drew on samples which were highly selective from the socio-economic point of view. It may be, as Bernstein (1971) has suggested, that sex differences in language performance are particularly characteristic of boys and girls from the lower socio-economic strata. Some support for this view may be derived from the finding that, during the early part of the secondary stage of the NFER evaluation, when the experimental sample was still relatively intact, the most marked sex differences in achievement in French occurred in the

7

secondary modern schools, whose intake was predominantly drawn from the lower socio-economic strata.

It is possible, of course, that if Britain's involvement in the European Economic Community eventually led to increased oportunities for boys to find employment which would demand a knowledge of foreign languages and so enhance the 'pay-off' value of foreign-language learning, there might be a marked diminution of sex differences in achievement. Some support for this view may be found in Morris's (1966) evidence that differences in boys' and girls' reading skills are attributable to motivational and environmental factors rather than to differences in ability, and in Preston's (1962) finding, arising from a comparative study of reading comprehension in the United States and in Germany, that although girls reach a higher level of achievement than boys in the United States, the reverse is true in Germany. Preston ascribes these results to the fact that 'reading and learning' are regarded as approved masculine activities in Germany, where the teaching force, even at the elementary level, is predominantly male, whereas in the United States reading skills are often 'associated with femininity'.

(v) *Achievement in the small school*

The schools involved in the NFER evaluation had a wide geographical distribution and varied greatly in size. The experimental sample included a number of small rural schools, the smallest of which had 16 pupils on roll, the largest 160 pupils. Throughout the primary stage of the experiment, the pupils in these small rural schools maintained a higher level of achievement in French than did those in the larger urban schools. This finding was an unexpected one. The classes in the small schools usually contained pupils differing widely in age and ability, and classroom conditions were often inimical to the teaching of French by audio-visual means. In spite of these apparently adverse circumstances, however, the test performance of the pupils in the small schools was consistently superior to that of the pupils in the large schools. At first, it was thought that this superiority might be partly attributable to the small size of the classes in which the pupils attending the small schools were taught French, but this did not prove to be the case: further analysis of the data revealed no association between size of class and level of achievement in French. The possibility remains that the high level of achievement in the small schools stems partly from the heterogeneous nature of their classes. If a given class contains pupils who vary greatly in age and ability, the individual pupil is not in direct competition with others of his own age-group: the concept of a 'standard' of achievement, which a pupil of a given age 'ought' to be able to reach, is difficult for either teacher or pupil to acquire. The classroom situation in the small school tends to encourage co-operative behaviour and to lack the negative motivational characteristics of the competitive classroom in which success for a few can only be achieved at the expense of failure for many.

In addition, findings reported earlier (Burstall, 1968) had indicated that teachers, as well as their classes, tended to have different characteristics in large and small primary schools. Teachers in small schools were, on average, older than those in large schools and therefore tended to have had greater teaching experience. Teachers in small schools also tended to have acquired all their teaching experience in the primary school, often in one school only, whereas teachers in large schools tended to have had a more varied teaching experience and to be considerably more mobile. Teachers in small schools tended to live in the village which the school served and to occupy a high-status role in the life of the community; teachers in large schools tended to live some distance from their place of employment and often had few points of contact with the community in which the school was situated. It was also observed that the head of a small school tended to carry a large part of the teaching load and to spend much of his day in direct contact with his pupils, whereas it was rare for the head of a large school to develop close relationships with his pupils. Recent research by Sumner and Warburton (1972) suggests that pupils in small schools regard the head as more important in their lives than do pupils in large schools and are also more responsive to evidence of 'teaching effort'. Such factors may well have contributed to the differences in level of achievement observed in the schools taking part in the experiment. That these differences are of a persistent nature has been demonstrated by a recent follow-up study (Burstall, 1974). It was found that, even after two years in a secondary school, pupils who had formerly attended small primary schools continued to achieve significantly higher scores on French tests than did their classmates who had formerly attended large primary schools.

There is some evidence (Barker-Lunn, 1970, 1971) that a pupil's attitude towards his own learning potential and towards life in school is positively associated with the way in which he perceives his relationships with his teachers. There is also evidence (Dale, 1969, 1971; Sumner & Warburton, 1972) that pupils in small schools tend to form closer relationships with their teachers than do pupils in large schools. The higher level of achievement in French of pupils in small schools may thus be at least partly attributable to the early establishment of good teacher–pupil relationships and the subsequent development of positive attitudes towards further learning.

(vi) *Teacher–pupil interaction*

The possibility that a pupil's level of achievement might to some extent be determined by the attitudes and expectations of his teacher has long been a matter of debate, but until recently there has been little direct experimental evidence on which to base judgement. In 1968, however, the issue was brought into sharp focus by the publication of a controversial study (Rosenthal & Jacobson, 1968) which purported to demonstrate the direct effect of teacher expectation on pupil performance. In this study, teachers in an elementary school were presented with test results that allegedly predicted which of the children in their classes were 'most likely to show an academic spurt'. The children concerned, who had actually been selected at random, were subsequently re-tested on three occasions: the authors claimed that the re-test results supported the proposition that the teachers' expectations had influenced the children's intellectual development. Unfortunately, this study is so open to criticism on methodological grounds (see, for instance, Thorndike, 1968; Jensen, 1969; Snow, 1969) that its findings can be given little weight. Nevertheless, the publication of the study has not been without value, since it has undoubtedly stimulated further research into the possible effects of teacher expectation on pupil performance. There have been two recent review studies in this field (Pidgeon, 1970; Rosenshine, 1971) and a number of experimental investigations. Attempts to replicate the original study, however, have met with little success. Claiborn (1969) followed the same procedures as Rosenthal and Jacobson, but over a somewhat shorter period, and found no evidence at all to support the earlier findings: the 'potential academic bloomers' stubbornly failed to bloom. José and Cody (1971) attempted a partial replication of the original study, with the addition of a teacher–pupil interaction analysis, but were unable to identify any effect of teacher expectation on pupil performance nor observe any differences in teachers' overt behaviour towards the pupils designated as 'potential bloomers'. A further investigation of the 'self-fulfilling prophecy' described by Rosenthal and Jacobson was carried out on a considerably larger scale by Fleming and Anttonen (1971), but with equally negative results. It was concluded that the teachers taking part in these last two studies had treated the experimenters' predictions with some scepticism and therefore had not actually modified their expectations for any given pupil.

Studies investigating teachers' attitudes and expectations which have been built up naturally over time rather than created in response to artificial circumstances have tended to produce more positive results. Palardy (1969), for example, found that the mean reading-test scores for boys in first-grade classes where the teachers expected boys to be less successful than girls in learning to read were significantly lower than those for comparable boys in classes where the teachers did not share this expectation. A large-scale study of the education of disadvantaged children (US Office of Education, 1970) also reported 'an extraordinarily consistent relationship between teacher expectations and the reading achievement gains of pupils'. The authors of this study reported that teachers' expectations and pupils' reading test scores were so closely related that 'teacher predictions of pupils' academic future could be used instead of test information in some analyses'. Dusek and O'Connell (1973) found that teachers' estimates of their pupils' learning potential, formed at the beginning of the school year, were closely related to the pupils' scores on language and arithmetic tests, given at the end of the school year. The teachers taking part in this study reported that they had based their estimates on the pupils' performance in previous classes and on their behaviour in class during the first few weeks of the year. Dusek and O'Connell had also attempted to bias the teachers' estimates by informing them that certain of their pupils, actually chosen at random, would show unusual gains in linguistic and arithmetical skills during the course of the school year: this attempt was without apparent effect.

To the findings reported above may be added those of the NFER evaluation of the teaching of French in primary schools. It was found that pupils' mean scores on each of the French tests used during the primary stage of the experiment differed significantly according to the attitude taken by the head of the school towards the experimental teaching of French to children of all levels of ability: pupils' mean scores were significantly higher in schools where the head had a favourable attitude towards the experiment than they were in those where the head's attitude was unfavourable (Burstall, 1970, 1974). These results are consistent with those reported by Anastasiow and Espinosa (1966) in their evaluation of the teaching of Spanish in Californian elementary schools. They found that pupils' scores on tests of Spanish were significantly higher in schools where the principal's attitude towards the language-teaching programme was 'supportive' than in schools where it was 'negative'. Further, during both the primary and the secondary stages of the French experiment, the pupils' level of achievement in French was consistently rated more highly in those classes where the French teacher's attitude towards the class was considered 'positive' than in those classes where it was considered 'non-committal' or 'negative'. Somewhat similarly, a recent study of classroom behaviour carried out by Aspy and Roebuck (1972) has produced evidence of an association between the extent of a teacher's 'positive regard for students' and the level of 'cognitive functioning' which the teacher was able to elicit. Hughes (1973) also found children's achievement test scores to be positively related to the teacher's 'positive' or 'minimal' reactions to the children's responses in class. Evidence from studies such as these, carried out within the normal classroom, lends considerable support to the view that a close association exists between the teacher's attitudes and expectations and the pupils' attitudes and achievement.

Some indication of the subtle processes by which such an association is brought about may be gleaned from recent studies of classroom interaction. Brophy and Good (1970), for instance, in a study of teacher–pupil interaction in four first-grade classes, found that teachers demanded better performance from those children for whom they had higher expectations and were also more likely to praise such performance when it occurred. In contrast, they were more likely to accept poor performance from pupils for whom they had low expectations and were less likely to praise the latter's good performance when it occurred, even though it occurred less frequently. Similarly, Rist (1970), carrying out a longitudinal study of a class of black children in an urban ghetto school, reported that children judged by the teacher (apparently on the basis of social class criteria) to be potential fast learners received the majority of the available teaching time and the bulk of the teacher's supportive behaviour. Those judged to be potential slow learners, on the other hand, were taught infrequently and were subjected to considerable disapproval and rejection by the teacher. The gap between the two groups with regard to the completion of their course material inevitably widened as the school year advanced. The pupils' divergent performance on achievement tests given at the end of the year was then used as supporting evidence for the teacher's initial judgement: a chilling example of the self-fulfilling prophecy.

Even in the most favourable circumstances, however, it must not be assumed that pupils' attitudes will remain constant over time: maturational factors may well exert a considerable influence on the development of pupils' attitudes towards foreign-language learning. The findings of a recent cross-national study of children's attitudes towards foreign peoples suggest, for instance, that favourable attitudes may reach their peak at about the age of ten and thereafter decline during the early years of adolescence, concomitant with an accelerated development of the stereotyping process and an increase in loyalty towards the peer-group (Lambert & Klineberg, 1967). Other studies (Morse & Allport, 1952; Jahoda, 1953; Allport, 1954) have indicated that close identification with the values of the peer-group, at its height during the adolescent period, may be a crucial factor in the formation of prejudice and the consequent rejection of the values characteristic of foreign cultures.

Evidence from studies of school achievement also contributes to the view that the early adolescent period may be particularly critical for the development of negative attitudes towards the self as well as towards others. A number of studies (Douglas, Ross & Simpson, 1968; Schools Council, 1968; Sumner & Warburton, 1972), have noted the increasing negativity of the attitudes of unsuccessful secondary-school pupils, but Ferri's recent follow-up study of pupils involved in Barker-Lunn's (1970) investigation into the effects of streaming indicates that even high-achieving pupils, and particularly girls, may show a deterioration in their attitudes to school work and a decrease in their levels of aspiration during the early years of secondary education (Ferri, 1971). It has elsewhere been suggested (Maccoby & Jacklin, 1973) that high-achieving girls develop a 'will to fail' at this time, in response to strong social pressures.

Further, a considerable body of experimental evidence now exists which lends support to the view that pupils' attitudes towards learning are positively and significantly related to their eventual level of achievement. Much of the research in this area (e.g. Kurtz & Swenson, 1951; Brookover, Thomas & Paterson, 1964; Robinson, 1964; Austrin, 1965; Wisenthal, 1965; Khan, 1969; Russell, 1969) has been concerned with relations between pupils' achievement motivation and their general academic success (as reflected, for example, in their grade-point average), but there are also a number of studies which have specifically investigated associations between pupils' attitudes and achievement in the field of foreign-language learning (e.g. Jordan, 1941; Pimsleur, Stockwell & Comrey, 1962; Lambert, Gardner, Barik & Tunstall, 1963; Carroll, 1967; Feenstra & Gardner, 1968; Gardner & Santos, 1970; Gardner & Lambert, 1972). All these studies, whether dealing with academic success in general or with a particular subject-area such as foreign-language learning, have produced findings which lend support to the view that a positive association exists between pupils' level of achievement and their attitudes towards learning. It has even been suggested that pupils' 'motivation for school work', if objectively measured, could be used to predict their future level of achievement (Russell, 1969). In the case of the NFER evaluation, it is certainly true that the findings repeatedly and consistently indicated a positive and significant association between attitudinal factors and achievement in the foreign-language learning situation. On each of the French tests, whether measuring spoken or written skills, mean scores for pupils with favourable attitudes towards learning French were significantly higher than those for pupils with unfavourable attitudes. These findings applied equally to pupils of either sex. However, although such findings indicate the existence of a positive association between pupils' attitudes and achievement in foreign-language learning and suggest a complex interaction process, they shed no light on the possible direction of causality. Gardner and Lambert (1972) argue that the major causative variable influencing foreign-language acquisition is the attitude of the learner towards the foreign culture, on the grounds that this attitude represents 'a more stable personal characteristic' than any previous experience of achievement. The findings of the NFER study, however, point in the opposite direction: early achievement in French affected later attitudes towards learning French and later achievement in French to a significantly greater extent than early attitudes towards learning French affected the subsequent development of either attitudes or achievement. This would suggest that the acquisition of foreign-language skills and the development of attitudes towards foreign-language learning during later years may be powerfully influenced by the learner's initial and formative experience of success or failure in the language-learning situation.

(vii) *The presentation of material*

In their study of under-achievement in foreign-language learning, Pimsleur and his co-workers found a positive association between success in foreign-language learning and preference for the auditory modality. This led them to suggest that the principal component of linguistic ability might be the 'ability to receive and process information through the ear' (Pimsleur, Sundland & McIntyre, 1963). Lambert (1963), however, pointed out that the audio-visual approach to foreign-language learning does not take into account individual differences in modality preference at different age-levels and might well, where older pupils are concerned, run counter to long-established patterns of achievement. Other studies of foreign-language learning have lent support to Lambert's view by highlighting the adverse effect that an uncongenial mode of presentation may have on pupils' attitudes towards learning the language in question. For instance, pupils may react negatively to the passive features of televised instruction (Moskowitz & Amidon, 1962; Moskowitz, 1964) or to the total reliance on the spoken word which the audio-visual approach initially entails (Mueller & Leutenegger, 1964). There is also evidence to suggest that the suitability of a given mode of presentation may vary with the nature of the material to be presented. In their early investigation of the use of radio as an educational medium, Cantril & Allport (1935) concluded that a face-to-face presentation of material was superior to a purely auditory presentation, if the material to be presented were of a complex verbal nature. These findings were subsequently confirmed by Krawiec (1946) and have received further support from more recent language-learning studies in which increased efficiency and enhanced motivation were reported to have followed the addition of visual components to an otherwise auditory presentation (Dodson & Price, 1966; Mueller & Harris, 1966).

Similarly, in the NFER study, it was observed that few of the pupils in the experimental sample were able to tolerate for long a purely auditory presentation of material: most pupils strongly disliked having to accept a passive listening role, a role which, as Gupta and Stern's (1969) findings indicate, is markedly less effective than active practice in the spoken language, if the objective to be achieved is that of oral fluency. The majority of the sample, but particularly the high-achieving pupils, expressed an increasing preference for a visually supported presentation of material as the experiment progressed. This point of view was particularly characteristic of the grammar-school pupils, who tended to reject the audio-visual approach to language learning, in favour of a more traditional textbook-based approach. Allied to this increasing preference for the written aspects of learning French was a growing anxiety regarding the necessity to speak in French, the most anxious group in this respect being the grammar-school girls. For these girls, fear of speaking French was almost invariably linked with fear of being exposed to the ridicule of other members of the class, particularly in a co-educational setting. The evidence would therefore seem to suggest that methods of presenting language-learning material should vary according to the stage of learning reached, the nature of the material, and the ability, maturity and modality preferences of the learner.

2. An 'optimum age' for foreign-language learning?

The belief that young children are better equipped than older children or adults to learn foreign languages with speed and efficiency underlies the recent expansion of foreign-language teaching at kindergarten and elementary-school level. Much of the impetus for the early introduction of foreign-language study can be attributed to the influence of Wilder Penfield's work. Penfield has frequently reiterated the view that the young child's brain is uniquely well adapted for language learning and that there is an 'optimum age' during which 'multiple languages may be learned perfectly, with little effort and without physiological confusion' (Penfield, 1953). Penfield situates this optimum age for language learning within the first decade of life, after which period 'a built-in biological clock' inexorably records the lost educational opportunity (Penfield, 1964). Further attempts to acquire foreign languages will be crowned with only modest success. The age of the learner is thus the most critical factor in the language-learning process: if it is to be successful, foreign-language learning must take place between the ages of four and ten, 'in accordance with the demands of brain physiology' (Penfield & Roberts, 1959).

Although Penfield's views have been extremely influential in stimulating the move towards the earlier learning of foreign languages, they are based on logical inference rather than on direct observation and lack the support of experimental evidence. Other studies which claim to have produced evidence in favour of an early introduction to foreign-language learning tend either to be anecdotal in nature (Dryer, 1956; Price, 1956; Kirch, 1956; Andersson, 1960) or severely limited in scope and deficient in control procedures (Larew, 1961; Brega & Newell, 1965, 1967; Durette, 1972). It is certainly worthy of note that, almost without exception, the research studies which have striven for a high degree of precision and control have failed to produce evidence favouring the younger learner. For example, Thorndike and his associates carried out a series of experiments on the learning of Esperanto, using subjects who ranged in age from 9 to 57, and found that the younger subjects learned more slowly than the older (Thorndike, Bregman, Tilton & Woodyard, 1928). Justman and Nass (1956) studied the foreign-language attainments of 100 matched pairs of high-school students and concluded that those who had studied a foreign language in the elementary school had no long-term advantage over those who had begun their studies later. Grinder and his associates (1961) investigated the relation be-

15

tween age and level of proficiency in Japanese as a second language, using the same audio-lingual course for one year in second-grade, third-grade and fourth-grade classes, and found age and proficiency in Japanese to be positively related: on tests measuring both expressive and receptive skills, the perform-ance of the older children was consistently superior to that of the younger (Grinder, Otomo & Toyota, 1961). In the same vein, Stern (1963) described an experiment in which English was taught to 40 classes of Swedish elementary-school pupils, aged from 7 to 11, and reported that, although subjective estimates of the younger children's progress were favourable, 'a more careful evaluation…by means of scientific procedures at the end of the experimental period led to the somewhat unexpected conclusion that pronunciation as well as understanding improved more rapidly the older the pupils were. Pupils of 11 years of age learnt more accurately and more quickly than the 7-year-olds' (Stern, 1963). Findings of a similar nature were reported by Asher and Price (1967), who compared the listening comprehension in Russian of adults and of children whose ages ranged from 8 to 14. After all subjects had received identical training in Russian, test results indicated that the adults 'dramatically excelled the children of any age-group tested', while the performance of the older children was significantly superior to that of the younger ones. The authors came to the conclusion that 'when adults learn a second language under the same conditions as children, the adults are superior' (Asher & Price, 1967). Even in the achievement of a native-like pronunciation, where the age of the learner has been held to play a particularly crucial role, the more recent evidence favours the older learner. In 1972, Olson and Samuels reported that, given equal exposure to instruction in German, older pupils achieved a significantly more accurate standard of pronunciation in the language than did younger pupils. Summaris-ing their results, the authors commented: 'The general assumption is that younger children learn to pronounce foreign words with a more native-like accent than older people. Not only is this assumption not supported by the test results but the trend is in a reverse direction favoring older students' (Olson & Samuels, 1972).

Carroll (1963 a) has suggested that one of the most important variables in the learning process is the total amount of time spent actively in the learning situation. If to this suggestion is added the assumption that the older learner has developed more efficient learning strategies than the younger, there is no need to seek further for a consistent interpretation of the bulk of the available evidence. To this evidence may be added without dissonance the findings of the NFER evaluation. For example, when the experimental pupils were compared at the age of 13 with a group of control pupils in comprehensive schools who were the same age but who had been learning French for a shorter period, the performance of the experimental pupils on all tests of achievement in French was consistently superior to that of the control pupils. However, when the experimental pupils were compared at the age of 13 with control pupils who had been learning French for an equivalent period of time, but who were, on average, two years older, the control pupils' performance on each of the French tests was consistently superior to that of the experimental pupils. There were also some indications that, with the passage of time, the influence of the age of the learner began to outweigh that of the length of the learning period. For instance, when the experimental pupils were compared at the age of 16 with pupils in schools untouched by the experiment who were the same age but who had been learning French for a shorter period, the experimental pupils scored significantly higher than the control pupils on French Listening and Reading tests, but there were no significant differences between the two groups on French Speaking or Writing tests. A similar 'diminishing returns' effect was observed when the experimental pupils' level of achievement in French was compared with that of control groups of 11-year-old beginners who were in the same secondary schools and, most frequently, in the same French classes as the experimental pupils. When the experimental and the control pupils were compared at the age of 13, the experimental pupils scored significantly higher than the control pupils on French Speaking and Listening tests, but the control pupils' performance on French Reading and Writing tests equalled or surpassed that of the experimental pupils. When the experimental and the control pupils were compared at the age of 16, the only test on which the experimental pupils still scored significantly higher than the control pupils was the Listening test. The two groups of pupils did not differ in their performance on the Speaking test, but the control pupils maintained their superiority on the Reading and Writing tests.

Thus, the most conservative interpretation which the available evidence would appear to permit is that the achievement of skill in a foreign language is primarily a function of the amount of time spent studying that language, but is also affected by the age of the learner, older learners tending to be more efficient than younger ones. Penfield's contention that the first ten years of life constitute a 'critical period' for foreign-language acquisition remains unsupported by direct experimental evidence. *January 1975*

References

Agard, F. B. & Dunkel, H. B. (1948). *An investigation of second-language teaching*. Boston: Ginn & Co.

Allport, G. W. (1954). *The nature of prejudice*. Reading, Massachusetts: Addison-Wesley Publishing Co.

Anastasiow, N. J. & Espinosa, I. B. (1966). Development of a Spanish listening comprehension test and evaluation of the elementary Spanish television instruction. *California Journal of Educational Research*, **17**, 1, 12–21.

Andersson, T. (1960). The optimum age for beginning the study of modern languages. *International Review of Education*, **6**, 298–306.

Asher, J. J. & Price, B. S. (1967). The learning strategy of the total physical response: some age differences. *Child Development*, **38**, 4, 1219–27.

Aspy, D. N. & Roebuck, F. N. (1972). An investigation of the relationship between student levels of cognitive functioning and the teacher's classroom behaviour. *Journal of Educational Research*, **65**, 8, 365–8.

Austrin, H. R. (1965). Cross validation of an attitude scale for the identification of high and low academic achievers. *Journal of Educational Research*, **58**, 9, 426–8.

Barker-Lunn, J. C. (1970). *Streaming in the primary school.* Slough: NFER.

Barker-Lunn, J. C. (1971). *Social class, attitudes and achievement.* Slough: NFER.

Bernstein, B. (1971). Language and roles. In R. Huxley and E. Ingram (eds.), *Language acquisition: models and methods.* London and New York: Academic Press.

Brega, E. & Newell, J. M. (1965). Comparison of performance by FLES program students and regular French III students on Modern Language Association tests. *French Review*, **39**, 433–8.

Brega, E. & Newell, J. M. (1967). High-school performance of FLES and non-FLES students. *Modern Language Journal*, **51**, 408–11.

Brookover, W. B., Thomas, S. & Paterson, A. (1964). Self-concept of ability and school achievement. *Sociology of Education*, **37**, 271–8.

Brophy, J. E. & Good, T. L. (1970). Teachers' communication of differential expectations for children's classroom performance. *Journal of Educational Psychology*, **61**, 365–74.

Burstall, C. (1968). *French from eight: a national experiment.* Slough: NFER.

Burstall, C. (1970). *French in the primary school: attitudes and achievement.* Slough: NFER.

Burstall, C., Jamieson, M., Cohen, S. & Hargreaves, M. (1974). *Primary French in the balance.* Slough: NFER.

Cantril, H. & Allport, G. W. (1935). *The psychology of radio.* New York and London: Harper.

Carroll, J. B. (1963 a). A model of school learning. *Teachers College Record*, **64**, 723–33.

Carroll, J. B. (1963 b). Research on teaching foreign languages. In N. L. Gage (ed.), *Handbook of research on teaching.* Chicago: Rand McNally & Co.

Carroll, J. B. (1966). Research in foreign language teaching: the last five years. In R. G. Mead (ed.), *Language teaching: broader contexts.* Report of the Northeast Conference on the Teaching of Foreign Languages.

Carroll, J. B. (1967). *The foreign language attainments of language majors in the senior year: a survey conducted in U.S. colleges and universities.* Cambridge, Mass: Laboratory for Research in Instruction, Graduate School of Education, Harvard University.

Central Advisory Council for Education (1967). *Children and their primary schools.* London: HMSO.

Claiborn, W. L. (1969). Expectancy effects in the classroom: a failure to replicate. *Journal of Educational Psychology*, **60**, 5, 377–83.

Dale, R. R. (1969). *Mixed or single-sex school?* Vol. 1: *A research study in pupil–teacher relationships.* London: Routledge & Kegan Paul.

Dale, R. R. (1971). *Mixed or single-sex school?* Vol. 2: *Some social aspects.* London: Routledge & Kegan Paul.

Dewart, M. H. (1972). Social class and children's understanding of deep structure in sentences. *British Journal of Educational Psychology*, **42**, 2, 198–203.

Dodson, C. J. & Price, J. E. (1966). The role of the printed word in foreign-language learning. *Modern Languages*, **47**, 59–63.

Douglas, J. W. B. (1964). *The home and the school: a study of ability and attainment in the primary school.* London: MacGibbon & Kee.

Douglas, J. W. B., Ross, J. M. & Simpson, H. R. (1968). *All our future.* London: Peter Davies.

Dryer, M. (1956). Grade school French students reach high school. *French Review,* **29,** 157–61.

Dunkel, H. B. & Pillet, R. A. (1962). *French in the elementary school: five years' experience.* Chicago and London: University of Chicago Press.

Durette, R. (1972). A five-year FLES report. *Modern Language Journal,* **56,** 23–4.

Dusek, J. B. & O'Connell, E. J. (1973). Teacher expectancy effects on the achievement test performance of elementary school children. *Journal of Educational Psychology,* **65,** 3, 371–7.

Feenstra, H. J. & Gardner, R. C. (1968). Aptitude, attitude, and motivation in second-language acquisition. *Research Bulletin No. 101,* University of Western Ontario.

Ferri, E. (1971). *Streaming: two years later.* Slough: NFER.

Fleming, E. S. & Anttonen, R. G. (1971). Teacher expectancy or My Fair Lady. *American Educational Research Journal,* **8,** 2, 241–52.

Gardner, R. C. (1966). Motivational variables in second-language learning. *International Journal of American Linguistics,* **32,** 24–44.

Gardner, R. C. & Lambert, W. E. (1959). Motivational variables in second-language acquisition. *Canadian Journal of Psychology,* **13,** 266–72.

Gardner, R. C. & Lambert, W. E. (1972). *Attitudes and motivation in second-language learning.* Rowley, Massachusetts: Newbury House Publishers, Inc.

Gardner, R. C. & Santos, E. H. (1970). Motivational variables in second-language acquisition: a Philippine investigation. *Research Bulletin No. 149,* University of Western Ontario.

Goodacre, E. J. (1968). *Teachers and their pupils' home background.* Slough: NFER.

Grinder, R. E., Otomo, A. & Toyota, W. (1961). *Comparisons between 2nd, 3rd and 4th grade children in the audio-lingual learning of Japanese as a second language.* Honolulu: Psychological Research Center, University of Hawaii.

Gupta, W. & Stern, C. (1969). Comparative effectiveness of speaking vs. listening in improving spoken language of disadvantaged young children. *Journal of Experimental Education,* **38,** 54–7.

Hughes, D. C. (1973). An experimental investigation of the effects of pupil responding and teacher reacting on pupil achievement. *American Educational Research Journal,* **10,** 1, 21–37.

Jahoda, G. (1953). Social class attitudes and levels of occupational aspiration in secondary modern school leavers. *British Journal of Psychology,* **44,** 95–107.

Jensen, A. R. (1969). Review of *Pygmalion in the classroom. American Scientist,* **51,** 44a–45a.

Johnson, C. E., Flores, J. S., Ellison, F. P. & Riestra, M. A. (1963). *The development and evaluation of methods and materials to facilitate foreign language instruction in elementary schools.* Urbana, Illinois: University of Illinois Foreign Language Instruction Project.

Jordan, D. (1941). The attitude of central school pupils to certain school subjects and the correlation between attitude and attainment. *British Journal of Educational Psychology,* **11,** 28–44.

José, J. & Cody, J. J. (1971). Teacher–pupil interaction as it relates to attempted changes in teacher expectancy of academic ability and achievement. *American Educational Research Journal,* **8,** 1, 39–49.

Justman, J. & Nass, M. L. (1956). The high school achievement of pupils who were and were not introduced to a foreign language in elementary school. *Modern Language Journal,* **40,** 120–3.

19

Khan, S. B. (1969). Affective correlates of academic achievement. *Journal of Educational Psychology,* **60,** 3, 216–21.

Kirch, M. S. (1956). At what age elementary school language teaching? *Modern Language Journal,* **40,** 399–400.

Krawiec, T. S. (1946). A comparison of learning and retention of materials presented visually and auditorially. *Journal of General Psychology,* **34,** 179–95.

Kurtz, J. J. & Swenson, E. J. (1951). Student, parent, and teacher attitude toward student achievement in school. *School Review,* **59,** 273–9.

Lambert, W. E. (1963). Psychological approaches to the study of language. Part I: On learning, thinking and human abilities. *Modern Language Journal,* **47,** 51–62.

Lambert, W. E., Gardner, R. C., Barik, H. C. & Tunstall, K. (1963). Attitudinal and cognitive aspects of intensive study of a second language. *Journal of Abnormal and Social Psychology,* **66,** 4, 358–68.

Lambert, W. E., Gardner, R. C., Olton, R. & Tunstall, K. (1961). *A study of the roles of attitudes and motivation in second-language learning.* McGill University Mimeo.

Lambert, W. E. & Klineberg, O. (1967). *Children's views of foreign peoples: a cross-national study.* New York: Appleton-Century-Crofts.

Lambert, W. E., Tucker, G. R. & d'Anglejan, A. (1973). Cognitive and attitudinal consequences of bilingual schooling: the St Lambert project through grade five. *Journal of Educational Psychology,* **65,** 2, 141–59.

Larew, L. A. (1961). The optimum age of beginning a foreign language. *Modern Language Journal,* **45,** 203–6.

Maccoby, E. E. & Jacklin, C. N. (1973). Sex differences in intellectual functioning. In *Assessment in a pluralistic society: proceedings of the 1972 Invitational Conference on Testing Problems.* Princeton, New Jersey: Educational Testing Service.

Morris, J. M. (1966). *Standards and progress in reading.* Slough: NFER.

Morse, N. C. & Allport, F. H. (1952). The causation of anti-semitism: an investigation of seven hypotheses. *Journal of Psychology,* **34,** 197–233.

Moscowitz, G. (1964). TV versus classroom instruction in foreign language: a study of elementary school children's attitudes. *Journal of Experimental Education,* **33,** 175–81.

Moscowitz, G. & Amidon, E. J. (1962). TV FLES versus live FLES: a study of student reactions. *Modern Language Journal,* **46,** 213–19.

Mueller, T. & Harris, R. (1966). The effect of an audio-lingual program on drop-out rate. *Modern Language Journal,* **50,** 133–7.

Mueller, T. & Leutenegger, R. (1964). Some inferences about an intensified oral approach to the teaching of French based on a study of course drop-outs. *Modern Language Journal,* **48,** 91–4.

Nisbet, J. D. & Welsh, J. (1972). A local evaluation of primary school French. *Journal of Curriculum Studies,* **4,** 2, 169–75.

Olson, L. L. & Samuels, S. J. (1972). The relationship between age and accuracy of foreign language pronunciation. Paper presented at the Annual Meeting of the American Educational Research Association, Chicago, 1972.

Palardy, J. M. (1969). What teachers believe – what children achieve. *Elementary School Journal,* **69,** 370–4.

Penfield, W. (1953). A consideration of the neuro-physiological mechanisms of speech and some educational consequences. *Proceedings of the American Academy of Arts and Sciences,* **82,** 201–14.

Penfield, W. (1964). The uncommitted cortex: the child's changing brain. *Atlantic Monthly,* **214,** 1, 77–81.

Penfield, W. & Roberts, L. (1959). *Speech and brain-mechanisms.* Princeton, New Jersey: Princeton University Press.

Pidgeon, D. A. (1970). *Expectation and pupil performance*. Stockholm: Almqvist & Wiksell.

Pimsleur, P., Stockwell, R. P. & Comrey, A. L. (1962). Foreign language learning ability. *Journal of Educational Psychology*, **53**, 15–26.

Pimsleur, P., Sundland, D. M. & McIntyre, R. D. (1963). *Under-achievement in foreign language learning*. Colombus, Ohio: The Ohio State University Research Foundation.

Poole, M. E. (1972). Social class differences in language predictability. *British Journal of Educational Psychology*, **42**, 2, 127–36.

Preston, R.C. (1962). Reading achievement of German and American children. *School and Society*, **90**, 350–4.

Price, B. (1956). Memories of French in elementary school. *French Review*, **29**, 245–9.

Riestra, M. A. & Johnson, C. E. (1964). Changes in attitudes of elementary-school pupils toward foreign-speaking peoples resulting from the study of a foreign language. *Journal of Experimental Education*, **33**, 65–72.

Rist, R. C. (1970). Student social class and teacher expectations: the self-fulfilling prophecy in ghetto education. *Harvard Educational Review*, **40**, 411–51.

Robinson, W. P. (1964). The achievement motive, academic success and intelligence test scores. *British Journal of Social and Clinical Psychology*, **4**, 98–103.

Robinson, W. P. (1971). Social factors and language development in primary school children. In R. Huxley & E. Ingram (eds.), *Language acquisition: models and methods*. London and New York: Academic Press.

Rosenshine, B. (1971). *Teaching behaviours and student achievement*. Slough: NFER.

Rosenthal, R. & Jacobson, L. (1968). *Pygmalion in the classroom*. New York: Holt, Rinehart & Winston, Inc.

Russell, I. L. (1969). Motivation for school achievement: measurement and validation. *Journal of Educational Research*, **62**, 6, 263–6.

Schools Council (1968). *Young School Leavers*, Enquiry 1. London: HMSO.

Snow, R. E. (1969). Unfinished Pygmalion. *Contemporary Psychology*, **14**, 4, 197–9.

Stern, H. H. (1963). *Foreign languages in primary education: the teaching of foreign or second languages to younger children*. Hamburg: UNESCO Institute for Education.

Sumner, R. & Warburton, F. W. (1972). *Achievement in secondary school*. Slough: NFER.

Taylor, L., Catford, J., Guiora, A. & Lane, H. (1971). Psychological variables and ability to pronounce a second language. *Language and Speech*, **14**, 2, 146–57.

Thorndike, E. L., Bregman, E. O., Tilton, J. W. & Woodyard, E. (1928). *Adult Learning*. New York: The MacMillan Company.

Thorndike, R. L. (1968). Review of *Pygmalion in the Classroom*. *American Educational Research Journal*, **5**, 4, 708–11.

United States Office of Education (1970). *Education of the disadvantaged*. Washington, DC: US Government Printing Office.

Vollmer, J. H. & Griffiths, R. E. (1962). *Evaluation of the effect of foreign language study in the elementary school upon achievement in the high school*. Somerville, New Jersey: Somerville Public Schools.

Wisenthal, M. (1965). Sex differences in attitudes and attainment in junior schools. *British Journal of Educational Psychology*, **35**, 79–85.

21

DISCOURSE ANALYSIS IN ENGLISH – A SHORT REVIEW OF THE LITERATURE

Malcolm Coulthard

Department of English, University of Birmingham

Introduction

For the purposes of this article I take as the concern of discourse analysis the identification and description of supra-sentential linguistic structure in written and spoken texts. The analytic concern is supra-sentential in that it focuses on the way in which 'sentences' combine into larger units to form coherent texts, although this does not exclude some consideration of the structure of individual sentences in order to discover firstly how given grammatical structures come to have given meanings in given contexts, and secondly how larger textual or topical constraints affect deletion possibilities, the choice of individual lexical, exophoric or anaphoric items, and so on, within a given clause. The analytic concern is linguistic in that it concentrates on the '"textual surface", the actual sentential forms that constitute a text' (Hendricks, 1973), and attempts to 'deal critically with...larger patterns without abandoning consideration of their linguistic composition' (Sayce, 1957). Thus textual analyses which rely on abstractions from the text, rather than the text itself (Propp, 1968; Lévi–Strauss, *passim*) are seen as describing non-linguistic structure.

Forty years ago Firth observed that 'neither linguists nor psychologists have begun the study of conversation, yet it is here that we shall find the key to a better understanding of what language really is and how it works' (1935), yet very little of the work in discourse analysis has been done by linguists. First Bloomfield led linguistics away from any consideration of meaning to a concentration on form and substance – there was an isolated attempt within this tradition by Harris (1952) to develop a formal method for analysing texts, which depended 'only on the occurrence of morphemes as distinguishable elements...not...on the analyst's knowledge of the particular meaning of each morpheme', but this method was difficult to apply to any but the most highly patterned texts and had little of interest to say about them – then Chomsky's competence/performance distinction and the resulting appeal pre-eminently to intuition, made any study of texts irrelevant. More recently there has been a realisation that verbal and non-verbal context are not merely relevant but essential for even a grammatical analysis of the clause (Karttunen, 1969;

Gordon & Lakoff, 1971; Lakoff, 1972; Fillmore, 1972), but nevertheless most of the work reported below has been done by researchers in other disciplines than linguistics.

Discourse units

Discourse does not consist simply of a string of grammatically well-formed utterances or sentences. The following examples from Labov (1970) are grammatically unexceptional yet noticeably odd:

A: What is your name?
B: Well, let's say you might have thought you had something from before, but you haven't got it any more.
A: I'm going to call you Dean.

A: I feel hot today.
B: No.

In both examples B's contribution obviously breaks rules for the production of coherent discourse. One of the fundamental aims of discourse analysis is to discover these rules, but an even more fundamental question is the nature of the units whose structure and occurrence the sequencing rules will describe.

Labov (1972) emphasises that the first and most important step is to distinguish '*what is said* from *what is done*'; that is, discourse analysis must be concerned with the functional use of language. Thus, for all discourse analysts the unit of analysis is not the grammatically defined 'clause' or 'sentence', although the unit may very frequently consist of one clause or sentence. Hymes (1972) labels the unit 'speech act' and insists that it 'represents a level distinct from the sentence and not identifiable with any single portion of other levels of grammar, nor with segments of any particular size defined in terms of other levels of grammar'. Labov (1970, 1972), Sacks (*passim*), Schegloff (1968, 1972) and Jefferson (1972, 1973) regard the 'utterance' as the basic unit of analysis, but this is almost certainly the result of working with simple and at times constructed data. Sinclair, Forsyth, Coulthard and Ashby (1972) observe that they also began with utterance as the basic unit, but, in dealing with examples like the following, came to feel the need for a smaller unit, which they called a 'move'. Moves can be co-extensive with utterances, but some utterances, like A's second, contain two moves:

A: Can you tell me why do you eat all that food?
B: To keep you strong.
A: To keep you strong, yes, to keep you strong. Why do you want to be strong?

Any attempt to apply the analyses suggested by Labov, Sacks, Schegloff and

Jefferson to the above example quickly demonstrates that in fact their analytic unit is not the utterance but something equivalent to the move.

Discourse function

The relations between the basic units of discourse are generally agreed to depend on their respective functions but there is as yet no consensus on how many different functions there are. The first serious attempt to analyse how speakers do things by saying was Austin's *How to do things with words*. He began with the obvious examples such as *I bet you five shillings* or *I name this ship Elizabeth* in which the action can only be performed through the uttering of the words, but then noticed that many utterances were also performing a speech act even though the performative verb was not present: (*I promise*) *I'll come tomorrow*. This led him to a consideration of how many senses there may be in which to say something is also, or is in essence, to do something. He concluded that there are three types of speech act: 'locutionary', which is roughly equivalent to uttering a sentence with a certain sense and reference, to 'meaning' something; 'illocutionary', that is performing an act *in* saying something, for example 'warning'; and 'perlocutionary', that is bringing about something *by* saying something, for example 'deterring'. All speech acts are both locutionary and illocutionary, but not necessarily perlocutionary. It is obviously the illocutionary acts which are important for discourse analysis, and Austin suggests that there are between one and ten thousand of them in English, groupable into five large classes. Austin's basic concern was not with discourse structure but simply with the isolated act, and therefore he does not discuss whether the acts are structurally as well as meaningfully distinct – that is, whether there are unique restrictions on what can follow or precede 'remarking' to distinguish it from 'mentioning', or 'informing' to distinguish it from 'telling'.

Analysts interested in structure have mainly chosen intuitively recognisable acts such as Request, Question and Invitation, and discussed the structural constraints on what can follow. The discussions have, however, been in the nature of the 'illustrative fragments' so familiar to linguists. There has been little attempt to show how various speech acts are similar or different, and to provide formal definitions. Labov (1972) recognises that 'there may be such a thing as premature formalisation', but argues that it is 'a fruitful procedure even when it is wrong: it sharpens our questions and promotes the search for answers'. Sinclair and Coulthard (1975) suggest that a piecemeal approach, which only describes parts of data, is potentially dangerous. They argue that until one can demonstrate that description is finite and can in some way describe all the data, the analyst may not be saying anything at all, but simply creating the illusion of classification. Sinclair *et al.* (ibid.) is one attempt to produce a system which will describe all the data. They draw on the linguistic concept of 'delicacy' (Halliday, 1961), and envisage a description with several degrees of delicacy, each describing all the data but in a progressively more detailed way. At primary delicacy they propose only three major all-inclusive functions or moves – Opening, Answering and Follow-up. These are defined in terms of their effect on and position in the discourse. An Opening move is prospective: it influences the production of another, Answering, move by a next speaker. Answering moves are defined reciprocally: they fulfil predictions and constraints set up by the Opening move. Answering moves create no prospective constraints, but may be followed by a Follow-up move, which, while not constrained, does refer to the preceding move. At secondary delicacy, Opening moves for instance are subdivided into Informing, Eliciting, Checking and Directing, and at tertiary delicacy distinctions such as those between ordering and requesting would be handled.

Realisation and interpretive rules

Regardless of whether one sees discourse as an independent linguistic level equal in status to grammar and phonology (Sinclair *et al.*, ibid.), or as higher ranks of grammar (Fawcett, forthcoming), the problem of realisation or recognition remains – how does the speaker encode his function in grammatical form, and how does the listener derive the correct function? There is a relationship between form and function: very frequently declarative mood realises statements, interrogative mood questions, imperative mood commands and moodless items responses, but this is by no means always the case. As Sinclair *et al.* (ibid.) point out, 'A native speaker who interpreted *Is that the mint sauce over there?* or *Can you tell me the time?* as *yes/no* questions, *Have a drink* as a command, or *I wish you'd go away* as requiring just a murmur of agreement, would find the world a bewildering place.' How then does a speaker recognise a question which is not realised by interrogative mood or a command not realised by imperative mood? It is now possible to explain how listeners arrive at correct interpretations in some instances, by considering features of the non-verbal context. Labov (1972) suggests a rule for distinguishing some declarative questions. He quotes an extract from a therapeutic interview:

Therapist: Oh, so she *told* you.
Patient: Yes.
Therapist: She didn't say for *you*.
Patient: No.

and asks why an utterance which is superficially a statement functions as a *yes/no* question. He suggests that, using the concept of 'shared knowledge', one can classify all reported events as A-events, B-events, or AB-events; that is, in any conversation, there will be events about which only one of the participants

25

knows, and events about which knowledge is shared. He then formulates a simple rule, which explains the example, 'If A makes a statement about a B-event it is heard as a request for confirmation.'

Brazil (forthcoming) suggests a linguistic rather than contextual explanation for data which looks similar. In the first extract below, the patient doesn't respond as if to a question; in the second he does:

Patient: Well I had 'm er a week last Wednesday.
Doctor: A week last Wednesday. How many attacks have you had?

Patient: I felt a tight pain in the middle of the chest.
Doctor: Tight pain.
Patient: You know like a dull ache...

In both instances the doctor repeats part of what the patient has said, but the crucial difference is in the intonation. Neither is marked by rising intonation, but the second is produced in a relatively high pitch or 'Key', while the first is in low Key. Brazil argues that it is the Key choice which affects the interpretation, and goes on to show that all declarative clauses in high Key occurring at positions where they could be heard as questions are heard as such.

Sinclair *et al.* (ibid.) examine declarative and interrogative utterances in the classroom to discover the conditions under which they realise commands. They find they need to use such contextual evidence as 'the predicate describes an action which is physically possible at the time of utterance'; 'it refers to an action or activity which is proscribed at the time of the utterance'; 'it refers to an action or activity which teacher and pupil(s) know ought to have been performed or completed and hasn't been'. The interpretation of utterances thus depends on the interpretation of the situational features. Sinclair *et al.* discuss the following example in which a pupil misunderstands the situation, assumes that laughing is a proscribed activity, and thus interprets the teacher's interrogative as a command to stop laughing, not a question about why she was laughing.

Teacher: Do you – what are you laughing at?
Pupil: Nothing.

Labov (1970) and Gordon and Lakoff (1971) make similar assumptions about the relative status of participants, their knowledge of the situation and the feasibility of activities, in order to explain similar examples. Lakoff (1972) uses relative status of participants in order to explain how the choice of the modals, *may, must, should*, in the sentence *you . . . have some cake*, can realise politeness, rudeness or degrees of coercion, while Coulthard, Sinclair and Forsyth (1972) note how politeness inside the classroom can be realised by choice of interrogative or declarative mood for commands and the use of 'softeners' such as *just*, modal verbs, and the inclusive *we*.

The verbal context of an item is equally important in its interpretation.

Sinclair *et al.* point out that many potential questions never actually function as such because the teacher rephrases, alters or in some other way removes them from an initiating position in the discourse, while Labov (1972) faces the problem of how an item comes to be heard as an answer to a preceding question. He takes the sequence

A: Are you going to work tomorrow? (U1)
B: I'm on jury duty. (U2)

and asks in what sense the second utterance is an answer to the first. Sacks (*passim*) asserts that the first constraint on any speaker is to produce recognisably relevant and coherent contributions, and Labov suggests that 'in answering A's request for information Q-S_1, with a superficially unrelated statement S_2, B is in fact asserting that there is a proposition known to both A and B that connects this with S_1...there is no direct connection between the two utterances Q-S_1 and S_2 and it would be fruitless to search for one.' The relevant proposition is likely to depend on assumed shared knowledge but the questioner may for various reasons not see the connection.

Linus: Do you want to play with me, Violet?
Violet: You're younger than me. [Shuts the door.]
Linus: [Puzzled.] She didn't answer my question.

Speaker change

For the analyst there is the problem of describing how utterances follow one another in a coherent way; for the speakers there is the problem of how to get in and out of the interaction, how to hold and yield the floor. In fairly formal situations – classrooms, doctor/patient interviews, media discussions, media interviews – one participant has an acknowledged right to direct the discourse and to have the floor whenever he wants it. Such discourse progresses mainly by question/answer sequences (Sinclair *et al.*, 1972; Pearce, 1973 *a*, *b*; Coulthard & Ashby, forthcoming). However, Sacks (*passim*) demonstrates that in ordinary conversation this is definitely not so.

Sacks (MS.) and Sacks, Schegloff and Jefferson (1974) describe a turn-taking system to handle change of speaker in conversation. They note that a basic rule of conversation is that one and only one speaker talks at a time – this is not an empirically observed rule because obviously sometimes speakers overlap and sometimes there is silence, but it is one which speakers 'orient to', that is, if two are talking one quickly stops, if there is silence someone tends to begin, if only to produce *um* or *er* noises and claim the silence as theirs. Sacks suggests two degrees of control which a speaker can have over the next part of the discourse. He can select the next speaker by nominating him, or he can select the next action but leave the next speaker to select himself – by asking a question or making a request or a complaint, he specifies what a next appropriate utterance will be but not necessarily who will answer it. His other alternative is simply to stop and place no constraints on the next speaker, who then selects himself and his contribution. Self-selection is much more frequent in interaction between equal participants, and, because normally turns to speak are valued, speakers often self-select before the current speaker feels he has finished. As Sacks observes, speakers can never know when another speaker has actually finished, even if he pauses; they can only know when he has reached a 'possible completion' and it is at points of possible completion that speakers most usually self-select. Self-selection does occur at points other than possible completions, but then it is heard as rudeness.

> A: but there aren't enough people who need that service at two thirty
>   at night ⌈ down to my particular sta
> B: ⌊ you talk like the chairman of British Rail   [Pearce, M.S.]

The ability to come in as soon as a speaker has reached a possible completion suggests a high degree of skill on the part of participants – they need to be able to analyse and understand an ongoing sentence in order to recognise when it is possibly complete and immediately produce a relevant next utterance. Jefferson (1973) demonstrates that the recipient of an ongoing utterance does have 'the technical capacity to select a precise spot to start his own talk "no later" than the exact appropriate moment'. She illustrates how speakers can add adjuncts and clauses immediately on to the end of another's apparently completed utterance; how speakers can come in in the middle of another's clause and produce a perfectly grammatical whole:

> A: a Soshe is someone who ⌈ is a carbon copy of their friend.
> B: ⌊ drinks Pepsi.

and how they can even say the same thing at the same time to complete a sentence,

> A: The guy who doesn't run the race doesn't win it but
>   'e doesn ⌈ 't lose it.
> B: ⌊ b't lose it.

Kendon (1967) suggests that one important factor enabling the smooth change-over of speaker is gaze. He notes that while listening A looks at B with fairly long gazes broken by very brief away gazes, but while speaking A looks at and away from B for more equal periods. Kendon suggests that the listener picks up clues from the speaker about when he will end. One set of clues is that 'usually the person who is bringing a long utterance to an end does so by assuming a characteristic head posture and by looking steadily at the auditor before he actually finishes speaking'. Kendon notes that while less than a third of utterances which ended with an extended look were followed by a silence or a delayed response, almost three-quarters of utterances that ended without the speaker looking up were followed by silence or no response. De Long (1974), in a detailed study of conversations between pairs of pre-school children, discovered 'predictable patterning and clustering of leftward and downward kinesic activity to signal an intention to terminate verbalisation'; while Duncan (1970) suggests six cues – lexical, syntactic, paralinguistic and kinesic – which singly or in combination offer the listener the chance to take over the speaking role.

All these are verbal and non-verbal techniques for the current speaker to pass on the role of speaker. There are, of course, times when the speaker wishes specifically not to pass on the speaking role. He can pre-structure a fairly large unit of speech by such devices as *I'd like to make two points* or simply *firstly*; he can claim the right to produce two more clauses by opening with a sub-ordinator, *although, because,* or he can simply indicate, by pausing after an 'incompletion marker' (Sacks, MS.), *and, but, so,* that he intends to continue. None of these devices can guarantee that he keeps the floor, but they force the other speaker into a position where he must interrupt and be seen to be interrupting. Speakers reject interuptions, if they choose not to yield the floor, by speaking more loudly, more quickly and in a higher pitch (Pearce, M.S.). A non-speaker who wishes to speak, and who is unable to find a suitable entry spot, has the option of simply interrupting or of indicating by means of short, one-tonic utterances, that he would like the floor (Pearce, M.S.). The non-speaker who is offered the floor but doesn't want it, may simply remain silent until the speaker continues (Kendon, 1969; de Long, 1974; Sinclair *et al.*, 1972), or produce the minimal response to confirm, agree or express interest, or use the whole of his turn to produce a 'possible pre-closing', *alright, okay, so, well* (Schegloff & Sacks, 1973), and thereby indicate that he has nothing further to add and is willing to close the topic.

Discourse structure

Any model for spoken or written discourse which attempts to show how the basic units of communication are related must consist of at least two units in a hierarchical relationship. Hymes (1972 a) proposes 'act' and 'event' – 'an event may consist of a single speech act, but will often comprise several'; Goffman (1955) 'move' and 'interchange' – 'an interchange will involve two or more moves and two or more participants'; Mathiot (1972) outlines three ranks, 'statements', 'motifs' and 'sections', to handle the structure of a myth. Bellack, Kliebard, Hyman and Smith (1966) propose four, 'move', 'cycle', 'subgame' and 'game', to describe the structure of classroom interaction; Sacks and Schegloff (*passim*) apparently five, 'turn', 'pair', 'sequence', 'topic' and 'conversation', although it is difficult to tell, because, as Labov (1972) observes, they are anxious to avoid premature formalisation; Sinclair *et al.* (1972) also propose five, 'act', 'move', 'exchange', 'transaction' and 'interaction'; and Coulthard and Ashby (1973) insert a sixth, 'sequence', between 'exchange' and 'transaction'. Despite the different labels, the units proposed by Sacks and Sinclair *et al.* are remarkably similar and one can often read 'move' for 'turn', 'exchange' for 'pair', and so on.

For Sinclair *et al.* the basic unit of interaction is not the single utterance, but the exchange, which consists of at least two contributions or 'moves' by different speakers. Each exchange begins with an 'initiating' move which is prospective, and by questioning, commanding or informing requires a reply, reaction or acknowledgement from the next speaker. The second 'responding' move is retrospective and fulfils the expectations or requirements of the first; moves in responding position which do not respond are noticed as anomalous:

B.B: Adam, which is right, 'two shoes' or 'two shoe'.
A: Pop goes the weasel.   [Brown & Bellugi, 1964]

Sinclair *et al.* note that classroom exchanges consist typically of three moves, with the third, 'follow-up' move, being necessary because of the nature of the situation. Teachers typically ask questions not to find out answers but to find out if the pupils know the answers, and thus once a pupil has produced the answer he needs to know whether it was the right one. The follow-up move, referring back and commenting on the answer, allows for the need.

T: Initiation: What did we call this picture?
P: Response: Piece of paper.
T: Follow-up: A piece of paper. Yes.
T: Initiation: What did we call this?

The analysis in terms of moves and exchanges proved applicable to discourse produced in other situations – radio and television interviews (Pearce, 1973 *a*), televised discussions (Pearce, 1973 *b*) and doctor/patient interviews (Coulthard & Ashby, 1973). However, perhaps significantly, these were also situations in which one participant has acknowledged control over the progress of the discourse. Problems were encountered in the description of committee meetings (Stubbs, 1973), where the participants were more equal, and where there appeared at times to be no recognisable exchange structure. Interestingly, Sacks in his work on conversation has isolated the Adjacency Pair, a two-part exchange-like structure, but this only describes some of his data; other parts apparently consist of related turns which appear to build directly into sequences. Further research is needed to discover whether a consistent exchange structure is only a feature of more formal interaction or whether the more abstract version of exchange structure suggested by Brazil and Coulthard (forthcoming) and Williams (1974), is applicable to all interactions.

Sacks (MS.) notes that 'sequences' can be built up from two or more question–answer pairs, in which the first one is often what he confusingly calls a 'presequence', a pair whose function is to establish what the state of affairs is, so that the speaker doesn't waste a Request, Invitation or Offer or mistakenly make a Challenge or Complaint.

Pre-invitation
{ Jack: Say what you doin'?
{ Judy: Well, we're goin' out. Why?
Jack: Oh I was just gonna say come out...

Schegloff (1972) notes that sometimes one question–answer pair is embedded inside another while Jefferson (1972) shows how three-part 'side-sequences' often occur in the middle of a continuing sequence.

Sinclair *et al.* (ibid.) postulate a unit above exchange, 'transaction', for which they are able to provide no internal structure, but whose limits are indicated by boundary exchanges, consisting of two items 'frame' and 'focus'. Frame is the name given to a small set of words – *well, right, now, okay, good* – spoken with a falling intonation and followed by silent stress, which do not have their usual lexical meaning, but indicate that the speaker considers one stage in the discourse to have ended and another to be beginning. Schegloff and Sacks (1973) note the use of similar items to end topics, and they are found with similar function, but less predictable occurrence, in job interviews (Silverman, MS.), media interviews (Pearce, 1973), doctor–patient interviews (Coulthard and Ashby, 1973) and committee meetings (Stubbs, 1973). The other item in boundary exchanges, focus, is almost certainly unique to teacher-dominated discourse – it consists of a metastatement, an indication by the teacher of what the transaction has been, or will be, about.

It is so far impossible to produce any structure for the largest unit of all, the 'conversation' or 'interaction'. Sacks (MS.) wonders whether one can use conversation as an analytic unit at all, and whether there are any features which all conversations share. He suggests that greetings are close to being universal in conversation because, although they sometimes do not occur, on some of these occasions their absence is noticeable. The openings to telephone conversations have been analysed by Schegloff (1968), and the closings by Schegloff and Sacks (1973). Pearce (1973 *a*) describes openings and closings in media interviews and Coulthard and Ashby (1973) in doctor/patient interviews. Scheflen (1964) argues that speakers signal kinesically boundaries in discourse. He suggests a hierarchical structure composed of four ranks, syntactic sentence, point, position and presentation, which seem to correspond roughly to move, sequence, topic and conversation. The end of a point – so named because, consisting of several syntactic sentences, it 'corresponds crudely to making a point in a discussion'

31

– is indicated by a change in the position of head and eyes; the termination of a presentation – the totality of positions in a given interaction – is a complete change of location. He observes that 'after an exit the re-entrant usually assumes a different role or engages in a new type of interaction'.

Lexical and referential cohesion

Sacks (1972 a) argues that the descriptive and referential items in successive utterances, or in successive parts of one utterance, are related in highly complex ways. He presents the story *The baby cried. The mommy picked it up* and suggests that most people will 'hear' the story in the same way and agree with the following 'facts'. Firstly that although there is no genitive in the story, the mommy who picks up the baby is the baby's mommy; secondly that the two events occur sequentially; and thirdly that the second event occurs because of the first event. He sets out to produce a descriptive apparatus which will account for these facts, and, because it is 'overbuilt', for similar facts in other stories. He introduces 'membership categorisation device', the name he gives to superordinate descriptive items like sex, family, stage of life, which in turn consist of sets of labels such as male, female, mother, father, son, daughter, baby, with which a speaker can subcategorise members of a group. Some labels have more than one 'meaning' and belong to more than one 'device': this baby belongs to both 'family' and 'stage of life'. Sacks then introduces an 'economy' rule, 'If two or more categories are used to categorise two or more members of some population, and those categories can be heard as categories from the same collection: hear them that way.' Thus mommy and baby are heard as being co-members of the same device, 'family', and *the mommy* is the baby's mommy.

The idea of membership outlined in this article is developed in Schegloff (1972). Schegloff points out that any speaker wishing to refer to a place or location has a relatively large number of possible formulations – as he writes he could describe the location of his notes as 'right in front of me, next to the telephone, on the desk, in my office, in the office...in Manhattan, in New York City...' While all these 'correctly' describe the location of the notes, on any occasion of actual use not all of them are 'correct'. The problem Schegloff poses is 'how is it that on a particular occasion of use some term from the set is selected and other terms rejected?' The answer depends partly on who one is talking to and partly on the topic. Whatever the topic of the conversation the speaker must 'membership' his listener, put him into one of two or more mutually exclusive boxes. Each time a topic changes the listener must be re-membershipped, and during a conversation the same person may be member-shipped as a doctor, a rugby player, a liberal, a gardener, a bridge player. (Membershipping is another way of describing the assumptions a speaker makes about what Labov (1972) refers to as Shared Knowledge.) Speakers usually membership their friends correctly but may make mistakes with strangers, and shoppers membershipped as shop-assistants can get annoyed. Sacks (1968) reports an exchange on an aeroplane:

Passenger: Do you have a cigarette?
Stewardess: No we don't. They don't provide that service any more.

It is a perfectly common event for strangers to ask for cigarettes but the stewardess assumes that she has been membershipped as a stewardess and that the question is addressed to her in that role. She indicates this in her use of *we* in the reply, and replies, on behalf of the organisation, that cigarettes aren't available any more. Had she taken it that the passenger was membershipping her as a stranger not a stewardess she might have offered him one of her own cigarettes.

The fact that there are several possible formulations for the same person, place or event allows the speaker to choose formulations which emphasise the coherence of the topic. Sacks (1968) and Schegloff (1972) quote the following telephone conversation:

Estelle: Well, I just though I'd – re – better report to you what's happen' at Bullock's today...Well I-v-got outta my car at five thirty I drove aroun' an' at first I had t'go by the front a' the store,
Jeanette: Eyeah.
Estelle: An' there was two p'leece cars *across the street*, andeh – colored lady wan'tuh go *in the main entrance* there *where the silver is an all the gifts an' things*,
Jeanette: Yeah,
Estelle: And they, wouldn' let 'er go in and he hadda gun he was holding a gun in 'is hand a great long gun
Jeanette: Yeh
Estelle: An'nen over on the other side, I mean to the right of *there* where the employees come out there was a whole oh musta been tenuh eight'r ten employees stanning there, because there musta been a – it seem like they had every entrance barred. I don' know what was going on.

Once Estelle has given the name of the store where the incident happened, all other places are described in relation to it. The police cars were 'across the street'; the coloured lady wanted to go 'in the main entrance', 'where the silver is'; the eight or ten employees were standing 'over on the other side', 'to the right of there'. The choice of location terms follows the consistency rule; Bullocks is the topic and the way in which the places are formulated emphasises its centrality. Had the teller, for instance, been coming out of the store across the road, the police cars would have been parked 'in front of the store' and the incident would have been 'across the street'. As Sacks observes, 'the phenomenon of being "parked across the street from" is obviously one sort of characterisation which turns on not only where you are but what it is that is being talked about and where *that* is'. Even linguists whose concern is primarily with the structure of the sentence are coming to realise that it is impossible to ignore the verbal context of which it is a part. Halliday's (1967) discussion of the information structure of the clause and Hasan's (1968) discussion of cohesion both use items outside the clause to explain features within it. Dressler (1970) suggests that modality can best be treated at the discourse rather than the sentence level, while Karttunen (1969) invokes the concept of 'discourse referent' to explain why the perfectly grammatical sentence *The kite has a long string* cannot occur in the sequence *Bill can make a kite. The kite has a long string*.

Application of discourse analysis

Until recently not only linguists but applied linguists also ignored suprasentential structure and language function – now there is a growing concern with 'communicative competence' (Hymes, 1972 *b*). Wilkins (1974), examining a three-week introductory course in Malay, observes that 'It is possible for some things to have been learned very well and yet, because what is known is a decidedly limited part of the whole system, one's communicative capacity will have remained virtually at zero.' He argues for courses structured so that all language taught will have 'maximal communicative value'. Jakobivits and Gordon (1974) in a theoretical book argue similarly that language teaching must be more communication-oriented, and suggest ways in which materials writers can benefit from current work in discourse analysis. Candlin, Leather and Bruton (1974) describe a research project which is examining the structure of interaction between hospital doctors and patients, and which intends to produce materials based on the findings, for use with immigrant doctors. Johns (forthcoming) outlines two sets of materials: one set, based on Sinclair *et al.* (1972), is intended to demonstrate to non-native teachers who are required to teach in English, how native teachers teach; the other set, based on an analysis of small group discussions, is intended to help foreign students participate more easily in seminars and tutorials.

Widdowson (1974 *a, b*) argues for the importance of translation in teaching students how to read scientific English – the problem for them, at least at first, should be seen 'not as the acquisition of new knowledge and experience, but as an extension or alternative realisation of what the learner already knows'. The students' concerns are not with grammatical equivalence but with functional equivalence, and they should therefore learn how 'certain acts of communication which are central to scientific enquiry' are realised. Allen and Widdowson (1974) is the first of a series of text books which exemplify this approach. While

Widdowson concentrates on discourse at the rank of act, Jones (forthcoming) in a suggestive paper points the way to an analysis of structure at higher ranks.

Psycholinguists investigating children's acquisition of language are moving from a concern with children's grammars to a concern with discourse. Most of the work currently concentrates on the lowest rank, with considerations of the ages at which children acquire the various speech acts (Bates, 1974; Bruner, forthcoming; Dore, MS.), at what age children begin to exploit the variety of grammatical realisations available for a given function (Ervin-Tripp, 1974), and of how successfully they decode discourse function from grammatical form (Shatz, MS.). Keenan (1974) is the first published attempt to describe the structure of interaction between young children, but this is very much a growth area. Surprisingly, sociolinguists involved with questions of language deprivation have not yet begun to examine the structure of interaction, though this is where the most valuable evidence will be found. *April 1975*

References

I know of no recent published bibliography of work in discourse analysis. I have therefore added to the cited works other useful references for those who wish to read further.

Allen, J. P. L. & Widdowson, H. G. (1974). *English in physical science.* London: Oxford University Press.

Austin, J. L. (1962). *How to do things with words.* Oxford: Clarendon.

Bates, E. (1974). Acquisition of pragmatic competence. *Journal of Child Language,* **1**, 2, 277–81.

Bates, E. (1976). *Language and context: the acquisition of pragmatics.* New York: Academic Press.

Bauman, R. & Sherzer, J. (eds.) (1974). *Explorations in the ethnography of speaking.* London: Cambridge University Press.

Bellack, A. A., Kliebard, H. M., Hyman, R. T. & Smith, F. L. (1966). *The language of the classroom.* New York: Teachers College Press.

Brazil, D. (forthcoming). *Intonation in discourse.*

Brazil, D. & Coulthard, R. M. (forthcoming). *Exchange structure.*

Brown, R. & Bellugi, U. (1964). Three processes in the child's acquisition of syntax. *Harvard Educational Review,* **34**, 133–51.

Bruner, J. (1975). The ontogenesis of speech acts. *Journal of Child Language,* **2**.

Campbell, R. & Smith, P. T. (eds.) (1977). *The Stirling Psychology of Language Conference.* London: Plenum Press.

Candlin, C. C., Leather, J. & Bruton, C. (1974). *English language skills for overseas doctors and medical staff: reports 1–4.* University of Lancaster mimeo.

Cole, P. & Morgan, J. L. (eds.) (1975). *Syntax and semantics, III: speech acts.* New York: Academic Press.

Coulthard, R. M. (1974). Approaches to the analysis of classroom discourse. *Educational Review,* **26**, 3, 229–40.

Coulthard, R. M. (1977). *An introduction to discourse analysis.* London: Longman.

Coulthard, R. M. & Ashby, C. M. (1973). Doctor–patient interviews. *Working Papers in Discourse Analysis,* 1. University of Birmingham mimeo.

Coulthard, R. M. & Ashby, C. M. (forthcoming). A linguistic description of doctor–patient interviews. In M. Wadsworth (ed.), *Medical sociology.*

Coulthard, R. M., Sinclair, J. McH. & Forsyth, I. J. (1972). Discourse in the classroom. Mimeo.

Dore, J. (MS.). On the acquisition of speech acts: a pragmatic description of early language development.

Dore, J. (1975). Holophrases, speech acts and language universals. *Journal of Child Language,* **2**, 21–39.

Dressler, W. (1970). Towards a semantic deep structure of discourse grammar. In *Papers from the sixth regional meeting of the Chicago Linguistic Society.* Chicago: Department of Linguistics, University of Chicago.

Duncan, S. (1972). Some signals and rules for taking speaking turns in conversation. *Journal of Personality and Social Psychology,* **23**, 2, 283–92.

Duncan, S. (1973). Towards a grammar for dyadic conversation. *Semiotica,* **9**, 1, 29–46.

Duncan, S. (1974). On the structure of speaker–auditor interaction during speaking turns. *Language in Society,* **3**, 2, 161–80.

Duncan, S. & Niederehe, G. (1974). On signalling that its your turn to speak. *Journal of Experimental Social Psychology,* **10**, 234–47.

Ervin-Tripp, S. (1974). The comprehension and production of requests by children. *Papers and reports on child language development.* Stanford: Stanford University.

Ervin-Tripp, S. (1976). Wait for me roller-skate. In C. Mitchell-Kernan & S. Ervin-Tripp (eds.), *Child discourse.* New York: Academic Press.

Fawcett, R. (forthcoming). Two concepts of function in a cognitive model of communication. In C. C. Candlin (ed.), *Proceedings of the 1973 BAAL Conference on the Communicative Teaching of English.* London: Longman.

Fillmore, C. J. (1972). May we come in. In D. M. Smith & R. W. Shuy (eds.), *Sociolinguistics in crosscultural perspective.* Washington: Georgetown University Press.

Firth, J. R. (1935). The technique of semantics. Reprinted in J. R. Firth (1957), *Papers in Linguistics 1934–51.* London: Oxford University Press.

Forsyth, I. J. (1974). Patterns in the discourse of pupils and teachers. In *The space between. . . . : English and foreign languages at school. CILT reports and papers 10.* London: CILT.

Goffman, E. (1955). On face-work: an analysis of ritual elements in social interaction. *Psychiatry,* **18**, reprinted in J. Laver & S. Hutcheson (eds.), *Communication in face to face interaction.* Harmondsworth: Penguin.

Gordon, D. & Lakoff, G. (1971). Conversational postulates. In *Papers from the seventh regional meeting of the Chicago Linguistic Society.* Chicago: Department of Linguistics, University of Chicago.

Grice, H. P. (1975). Logic and conversation. In P. Cole & J. L. Morgan (eds.).

Gumperz, J. J. & Herasimchuk, E. (1972). The conversational analysis of social meaning: a study of classroom interaction. In R. W. Shuy (ed.), *Sociolinguistics: current trends and prospects.* Washington: Georgetown University Press.

Gumperz, J. J. & Hymes, D. (eds.). (1972). *Directions in sociolinguistics.* New York: Holt, Rinehart & Winston.

Halliday, M. A. K. (1961). Categories of the theory of grammar. *Word,* **17**, 241–92.

Halliday, M. A. K. (1967). Notes on transitivity and theme. *Journal of Linguistics,* **3**, 37–81, 199–244.

Halliday, M. A. K. (1975). *Learning how to mean.* London: Arnold.

Harris, Z. (1952). Discourse analysis. *Language,* **28**, 1–30.

Hasan, R. (1968). *Grammatical cohesion in spoken and written English.* Paper 7, Schools Council programme in linguistics and English teaching. London: Longman.

Hendricks, W. O. (1967). On the notion 'beyond the sentence'. *Linguistics*, **37**, reprinted in Hendricks (1973). .

Hendricks, W. O. (1973). *Essays on semiolinguistics and verbal art.* The Hague: Mouton.

Hymes, D. (1972 *a*). Models of the interaction of language and social life. In G. G. Gumperz & D. Hymes (eds.), *Directions in sociolinguistics.* New York: Holt, Rinehart & Winston.

Hymes, D. (1972 *b*). On communicative competence. In J. B. Pride and J. Holmes (eds.), *Sociolinguistics.* Harmondsworth: Penguin.

Hymes, D. (1974). Ways of speaking. In R. Bauman & J. Sherzer (eds.).

Jakobovits, L. A. & Gordon, B. (1974). *The context of foreign language teaching.* Rowley, Mass.: Newbury House.

Jefferson, G. (1972). Side sequences. In D. Sudnow (ed.), *Studies in social interaction.* New York: The Free Press.

Jefferson, G. (1973). A case of precision timing in ordinary conversation: overlapped tag-positioned address terms in closing sequences. *Semiotica*, **9**, 1, 47–96.

Jefferson, G. (1974). Error correction as an interactional resource. *Language in Society*, **3**, 2, 181–99.

Johns, T. F. (forthcoming). Some implications of discourse analysis for the teaching of spoken English for Academic Purposes.

Jones, K. (forthcoming). The role of discourse analysis in devising undergraduate reading programmes in EST. Mimeo available from ETIC.

Karttunen, L. (1969). Discourse referents. Preprint 70, International Conference on Computational Linguistics, Stockholm; quoted in Hendricks (1973).

Keenan, E. O. (1974). Conversational competence in children. *Journal of Child Language*, **1**, 2, 163–83.

Keenan, E. O. & Klein, E. (1975). Coherency in children's discourse. *Journal of Psycholinguistic Research*, **4**, 365–80.

Kendon, A. (1967). Some functions of gaze direction in social interaction. *Acta Psychologica*, **26**, 22–63.

Labov, W. (1970). The study of language in its social context. *Studium Generale*, **23**, 30–87.

Labov, W. (1972). Rules for ritual insults. In D. Sudnow (ed.), *Studies in social interaction.* New York: The Free Press.

Lakoff, R. (1972). Language in context. *Language*, **48**, 4, 907–27.

Laver, J. (1974). Communicative functions of phatic communion. In *Work in Progress 7.* Edinburgh: Department of Linguistics, University of Edinburgh.

Li, C. (ed.) (1976). *Subject and topic.* New York: Academic Press.

de Long, A. J. (1974). Kinesic signals at utterance boundaries in preschool children. *Semiotica*, **11**, 1, 43–73.

Mathiot, M. (1972). Cognitive analysis of a myth: an exercise in method. *Semiotica*, **6**, 2, 101–42.

Mishler, E. (1972). Implications of teacher-strategies for language and cognition: observations in first-grade classrooms. In C. Cazden, V. P. Johns & D. Hymes (eds.), *Functions of language in the classroom.* New York: Teachers College Press.

Morgan, J. O. (1967). English structure above the sentence level. *Monograph series on Languages and Linguistics*, 20.

Pearce, R. D. (1973 *a*). *The structure of discourse in broadcast interviews.* Unpublished M.A. thesis, University of Birmingham.

Pearce, R. D. (1973 *b*). The television discussion programme. *Working Papers in Discourse Analysis*, 3. University of Birmingham mimeo.

Pearce, R. D. (MS.). Discourse structure in the television discussion programme.

Propp, V. (1968). *Morphology of the folk tale*, 2nd edn. Austin: University of Texas Press.
Ross, J. R. (1975). Where to do things with words. In Cole and Morgan (eds.), 233–256.
Sacks, H. (1967–72). Mimeo lecture notes.
Sacks, H. (1972 a). On the analysability of stories by children. In J. J. Gumperz and D. Hymes (eds.), *Directions in sociolinguistics*. New York: Holt, Rinehart & Winston.
Sacks, H. (MS.). *Aspects of the sequential organisation of conversation*.
Sacks, H., Schegloff, E. A. & Jefferson, G. (1974). A simplest systematics for the organisation of turn-taking for conversation. *Language*, **50**, 4, 696–735.
Sayce, R. A. (1957). Literature and language. *Essays in Criticism*, **7**.
Scheflen, A. E. (1964). The significance of posture in communication systems. *Psychiatry*, **27**, 316–21.
Schegloff, E. A. (1968). Sequencing in conversational openings. *American Anthropologist*, **70**, 6, 1075–95.
Schegloff, E. A. (1972). Notes on a conversational practice: formulating place. In D. Sudnow (ed.), *Studies in social interaction*. New York: Free Press.
Schegloff, E. A. & Sacks, H. (1973). Opening up closings. *Semiotica*, **8**, 4, 289–327.
Schlesinger, I. M. (1974). Towards a structural analysis of discussions. *Semiotica*, **11**, 2, 109–22.
Searle, J. R. (1965). What is a speech act? In M. Black (ed.), *Philosophy in America*, 221–39. Ithaca: Cornell University Press.
Searle, J. R. (1969). *Speech acts*. London: Cambridge University Press.
Searle, J. R. (1975). Indirect speech acts. In P. Cole & J. L. Morgan (eds.), 59–82.
Shatz, M. (1974). The comprehension of indirect directives: can two year olds shut the door? Paper presented the summer meeting of the LSA.
Siegman, A. W. & Pope, B. (eds.). (1972). *Studies in dyadic communication*. New York: Pergamon.
Silverman, D. (1973). Interview talk: bringing off a research instrument. *Sociology*, **7**, 1, 31–48.
Sinclair, J. McH., & Coulthard, R. M. (1975). *Towards an analysis of discourse*. London: Oxford University Press.
Sinclair, J. McH., Forsyth, I. J., Coulthard, R. M. & Ashby, M. C. (1972). *The English used by teachers and pupils*. Final Report to SSRC. University of Birmingham mimeo.
Stubbs, M. (1973). Some structural complexities of talk in meetings. *Working Papers in Discourse Analysis*, **5**. University of Birmingham mimeo.
Turner, R. (1970). Words, utterances and activities. In J. Douglas (ed.), *Understanding everyday life*. New York: Aldine.
Widdowson, H. G. (1973). An applied linguistic approach to discourse analysis. University of Edinburgh, unpublished PhD thesis.
Widdowson, H. G. (1974 a). The deep structure of discourse and the use of translation. In S. P. Corder & E. Roulet (eds.), *Linguistic insights in applied linguistics*. Second Neuchâtel Colloquium in Applied Linguistics. Brussels: AIMAV; Paris: Didier.
Widdowson, H. G. (1974 b). An approach to the teaching of scientific English discourse. *RELC Journal*, **5**, 27–40.
Widdowson, H. G. (1977). Approaches to discourse. In C. Gutknecht (ed.), *Grundbegriffe und Hauptströmungen der Linguistik*. Hoffmann und Campe.
Wilkins, D. Notional syllabuses and the concept of a minimum adequate grammar. In S. P. Corder & E. Roulet (eds.), *Linguistic insights in applied linguistics*. Second Neuchâtel Colloquium in Applied Linguistics. Brussels: AIMAV; Paris: Didier.
Williams, S. (1974). *A sociolinguistic analysis of the general practice interview*. University of Birmingham, unpublished MA thesis.

SOCIOLINGUISTICS AND THE PROBLEM OF 'COMPETENCE'.

R. B. Le Page

Department of Language, University of York

1. A central problem for sociolinguists is to evolve a theory of language in which consideration of the formal properties of the abstraction 'language' as a mediating system, the properties of *langue* as inherent in social institutions and the behaviour of groups, the property of the individual generally referred to as his linguistic competence, and the social beliefs of people about the nature of language, can all be related to one another in an illuminating way. In this paper I examine the concept of 'competence' in relation to various kinds of sociolinguistic investigation so as to bring out some aspects of this central problem. The headings are: the sociology of language (2); education, literacy and 'competence' in multilingual situations (3); intralanguage variation (4); pidgins, creoles and 'Black English' (5); communicative competence and the ethnography of speaking (6). I have tried to give a bibliographical guide for each.

1.1. *Theoretical framework.* Consideration of the problem over a number of years since starting work on the Linguistic Survey of the British Caribbean in 1951 has led me to the view that the integrating unit of our theory should be the act of identity made by people and groups of people in interactional situations. One must therefore try to understand the psychological and social needs which these acts serve.

The general rules which govern the acts of identity of groups have been codified to some extent by Sprott (1958), although he does not deal with language. I have elsewhere (Le Page, 1968, 1974) stated a general hypothesis about the rules which govern individual language behaviour: 'Each individual creates the systems for his verbal behaviour so that they shall resemble those of the group or groups with which from time to time he may wish to be identified, to the extent that: (*a*) he can identify the groups; (*b*) he has both opportunity and ability to observe and analyse their behavioural systems; (*c*) his motivation is sufficiently strong to impel him to choose, and to adapt his behaviour accordingly; (*d*) he is still able to adapt his behaviour.' Rider (*c*) of this hypothesis should take account of the cues which social groups feed back to the individual about his likelihood of being allowed to identify with them; this feedback affects his motivation. It must be remembered also that the hypothesis can cover aversive, as well as imitative, behaviour – that is, the motivation may be negative. Finally, it must be remembered that motivation is always complex, and will have to take account of one's wish to preserve one's personal identity as well as one's wish to be accepted in a variety of social roles.

For general introductory work about the psychological and social functions of language see Malinowski (1934), Roger Brown (1965, 1970), Le Page (1973), Robinson (1972), Pride (1971), Trudgill (1974), Fishman (1971/2), vol. 1.

1.2. We may conveniently illustrate some of the many parameters of sociolinguistic investigation and of the problem of 'competence', by referring to the case of East Africa (see Whiteley, 1969, 1971; Mohamed Bakari, 1975). Swahili has over the centuries developed as a *lingua franca* between Arabic traders and the coastal Bantu; then as the native language of the ethnically mixed population of the trading ports such as Mombasa and Zanzibar; as the literary language of the Mombasan community; as a language used by some missionaries – though eschewed by others because of its Islamic associations; as the administrative and army language under the Germans and then the British in Tanganyika; as the post-colonial national language of Tanzania; as the trading *lingua franca* today of parts of the Congo (see Polomé, 1971). It has as many 'dialects' as there are Bantu and Nilotic languages whose speakers adopt it. The Bantu language-area itself is a linguistic continuum (see Évrard, 1966; Guthrie, 1970); Swahili is in most grammatical respects a Bantu language, at least as it is spoken in the Bantu areas; the varieties of Swahili form a continuum; nor are they to be sharply distinguished from the Bantu vernacular in each case (see Abdulaziz, 1971). The official 'Standard Swahili' is the product of a succession of committees, ever since the East African International Language Committee was set up in 1930 and took the educated usage of Zanzibar as its basis; it is the vehicle of primary education in Tanzanian schools. But unofficial 'standardising' is occurring through such natural agencies as the campus of the University in Dar es Salaam and the usage of young African announcers and disc-jockeys on the radio. The Mombasan community still feels that *it* speaks the best, the authentic 'standard' Swahili.

I have been told by the teachers in one Tanzanian village that the village has in three generations changed from being monolingual in their vernacular to being monolingual in 'Swahili', via one bilingual generation. But what does this statement mean? The grandparents know many Swahili words; the parents' Swahili contains vernacular words and grammatical constructions; the children, out of respect, do not use Swahili to the grandparents but behave as if they at least understand the vernacular and, out of respect, purge their Swahili of the vernacular to their teachers.

Thus the situation can be surveyed at many levels and along many parameters: what people actually do, when, where and with whom, in language use; what they say they do; what they think they ought to do; what various groups do;

what Governments do, or say should be done; what economic, social, political, physical and cultural forces are at work to affect linguistic behaviour, attitudes towards language, and so on. All of this investigation is the work of socio-linguistics. Moreover, although the description of languages is the work of descriptive linguists, the selection of the data on which such a description can be based is itself a sociolinguistic act, as was the selection of the usage of educated Zanzibarians as the basis of standard Swahili. When we come to the central question of 'competence', we have to ask: 'What is it an individual needs to know, in order to operate as a member of this society?' A society only exists in the competence of its members to make it work as it does; a language only exists in the competence of those who use and regard themselves as users of that language; and the latter competence is the essential mediating system for the former.

2.0. The term 'sociology of language' has been used by J. A. Fishman (q.v.) to distinguish certain kinds of study within sociolinguistics. These tend to keep 'the language' a constant, and map the use of different languages for different purposes or by different groups; or else they concentrate on the social rather than the linguistic aspects of language variation; that is, they are initially directed towards understanding social rather than linguistic systems. Many language surveys come under this heading, being concerned less with intra-language than with inter-language mapping. Several are discussed in Ohannessian, Ferguson and Polomé, *Language surveys in developing nations* (1975). The *Linguistic survey of India*, undertaken by George Grierson between 1887 and 1927, is an early example (see Pandit, 1975); the *Survey of language use and language teaching in Eastern Africa*, carried out between 1967 and 1971 (see Prator, 1975), a very recent one. Grierson set out to 'make a collection of specimens of every language and dialect spoken in India' together with the names of these; to locate them, and to estimate the numbers of speakers, by linking the work with an analysis of the census returns. The specimen consisted of a translation of the Parable of the Prodigal Son, together with a skeleton grammar.

2.1. Any census, as Kelkar (1975) observes, may by including some questions on language use become a crude linguistic survey. E. Glyn Lewis gave an historical dimension to such studies in his 'Migration and language in the USSR' (1971), using official Soviet sources based largely on census returns; and such social statistics underlie a great many studies with political significance – e.g. of the use of Welsh in Wales, Gaelic in Ireland or Scotland, French in Quebec, or in Belgium; a number of political scientists (e.g. Kloss, Rustow, Lieberson, Deutsch) concerned with the sociology of language tend to rely very largely on censuses and official returns. Nevertheless, without any reference to a linguistic description (as in Grierson's survey) or a careful definition of 'competence', census questions and official statistics about language names, proficiency and use can be (and frequently are) meaningless or misleading (see Le Page, 1975*b*).

2.2. Either in conjunction with language surveys, or independently, micro-studies are made of the *use* of named languages within various smaller communities – for example, David Parkin's (1971) study of 'Language choice in two Kampala housing estates'. Such work frequently combines both political and social anthropology, as for example in Fishman, Cooper and Ma's (1971) *Bilingualism in the Barrio*, relating to Puerto Ricans in New York; Whiteley's (1971) *Language use and social change*; A. Tabouret-Keller's (1971) study of the influence of urbanisation on language use in Africa; the reports of the Canadian Royal Commission on Bilingualism; in Roger M. Thompson's (1974) 'Mexican American language loyalty and the validity of the 1970 census'. Fern Seckbach's (1974) 'Attitudes and opinions of Israeli teachers and students about aspects of modern Hebrew' brings the sociology of language at the micro-level to focus on dialects or types of Hebrew, and analyses the opinions of informants as to what categories comprise the 'varieties' of Hebrew in use, and who uses 'good', and who 'poor' Hebrew. Although no linguistic analysis is involved it is obvious that such judgements in a community must affect which speakers of the language are likely to be selected as models by the younger generation, and hence will affect the linguistic character of the language in the future.

2.3. We see therefore that work on 'the sociology of language' has frequent implications for policy-makers studying the likely effects of the implementation of language policies (or the lack of policies), and it has implications for the linguist too. Policy decisions and educational decisions may well affect the nature of languages themselves; these are in any case constantly changing. (The nature of the linguist's abstractions about them also changes, as he selects data first from this level of behaviour and then from that, e.g. from informal conversation, from formal interview data, from written records or from oral or written literature.)

Policy decisions regarding the use of Welsh in Wales – increasing, for example, education and broadcasting in Welsh – will affect the nature of the Welsh language and so the very rules of 'competence' in Welsh. There has to date been comparatively little explicit work on this kind of feedback, but it is a process central to the evolution of languages as social properties and to the properties of socially defined languages. An understanding of this fact has often been shown by historical linguists, whose work (sometimes unwittingly) rests as much upon social history as upon linguistics. Basically we are concerned with how a sense of social identity expresses itself in each individual's concept of his community's *langue*. A dimension is therefore missing from Whiteley's book, *Language use and social change* (1971), arising from sociolinguistic studies in

Africa; a companion volume entitled *Social use and language change* is needed to complete the picture.

3. *Education, literacy, and 'competence' in multilingual situations.* Many studies in the sociology of language have been concerned with the feasibility and desirability of education (at primary, secondary or tertiary level) in a local vernacular, or in a language of wider use, or in an international language (for general surveys see UNESCO, 1953; Rice, 1962; Spencer, 1963; Le Page, 1964; CCTA/CSA, 1964; Ohannessian & Ansré, 1975). These concerns tie up with social and linguistic questions about literacy, the devising of writing-systems, the preparation and publication of reading materials. The abstraction 'competence' reflects different dimensions of knowledge in a non-literate as compared with a part-literate or with a highly literate society. For example, the related roles of language and memory differ; in a non-literate society the social memory is stored to a much greater extent in the members of the society, whose language especially in formal and ritual use must therefore have mnemonic properties not essential in a literate society whose social memory is stored in books. Any attempt to teach through the vernacular, with an orthography being provided for a hitherto unwritten language, changes the nature of 'competence' in that language. (Very little work has been done on this question, but see Ferguson (1971) and Basso (1974) for two suggestive sketches.) Valdman (1968) discusses the relative virtues of 'idealising' the broad Creole French of rural Haiti and eliminating as far as possible the continuing influence of French, as was intended in devising the McConnell-Laubach phonemic orthography for Haitian Creole; or, on the other hand, recognising the continuing prestige of French as a medium of higher education, particularly in the capital Port-au-Prince, and devising an 'ethnophonemic' writing system which would provide the newly literate with a bridge towards written French. Valdman claimed that not only did the McConnell–Laubach system earn ridicule in Haiti by attempting to give prestige to the least prestigious dialect; it was phonemic rather than morphophonemic, and therefore failed to give regular morphemic and lexical forms; and its use would have involved the learner in learning to read for a second time when he came to French. The use of the Pressoir 'ethnophonemic' system, it was said, recognised the sociolinguistic realities; the urban, more Gallicised, creole was the prestige form, and in any case an orthography – which gave representation to the underlying form of 'the language' – rather than a system of transcription, was needed. But, of course, the choice of the Pressoir orthography, with the urban variety as its base, for use in schools has itself influenced what constitutes 'competence' among literate Haitian Creole speakers.

3.1. The sociolinguistics and sociology of literacy, and advances in linguistic theory, are here closely inter-dependent. Generative phonology, as developed by, for example, Chomsky and Halle (1968) and, in diachronic linguistics, by Roger Lass (1975), relies on the concept of 'competence' in underlying forms in the speaker–hearer's lexicon from which related surface forms can be generated. The underlying forms thus provide links between derived surface forms; for example, in English between nouns and derived adjectives (*person, personal*; *medicine, medicinal*), or between adjectives and derived nouns (*serene, serenity*) or verbs and derived nouns (*correct, correction*), etc. The underlying forms postulated may often closely resemble historically antecedent forms in the language. These, in the case of English, are often enshrined in the spelling. Thus it has come to be more clearly understood that English spelling preserves connections between words, and may therefore reflect an aspect of the user's competence, his knowledge of his language, which a phonemic or even a morphophonemic orthography may not. But sometimes the reflection is of the competence only of a fairly advanced and highly literate user. At the other end of the scale, the child learning to read is sometimes baffled by the lack of a clear and regular morphophonemic correspondence between his spoken and the written units; for this reason the Initial Teaching Alphabet (see Pitman & St John, 1969) was devised to help him. Not all children learn to read in a phonic or phonemic way – some appear to become morphographic readers almost immediately. We see therefore that it is possible that one kind of orthography will tend to favour educational élitism and the development and perpetuation of a mandarin class in society, while another will favour egalitarianism at the local level while being less efficient at an advanced level for use among an international and very widespread language community. A choice of orthography thus has political implications. The present struggle of the Chinese Government to find an effective *alphabet* for writing Chinese, to make universal literacy more easily attainable than the logographic system of Chinese characters can, reflects their ideological concerns. In India, one of the obstacles in the way of effective universal primary education is that non-Hindi-speaking children are likely to have to learn not only three languages but three different scripts. The case of the Maldivian writing-system has been discussed by De Silva (1969).

3.2. These considerations bring us to the general question of education and 'competence' in diglossic and other similar multilingual situations, to which we shall have to return in paragraph 5 below. Ferguson's well-known paper introducing the term 'diglossia' (1959) was concerned with speech-communities where 'two or more varieties of the same language are used by some speakers under different conditions'. Ferguson referred in each case to the High (H) and Low (L) varieties of the language, and in his analysis of the Haitian situation regarded Haitian Creole as the Low variety of French. In each case, the High variety is said to be used in more formal, or public, or rhetorical or literary contexts; the Low variety in more familiar, relaxed contexts. Education is normally concerned in such countries with gaining a command of H, but 'The situation in formal education is often more complicated...In the Arab world, for example, formal university lectures are given in H, but drills, explanations and section meetings may be in large part conducted in L, especially in the natural sciences as opposed to the humanities. Although the teachers' use of L in secondary schools is forbidden by law in some Arab countries often a considerable part of the teacher's time is taken up with explaining in L the meaning in H which has been presented in books and lectures.' Many diglossic speakers are unwilling to admit to knowledge or use of L; even where they do, there is still a tendency to insist that H is the 'real language', the only one worth describing, that which must be kept pure and so forth. (The question of 'purism' in the diglossic Sinhalese-speaking community of Ceylon has been examined in detail by De Silva, 1967.) L is acquired as a mother tongue; H chiefly through formal education, with an explicit study of its grammatical 'rules'. Thus, the only overt concept of grammaticality which a diglossic speaker has is that relating to H, and this is bolstered by a strong tradition of grammatical study. Diglossic situations can be stable over many centuries if the supporting mechanisms are strong enough – a scriptural tradition, for example, as in the case of Arabic. The actual grammar of L tends to be 'simpler' than that of H, in that there are fewer morpheme-alternants, fewer obligatorily marked categories, the paradigms are more symmetrical, etc. H and L tend to have overlapping lexicons, but H will have many technical and learned terms lacking in L, and L many homely or localised terms lacking in H. The sound-systems of H and L constitute a single phonological structure. For examples of diglossia Ferguson cited Arabic, Modern Greek, Swiss German, Haitian Creole, Tamil; Latin and emergent Romance in the early Middle Ages in Europe; and Chinese.

3.3. Since that paper was published the term has been very widely extended in its use as sociolinguists identified some elements of his defining characteristics in communities they were investigating (for a general survey see Fishman, 1968 *a, b*). Moreover, it has become clear that in one sense Ferguson's original analysis obscured the fact that the definition of a language and of varieties of a language is more social than linguistic. That is, such statements as 'H is used on formal occasions' should often be re-phrased as 'people think they use, or intend to use, H on formal occasions'. A description of H may well be based on prescriptive grammars and literary texts, rather than on the competence of any informant; yet the exploration of the grammar of L through the intuitions of native speakers will be biased by the fact that the only grammatical categories and the only standards of 'correctness' or 'acceptability' known to them are associated with H. The position here is similar to that obtaining in many Creole-speaking and Black English communities, further discussed below in paragraph 5. See also Le Page (1973, 1975).

With the consideration of diglossic communities our discussion of multilingual situations has converged with that appropriate to more homogeneous communities, to which I shall now turn.

4. *Intra-language variation.* Studies under this heading may be divided into (*a*) those which are concerned with correlating linguistic variation with non-linguistic factors (geography, social class, age, sex, etc.) within communities assumed to be in some sense monolingual, and (*b*) those which do not make this assumption but explore what I have called processes of focussing and diffusion (see Le Page, 1975) within geographical or social communities in order to understand how the concept of membership of a language community, with the accompanying notion of norms of behaviour, comes into being or dissolves.

4.1. *Dialectology.* Under (*a*), classically we must begin with the linguistic atlases which have been such a feature of both historical and synchronic dialectology. The parameter they explore is geographical, but in doing so they reflect the migratory history both of people and of cultural artefacts and ideas. Cultural contact leads to externally motivated linguistic innovation, which in turn leads to internally motivated adjustment in linguistic systems (see especially Samuels, 1972; Weinreich, Labov & Herzog, 1968). The results of contact spread with time along the paths of communication within a community; no two parts of the community are equally affected by each result, nor coevally by the interaction between different internal adjustments in their dialect systems resulting from different contacts, and hence we have dialect differentiation. At the same time, other social, political, demographic, cultural and economic forces work towards standardisation and homogeneity, and affect different age, sex, geographical and social groups differentially.

The synchronic *mapping* of dialects usually sets out to reify the relational concepts about their similarities and differences that subgroups within a language community have about each other. (It has been the initial concern of The Tyneside Linguistic Survey, based on Newcastle University, to test the validity of the diagnostic criteria which people in the street use about each other's language as clues to place of origin, age, social class, etc. – see Pellowe, 1967.) Selected features have to be taken as a surrogate for linguistic descriptions: phonological, morphological, syntactic, lexical or semantic. One or two informants have to be taken as representative of each subgroup – typically, in the idealising dialectology of the late nineteenth or early twentieth century, the oldest untravelled man in each village. The techniques of elicitation of systematic linguistic features have ranged from postal questionnaires directed to local schoolmasters and parsons (the basis of Joseph Wright's *English dialect dictionary*, of the *Deutscher Sprachatlas* (Wenker & Wrede), and of the Linguistic Survey of Scotland – see McIntosh, Uldall & Jackson, 1951; McIntosh, 1961) to interviews between fieldworkers and informants (see, for example, Gillieron-Edmont, *passim*; Kurath, 1939, 1949; Cassidy, 1961) and the collection of texts for analysis from informants either in writing (see Grierson, 1903–28) or by mechanical recording (see Orton & Wright; Kolb, 1966; Orton & Dieth). (A convenient guide to all but the most recent of these surveys is contained in Sever Pop's *La dialectologie* (1950).) The material collected has been published in the form of both lists and maps; on the latter, isoglosses – geographical boundaries separating the locale of the users of one form or meaning from that of users of another are plotted, and where they coincide for a number of features are felt to represent dialect boundaries. In Kurath and McDavid (1961) variant pronunciations were for the first time (to my knowledge) plotted both on maps – to show geographical distribution – and on grids (phonetic variety against lexemes in which they occur) to show the functional load of phones within a local speech-variety.

4.2. The concepts 'isogloss' and 'bundles of isoglosses' are held to be relational properties of the communities whom the informants represent – that is, they divide geographically from one another groups of people whose linguistic behaviour differs in one or more respects. Their validity rests to some extent on a concept of relative homogeneity of usage *within* each group, whose behaviour the informants represented. Kurath and McDavid's grids reflect supposed properties of the communal *langue* in each community – properties of the system, rather than of communities. More recent sociolinguistic surveys have sought (*a*) to take account of the well-known *lack* of homogeneity of usage within all except the most isolated communities, by exploring along the further parameters of social and economic class, age groups and sex; (*b*) to take account of the knowledge that one group has of the usage of adjacent groups, as reflected in their variable usage, and to find a place therefore for variation as a property of the social system; (*c*) to take account of lack of regularity in the behaviour of individuals; (*d*) to reflect the theoretical position that all concepts of *langue* are in fact abstractions made by the observer – either the participant–observer, that is, the individual member of the speech-community, or the linguist–observer – from the behaviour of the members of the community and from its social artefacts (e.g. books, patterns of social intercourse, explicit and implicit rules and regularities, etc.).

The surveys discussed below and in paragraph 5 reflect one or more of these concerns, and serve to illustrate the problem of what 'competence' can mean, and how it can be described, when full account is taken of observed irregularities.

4.3. In his 1966 study, *The social stratification of English in New York City*, Labov accepted a socio-economic classification already carried out by social welfare workers with the inhabitants of the Lower East Side of the city, and showed that, in respect of selected phonological features such as the presence or absence of post-vocalic *r*, each group had at least two modes of behaviour. In their more formal behaviour – as elicited by himself as a fieldworker – they gave a phonetic value to the feature which approached more closely that of a higher socio-economic group, or that indicated by the spelling, than in their relaxed informal behaviour. Labov's statements now incorporated two relatively new features in dialect research: the concept of the sociolinguistic variable as a systematic feature in *langue*, and as part of the competence of individual speakers; and, latterly, the use of statistical statements to show the *extent* to which speakers, and their socio-economic groups, used one exponent of a variable rather than another in given contexts. Thus, the either/or statements of dialect geography, with boundaries of usage running between groups, were replaced by statements about social class tendencies – with each individual member of a class partaking of the tendencies of his class to a quantifiable extent. The sociolinguistic variable has been envisaged as having the same kind of systematic status in the description of the language of a stratified community as units such as 'phoneme' had in the description of a Saussurean *langue*. Subsequent refinements and modifications by Labov and others both of his theory and his elicitation techniques are referred to in paragraph 5. Here we may simply note that Labov's 1966 graphs present visually the adaptive mechanisms in the competence of various groups of speakers; they are statistical abstractions from many observed performances; we may infer from them something about the competence of individual speakers in different modes of behaviour but they are not descriptions of that competence.

Trudgill based his (1974) study of social class differentiation in the use of English in Norwich on techniques very similar to those of Labov. He explored more fully than Labov the sex variable (see especially Trudgill, 1972), showing that women are generally more strongly motivated to adapt to the model behaviour of a higher social class than men; and he sought to give a base within linguistic theory and description for the competence of Norwich speakers not only in their own dialect but – passively at least – in the phonological systems of speakers of other Norwich dialects. He made use of a variety of theoretical approaches in 'attempting to establish a common framework that will, in some sense, incorporate all types of Norwich English. We hope to show that these different types are derived from a single underlying framework that is the same for the whole community. We shall call this... (together with the rules which produce the different types and relate them to each other) the Norwich "diasystem"...constructed...within the theoretical framework of generative phonology. The diasystem...should provide a model of the linguistic competence of the individual as a native speaker of Norwich English *and* as a member of the Norwich speech community' (Trudgill, 1974, pp. 133–4). The technical details of the diasystem, by means of which the phonetic output of Norwich speakers of all varieties is generated from a common underlying inventory through rules marked for such social categories as age group and social class, are set out at length in his final chapter (8, pp. 133–93). Whereas, therefore,

Labov's 1966 statements were very much statistical analyses of performance, Trudgill's was an attempt at a 'competence' statement in a more closely Chomskyan sense.

5. *The sociolinguistic study of pidgins, creole languages and 'Black English'.* Although Creole language studies have a very respectable nineteenth-century ancestry in the work of Schuchardt, the first half of the present century saw only isolated figures at work – notably Robert A. Hall and John Reinecke. With the establishment of the Linguistic Survey of the British Caribbean in 1951 and the work (surveyed in DeCamp, 1971) that led to the first International Conference on Creole language studies in Jamaica in 1959 (Le Page, 1961), however, interest spread, especially in the United States; this quickened when parallel work began on 'Black English' in the 1960s.

5.1. Both areas of work (on Creole and on Black English) have been stimulated by the practical need to find answers to the problems of disadvantaged children in diglossic and comparable societies, where they happen to be black and the educational road to success is through acquiring a command of a High variety which is a property of whites. The failure of various remedial programmes relying on attempts to deal directly with the linguistic symptoms of underprivilege – that is, to teach the High variety to underprivileged children so that they can compete on equal terms in education – has led to a much needed reappraisal of sociolinguistic and psycholinguistic theory.

5.2. The terms 'pidgin', 'pidginisation', 'creole' and 'creolisation' have been defined in the following ways: (i) with respect to the linguistic properties of pidgin and creole languages; (ii) with respect to the social functions of these languages; (iii) with respect to the historical linguistic processes that gave shape to them; (iv) with respect to the social processes that gave rise to them. Frequently all four kinds of definition are involved, and for good reason therefore the study of these languages is seen as *necessarily* involving both linguistic and social, diachronic and synchronic considerations. The processes of pidginisation and creolisation have now been identified as occurring or having occurred in very many parts of the world where particular contact-situations have existed (see Le Page, 1957–8; Hall, 1966; Hymes, 1971 *passim*, and ICPCL *passim*). Creole languages are most frequently the broad vernaculars in situations similar to diglossic situations, except that the prestige language may or may not be another variety of the 'same language', and that there may be more or less of a continuum between the creole and the prestige or model language. Commonly within such communities there are individuals who can command any part of the linguistic continuum and others whose range is more limited. The extent to which the Black English situation can be considered in this category has been the subject of controversy (see, for example, Dillard, 1972).

5.3. Such situations are at an extreme from Chomsky's idealised speaker-hearer in a homogeneous community. How then can the 'competence' of members of such communities be described? What meaning will the term have? Can we retain the general theoretical framework of transformational–generative grammar, with its claims to offer the possibility of unique insights into learning and psychology? Or were these claims always illusory? It is my own belief that they were, and the *Sociolinguistic survey of multilingual communities*, which I shall come to last, has reinforced that belief and relies on quite different concepts of competence. On the other hand, Labov and G. Sankoff have so modified the Chomskyan framework while trying to stay inside it that it becomes almost unrecognisable, while scholars like DeCamp and Bickerton, who arrange sequences of grammars differing from one another by one rule at a time on implicational scales and find representatives among their informants for each grammar in the sequence, still do not manage thereby to capture the variable performance of the individual and to find 'rules' which describe either his competence or his motivation to shift from one grammar to another.

5.4. Labov, coming fresh to the creole situation at the 1968 Jamaican conference, acknowledged the challenge; in his paper ('The notion of "system" in creole studies', 1971) he finds, as have other linguists, that creoles and pidgins offer a number of challenges to the central linguistic concept of system, and he returns via creoles to Black English Vernacular with the observation that 'much of the behavior of young [Black American] children which can be cited as possible evidence for a Creole substratum shows *non-systematic* linguistic behavior...There is no regular rule to predict which of the various forms will be selected or distinguished...The use of a form of language for communication does not make it automatic that it forms a system (in the normal linguistic sense); the degree of systematicity is an empirical matter...there are enormous implications for linguistic theory in Creole studies; for developing our concept of system, and for the treatment of systematic variation' (pp. 447–9). It is illusory, he feels, to believe that all cases of variation can be resolved into invariant rules, dialect mixture or free variation. In some cases DeCamp's solution of invariant rules which differ from individual to individual in an implicational array is satisfactory; in some cases optional rules are an adequate account. 'But more often, we find that the optional or variable rules show considerable internal structure, and only by describing such structure in the form of variable constraints can we solve...the questions...' (p. 468). To reject these variable relationships from grammar on the grounds that they are matters of 'performance' rather than 'competence' is unhelpful. Chomsky's definition of linguistics (in *Aspects*, 1965) is too restricted; the distinction between competence and performance, Labov concludes, becomes less clear the more we consider its implications.

5.5. Gillian Sankoff ('A quantitative paradigm for the study of communicative competence', 1974) begins with a very capable survey of the various attempts which have been made to resolve problems of the kind she herself has confronted in the behavioural data in speakers of both Montreal French and of New Guinea Pidgin. 'It is my contention...that quantitative techniques can be fruitfully used in demonstrating not only the general patterns existing within a speech community, but also the subtle distinctions internalised by individuals which are based on the human ability to deal with differences of degree, both in producing speech and in interpreting the speech of others. A meaningful and realistic framework need not imply that if only the analyst could exercise enough ingenuity, all variation could be accounted for, deterministically, by specifying long enough lists of constraints' (pp. 19–20). There is no space here for a detailed discussion of the procedures by which she incorporates statistical information about the incidence of sociolinguistic variables into a competence model through a development of Labov's variable rules. (She rebuts Bickerton's (1971) criticism of variable rules, that it is difficult to demonstrate the mental processes which would have to exist to mediate a rule such as 'When you recognise environment X, use feature Y Z% of the time', by claiming that there is no evidence that the human brain can only work in all-or-nothing terms.) Her paper is important and calls for careful and detailed study. In the final analysis, however, it does build on a narrowly linguistic base: sociolinguistic competence resides in having *linguistic* rules, and in knowing when or with what frequency to apply them. Somewhat similar concepts underlie many other approaches to sociolinguistics: ideas of code (Hymes, 1967; Bernstein, 1958, 1970), of register (Halliday, 1973; Ellis & Ure, 1975), of linguistic repertoire (Gumperz, 1971 *passim*).

5.6. The concepts which underlie the *Sociolinguistic survey of multilingual communities* (see bibliography, Le Page, Tabouret-Keller *passim*) seek to develop a 'quantum linguistics' to avoid these problems, seen as arising from the Newtonian character of Chomskyan models of competence. A distinction is drawn between the theoretical 'rules' which are supposed to govern the behaviour of an individual when we consider him as an isolate, those rules which govern his behaviour in interaction with others, and those which the linguist–observer abstracts. The first, 'Language One' rules, are inaccessible to the observer and to the speaker's own intuition, since the moment he is asked about them he will be concerned not with his actual behaviour but with the rules he has created for some model group's supposed behaviour; but they would be semantically based – meaning being a property of language-in-use and not of codes – and not necessarily 'linguistically systematic' in the usual sense. The second, 'Language Two', is evidenced by a series of speech acts which are seen as acts of identity in which the individual proclaims both his individual identity and the social roles he wishes to adopt; these acts have the linguistic characteristics of 'instant pidgins', the rules for which are inherent not in any one individual but in the members of the interacting group. If one asks the actor

51

about his 'language' he is likely to reply with reference to Language Two, the rules of his model groups.

Using these concepts, the survey does not require that the linguistic features quantified from speech acts should be regarded as variables of linguistic units within grammars, since grammars in the Chomskyan sense are properties of Language Three, the linguist's artefact. It does, however, require that they are socially as well as linguistically significant; it is assumed, that is, that they are used because they are properties of the user's Language Two, and identified by him with one or other of his model groups. They are therefore felt to be sociolinguistic features from the outset. The approach is bound up with a socio-psychological theory of language which concentrates on the speaker's need to project his inner concepts on to the social screen by talking about them, by getting others to recognise them, by bringing them into focus with the concepts of others through the feedback provided by language. Individuals living in a homogeneous society may therefore have a highly focussed language, their Language One and Language Two may be closely similar, and the linguist may be reasonably safe in transferring to 'competence' systematic rules which he abstracts from Language Two. Those who live in a very heterogeneous society, however, may have a much more diffuse language, and the linguist then encounters the problems outlined in this section.

6. *Communicative competence, the ethnography of speaking; theories of learning.* Dell Hymes was responsible for introducing the terms 'communicative competence' and the 'ethnography of speaking' in order to continue the long American tradition of linguistically oriented anthropology within the theoretical concepts provided by linguists such as Labov. Among the papers reprinted in his *Language in culture and society* (1964) were classics by Boas, Sapir, Kroeber, Bloomfield, Malinowski, Firth, Whorf and Pike. He set out his approach to sociolinguistics in 'Sociolinguistics and the ethnography of speaking' in Ardener, 1971. Taking part in, and editing the papers of, the Jamaican pidginisation and creolisation conference of 1968 (Hymes, 1971) strongly influenced his views, as also Labov's. Even within some kind of Chomskyan or Saussurean theoretical framework, it is evident that one must not only know the grammar of one's language and of its subdivisions (e.g. dialect, styles, registers) but one must know how to use each grammar 'appropriately' and 'meaningfully'.

6.1. The conference which gave rise to the collection of papers *Social anthropology and language* (Ardener, 1971) was held to try to remedy what was felt to be a general neglect of linguistics by anthropologists in Britain (a neglect however disputed by Leach, 1974). The linguistic theories which most held Ardener's own attention ('Social anthropology and the historicity of historical linguistics', pp. 209–41) were 'generative' and 'transformational', building on Neogrammarian historical linguistics; the ideas which lay behind these linguistic theories were felt to be of importance to social anthropology and of general application in the study of society and social behaviour. Within the same volume, however, we find illustrated a distinctly non-Saussurean, non-Chomskyan approach: R. H. Robins discusses 'Malinowski, Firth and the context of situation' (pp. 33–46). An extended critique of Firth's theories from a Chomskyan point of view has been provided by Langendoen (1968); an exemplification, by Mitchell (1957); they underlie the approach of M. A. K. Halliday, whose systemic grammar has provided the linguistic framework both for his own work on learning (e.g. Halliday, 1973 *a*, *b*), that of Bernstein (q.v.) on the contrasting 'competence' of children of different social classes, and that of Ellis and Ure (q.v.) on language registers.

6.2. Linguistic anthropology, like the sociology of language, forces us to extend the concept of competence very considerably. I would instance not only the papers in Ardener (1971) but those in Bauman and Sherzer (1974) – for example, James J. Fox's '"Our ancestors spoke in pairs": Rotinese views of language, dialect and code' (pp. 65–85), which describes the antiphonic nature of Rotinese rhetorical usage and relates it to the distribution of dialects in the island. The anthropologists have not on the whole been as concerned as the psychologists or linguists with the question of how the child acquires his competence, and perhaps the fact that the 'rules' of communicative competence – apart from a few rather simple cases which have been investigated such as rules of address (see, for example, Brown & Gilman, 'The pronouns of power and solidarity', 1970; S. Ervin-Tripp, 'Sociolinguistics' in Fishman (1971), vol. 1) – are rather difficult to formulate concisely compared with grammatical rules, makes a model for the acquisition of these rules seem less tidy than a 'language acquisition device'. Nevertheless, attention today is constantly being drawn to parameters of variation in linguistic behaviour which transformational–generative grammar leaves out of account and which any viable theory of learning must take into account. This essay is intended to illustrate some of these; I am only too well aware that limitations of space have compelled me to leave out almost as much as I have been able to include.   *July 1975*

Addendum, July 1977

6.21. Social psychologists have recently developed their view of 'competence'. Gumperz (1971) and others had already designated as a 'linguistic repertoire' the range of linguistic systems, part-systems, codes or registers available to individuals for use in appropriate circumstances. To this Giles and Powesland (1975) and others add, *manner of speaking*; their 'social psychological model of speech diversity' is basically very similar to our own as set out in 5.6

R. B. Le Page

above (Le Page, 1968, 1975a, etc.). Speakers are seen as accommodating to each other in discourse, assuming relational roles, sharing a knowledge of the linguistic and paralinguistic cues of that accommodation.

6.22. Three further embryonic areas of study are in need of development. The first contextualises grammatical theory by re-integrating the relevant prosodic features (as had A. A. Hill in 1961) – those bases of our syntax which we learn first and are most reluctant to discard in second language learning. The study of code-switching or mixing in bilingual children may reveal a great deal about how they have processed incoming data to assign it either to distinct codes or to one mixed code; prosodic features may prove to be a key to help unlock this problem. The second I have already mentioned above: the relationship of literate to non-literate 'competence' (see e.g. De Silva, 1976a, b). It may be that there is no universality about any narrowly defined abstraction 'the language'; De Silva's studies of purism (still in progress) especially in India and Sri Lanka, are most suggestive on this point. In the third case, recent work on both pidgins (e.g. Sankoff & Brown, 1976) and sign languages (Deuchar, 1977) illuminates the evolution of linguistic systems from those which must be related to the immediate context towards the idealised 'context-free'; from a semantic and deictic base to a syntactic base; from concrete to abstract; from idiosyncratic to generalised; from the expressive and poetic towards the communicative and logical. Much of the weakness of linguistic theory lies in its preoccupation with the idealised; sociolinguistics must concern itself with the whole process.

References

Journals and other abbreviations
ICPCL   Papers presented at the International Congress on Pidgin and Creole Languages, Department of Linguistics, University of Hawaii, 6–10 January 1975.
IJSL   *International Journal of the Sociology of Language.* The Hague: Mouton.
JLAEA   *Journal of the Language Association of East Africa.* Nairobi: East African Publishing House.
LinSoc *Language in Society.* Cambridge University Press.
YPL   *York Papers in Linguistics.* University of York, Department of Language.

Abdulaziz, M. H. (1971). Tanzania's national language policy. In Whiteley, 160–78.
Ardener, Edwin (ed.) (1971). *Social anthropology and language.* London: Tavistock Publications.
Basso, K. (1974). The ethnography of writing. In Bauman & Sherzer, 425–32.
Bauman, Richard & Sherzer, Joel (1974). *Explorations in the ethnography of speaking.* Cambridge University Press.
Bernstein, Basil (1958). Some sociological determinants of perception. *British Journal of Sociology,* **9**, 159–74.
Bernstein, Basil (1970). A sociolinguistic approach to social learning. In Williams, *Language and poverty.* Markham.
Bickerton, Derek (1971). Inherent variability and variable rules. *Foundations of Language,* **7**, 457–92.

Bickerton, Derek (1975). *Dynamics of a creole system.* Cambridge University Press.

Brown, Roger (1965). *Social psychology.* New York: Free Press.

Brown, Roger (1970). *Psycholinguistics.* New York: Free Press.

Brown, Roger & Gilman, A. (1970). The pronouns of power and solidarity. In Brown, 302–35.

Canada (1967–70). *Report of the Royal Commission on bilingualism and biculturalism.* 5 vols. Ottawa: Queen's Printer.

Cassidy, F. G. (1961). *Jamaica talk.* London: Macmillan, for Institute of Jamaica, Kingston.

CCTA/CSA (1964). *Symposium on multilingualism, Brazzaville 1962.* London: CCTA/ CSA (Scientific Council for Africa South of the Sahara) Publication no. 87.

Chomsky, N. (1965). *Aspects of the theory of syntax.* Cambridge, Mass.: MIT Press.

Chomsky, N. & Halle, M. (1968). *The sound pattern of English.* New York: Harper.

DeCamp, David (1971). The study of pidgin and creole languages. In Hymes, 13–42.

De Silva, M. W. S. (1967). Effects of purism on the evolution of the written language: case history of the Sinhalese situation. *Linguistics,* **36,** 5–17.

De Silva, M. W. S. (1969). The phonological efficiency of the Maldivian writing system. *Anthropological Linguistics,* **11,** 199–209.

De Silva, M. W. S. (1976 *a*). *Diglossia and literacy.* Mysore: Central Institute of Indian Languages.

De Silva, M. W. S. (1967 *b*). *Linguistic diversity.* Annamalai University Press.

Deuchar, Margaret. (1977). Sign Language diglossia in a British deaf community. Linguistics Association of Great Britain Spring Meeting – mimeo.

Deutsch, K. W. (1953). *Nationalism and social communication.* New York: John Wiley.

Dillard, J. L. (1972). *Black English.* New York: Random House.

Ellis, J. & Ure, Jean (1974). The contrastive analysis of language registers. To appear in Nemser (ed.), *Trends in contrastive linguistics.* Prepublication draft, mimeo, Edinburgh University, Department of Linguistics.

Ervin-Tripp, Susan (formerly Susan Ervin) (1971). Sociolinguistics. In Fishman, vol. 1, 15–91.

Ervin-Tripp, Susan (1972). On sociolinguistic rules: alternation and co-occurrence. In Gumperz & Hymes (eds.), 213–50.

Évrard, E. (1966). Étude statistique sur les affinités de cinquante-huit dialectes bantous. In *Statistique et analyse linguistique.*

Ferguson, Charles A. (1959). Diglossia. *Word,* **15,** 325–40, reprinted in Hymes (1964), 429–39.

Ferguson, Charles A. (1971). Contrasting patterns of literacy acquisition in a multilingual nation. In Whiteley, 234–52.

Fishman, Joshua (1968 *a*). Societal bilingualism: stable and transitional. In Fishman (1973), 135–52.

Fishman, Joshua (1968 *b*). The description of societal bilingualism. In Fishman (1973), 153–61.

Fishman, Joshua (ed.) (1971/2). *Advances in the sociology of language.* 2 vols. The Hague: Mouton.

Fishman, Joshua A. (1973). *Language in sociocultural change: collected essays.* Stanford University Press.

Fishman, J., Cooper, R. L. & Ma, R. (eds.) (1971). *Bilingualism in the Barrio.* Indiana University Language Science Monographs, 7.

Fishman, J., Ferguson, C. A. & Das Gupta, J. (eds.) (1968). *Language problems of developing nations.* New York: John Wiley.

Fox, James J. (1974). 'Our ancestors spoke in pairs': Rotinese views of language, dialect and code. In Bauman & Sherzer, 65–85.

Giles, H. & Powesland, P. F. (1975). *Speech style and social evaluation.* London: Academic Press.

Gillieron, J. & Edmont, E. (1902–20). *L'atlas linguistique de la France.* (35 fasc.+ table+supplement). Paris: Champion.

Grierson, Sir George A. (1903–28). *Linguistic survey of India.* 11 vols. Calcutta; reprinted 1967. Delhi: Motilal Banarsidass.

Gumperz, J. J. (1964). Linguistic and social interaction in two communities. In Gumperz & Hymes, 137–53.

Gumperz, J. J. (1971). *Language in social groups: collected essays.* Stanford University Press.

Gumperz, J. J. & Hymes, Dell (1964). The ethnography of communication. Menasha, Wisconsin: *American Anthropologist*, 66.

Gumperz, J. J. & Hymes, Dell (eds.) (1972). *Directions in sociolinguistics.* New York: Holt.

Guthrie, Malcolm (1970). *An introduction to the comparative linguistics and prehistory of the Bantu languages.* 4 vols. London: Gregg.

Hall, Robert A., Jr. (1966). *Pidgin and Creole languages.* Ithaca: Cornell University Press.

Halliday, M. A. K. (1973 a). *Explorations in the functions of language.* London: Arnold.

Halliday, M. A. K. (1973 b). Language as social semiotic: towards a general sociolinguistic theory. Preprint, to appear in Makkai & Heilman, *Linguistics at the crossroads.* The Hague: Mouton.

Houis, M. (1971). *Anthropologie linguistique de l'Afrique noire.* Paris: Presses Universitaires de France.

Hymes, Dell (ed.) (1964). *Language in culture and society: a reader in linguistics and anthropology.* New York: Harper & Row.

Hymes, Dell (1967). Models of the interaction of language and the social setting. *Journal of Social Issues,* **23**, 8–28.

Hymes, Dell (ed.) (1971). *Pidginization and creolization of languages.* Cambridge University Press.

Itebete, P. A. N. (1974). Language standardization in Western Kenya: the Luluyia experiment. In Whiteley, 87–114.

Kelkar, Ashok R. (1975). The scope of a linguistic survey. In Ohannessian, Ferguson & Polomé, 7–12.

Kolb, E. (1966). *The phonological atlas of the Northern Region* [of England]. Bern: Francke Verlag.

Kloss, Heinz (1968). Notes concerning a language–nation typology. In Fishman, Ferguson & Das Gupta, 69–85.

Kurath, Hans (1939). *Handbook of the linguistic geography of New England.* Washington, D.C.: American Council of Learned Societies.

Kurath, Hans (1949). *A word geography of the eastern United States.* University of Michigan Press.

Kurath, H. & McDavid, R. (1961). *The pronunciation of English in the Atlantic States.* Ann Arbor: University of Michigan Press.

Labov, William (1966). *The social stratification of English in New York City.* Washington, D.C.: Center for Applied Linguistics.

Labov, William (1971). The notion of 'system' in creole studies. In Hymes, 447–72.

Langendoen, D. T. (1968). *The London school of linguistics: a study of the linguistic theories of B. Malinowski and J. R. Firth.* Cambridge, Mass.: MIT Press.

Lass, Roger (1975). *English phonology and phonological theory.* Cambridge University Press (to appear).

Leach, Edmund (1974). Review of Hilary Henson, *British social anthropologists and language. Times Literary Supplement,* 19 July.

Le Page, R. B. (1957-8). General outlines of Creole English in the Caribbean. *Orbis,* **6,** 373-91, and **7,** 54-64.

Le Page, R. B. (ed.) (1960, 1961). *Creole Language Studies,* 2 vols. London: Macmillan.

Le Page, R. B. (1964, 1966, 1971). *The national language question.* Oxford University Press.

Le Page, R. B. (1968). Problems of description in multilingual communities. *Transactions of the Philological Society,* 189-212.

Le Page, R. B. (1973). The concept of competence in a creole/contact situation. YPL, **3,** 31-50.

Le Page, R. B. (1975 a). 'Projection, focussing and diffusion', or, steps towards a sociolinguistic theory of language. To appear in *Journal of Creole Studies,* **2,** 2 (1978).

Le Page, R. B. (1975 b). Polarising factors: political, social, economic, operating on the individual's choice of identity through language use in British Honduras. In Jean-Guy Savard & Richard Vigneault (eds.), *Les états multilingues/Multilingual political systems.* Quebec: Les presses de l'Université Laval.

Le Page, R. B. (1977). Processes of pidginization and creolization. In A. Valdman (ed.), *Pidgin and Creole linguistics.* Bloomington: Indiana University Press.

Le Page, R. B., Christie, P., Jurdant, B., Weekes, A. J. & Tabouret-Keller, A. (1974). Further report on the sociolinguistic survey of multilingual communities. LinSoc. **3,** 1-32.

Lewis, E. Glyn (1971). Migration and language in the USSR. *International Migration Review,* **5,** 147-79, and Fishman, vol. 2.

Lieberson, Stanley (1966 a). Language questions in censuses. In Lieberson (1966 b), 134-51.

Lieberson, Stanley (ed.) (1966 b). *Explorations in sociolinguistics.* The Hague: Mouton.

McIntosh, Angus (1961). *An introduction to a survey of Scottish dialects.* Edinburgh: Nelson.

McIntosh, A., Uldall, H. J. & Jackson, K. (1951). Postal questionnaire for *The linguistic survey of Scotland.* University of Edinburgh, Department of English Language and General Linguistics, Department of Celtic.

Malinowski, B. (1934). *Coral gardens and their magic.* London.

Mitchell, T. F. (1957). The language of buying and selling in Cyrenaiaca. *Hespéris,* **44,** 31-71.

Mohamed Bakari Mohamed (1975). *The political sociology of language in East Africa.* University of York Department of Language: unpublished B.Phil. dissertation.

Ohannessian, Sirarpi & Ansré, G. (1975). Some reflections on the uses of sociolinguistic surveys. In Ohannessian, Ferguson & Polomé (1975), 51-69.

Ohannessian, Sirarpi, Ferguson, C. A. & Polomé, E. (1975). *Language surveys in developing nations.* Arlington, Virginia: Center for Applied Linguistics.

Orton, H. & Dieth, E. (eds.) (1962 on). *Survey of English dialects.* Leeds: Arnold (publication of volumes still in progress).

Orton, H. & Wright, Nathalia (1974). *A word geography of England.* London: Seminar Press.

Pandit, P. B. (1975). The linguistic survey of India – perspectives on language use. In Ohannessian, Ferguson & Polomé (1975).

Parkin, David J. (1971). Language choice in two Kampala housing estates. In Whiteley, 347-63.

Pellowe, J. (1967). *Studies towards a classification of varieties of spoken English.* Department of English, University of Newcastle upon Tyne: unpublished M.Litt. thesis.

Pitman, Sir James & St John, John (1969). *Alphabets and reading.* London: Pitman.
Polomé, Edgar (1971 a). Multilingualism in an African urban centre: the Lubumbashi case. In Whiteley, 362–75.
Polomé, Edgar (1971 b). The Katanga (Lubumbashi) Swahili creole. In Hymes, 57–60.
Pop, S. (1950). *La dialectologie.* 2 vols. 1, *Dialectologie Romane*; 2, *Dialectologie non Romane.* Louvain, chez l'auteur: 185 avenue des Alliés.
Prator, Clifford H. (1975). The survey of language use and language teaching in Eastern Africa in retrospect. In Ohannessian, Ferguson & Polomé.
Pride, J. B. (1971). *The social meaning of language.* Oxford University Press.
Rice, Frank A. (ed.) (1962). *Study of the role of second languages in Asia, Africa and Latin America.* Washington, D.C.: Center for Applied Linguistics.
Robins, R. H. (1971). Malinowski, Firth and the concept of situation. In Ardener (1971), 33–46.
Robinson, W. P. (1972). *Language and social behaviour.* Penguin Books.
Rustow, D. A. (1968). Language, modernization, and nationhood – an attempt at a typology. In Fishman, Ferguson & Das Gupta, 87–105.
Samuels, M. L. (1972). *Linguistic evolution, with special reference to English.*
Sankoff, Gillian (1974). A quantitative paradigm for the study of communicative competence. In Bauman & Sherzer.
Sankoff, G. & Brown, P. (1976). The origins of syntax in discourse. *Language,* **52,** 3, 631–66.
Schuchardt, Hugo E. M. (1882–8). *Kreolische studien,* 1–8. Vienna.
Seckbach, Fern (1974). Attitudes and opinions of Israeli teachers and students about aspects of modern Hebrew. IJSL, 105–24.
Spencer, John (ed.) (1963). *Language in Africa – Papers of the Leverhulme conference on universities and the language problems of tropical Africa.* Cambridge University Press.
Sprott, W. J. H. (1958). *Human groups.* Penguin Books.
Statistique et analyse linguistique (1966). Colloque de Strasbourg, Faculté des Lettres et Sciences Humaines, Centre de philologie et de littératures romanes, 1964. Paris: Presses Universitaires de France.
Tabouret-Keller, Andrée (1968). Sociological factors of language maintenance and language shift. In Fishman, Ferguson & Das Gupta, 107–18.
Tabouret-Keller, Andrée (1971). Language use in relation to the growth of towns in West Africa: a survey. *International Migration Review,* **5,** 2, 180–203.
Tabouret-Keller, Andrée (1972). A contribution to the sociological study of language maintenance and language shift. In Fishman, vol. 2, 365–76.
Tabouret-Keller, Andrée (1975). Un champ sémantique: les noms d'identité raciale au Honduras Britannique (Cayo District). *La Linguistique,* **1.**
Tabouret-Keller, Andrée & Le Page, R. B. (1971). L'enquête sociolinguistique à grande échelle. Un exemple: Sociolinguistic survey of multilingual communities, part I, British Honduras survey. *La Linguistique,* **6,** 103–18.
Thompson, Roger M. (1974). Mexican American language loyalty and the validity of the 1970 census. IJSL, **2,** 7–18.
Trudgill, P. (1972). Sex, covert prestige and linguistic change in the urban British English of Norwich. LinSoc, **1,** 179–96.
Trudgill, P. (1973). *The social differentiation of English in Norwich.* Cambridge University Press.
Trudgill, P. (1974). *Sociolinguistics.* Pelican Books.
UNESCO (1953). *Monographs on fundamental education,* VIII: *The use of vernacular languages in education.* Paris.

Valdman, Albert (1968). Language standardization in a diglossic situation: Haiti. In Fishman, Ferguson & Das Gupta.

Weinreich, Uriel, Labov, W. & Herzog, Marvin I. (1968). Empirical foundations for a theory of language change. In Lehman & Malkiel, *Directions for historical linguistics.* University of Texas Press.

Wenker, Georg & Wrede, Ferdinand (1928). *Deutscher Sprachatlas.* Marburg (Lahn): N.G. Elwert'sche Verlagsbuchhandlung (G. Braun).

Whiteley, W. H. (1969). *Swahili: the rise of a national language.* London: Methuen.

Whiteley, W. H. (ed.) (1971). *Language use and social change; problems of multilingualism with special reference to Eastern Africa.* Oxford University Press for International African Institute.

Whiteley, W. H. (ed.) (1974). *Language in Kenya, Ethiopia, Tanzania, Uganda, Zambia.* Nairobi: Oxford University Press.

Wright, Joseph (1961). *English dialect dictionary.* Oxford University Press.

ERROR ANALYSIS, INTERLANGUAGE AND SECOND LANGUAGE ACQUISITION

S. P. Corder
University of Edinburgh

1.

In the course of learning a second language, learners regularly produce utterances in speech and writing which judged by the rules of the second language are erroneous, or ill-formed. Traditionally the attitude to errors was that they were a sign that the learner had not yet mastered the rules he was taught and that they were therefore to be dealt with by repeating the explanations until they disappeared. If learning were efficient errors would not occur. This point of view gave way later to the notion that errors were an indication of the difficulties the learners had with certain aspects of the language, which could be explained by the persistence of the habits of the mother tongue and their transfer to the new language (Lado, 1957). In this case they were to be dealt with not by further explanation of the target language rules but by more intensive drilling of the sound patterns and sentence structure of the language. Errors were the result of interference and in an ideal teaching situation could be avoided. The difficulties of learners could be predicted by a comparison or contrast between the structures of the mother tongue and the target language and appropriate steps could then be taken to minimise the difficulty and reduce the interference. From this notion has developed the whole industry of 'contrastive linguistics', with research projects and regular publications of results in a number of countries. The body of literature in this field is very large and although increasingly seen as related to the field here being reviewed, merits separate treatment. Several bibliographies on the topic are available (cf. Thiem, 1969). For an authoritative recent statement of the 'classical' position see Nickel (1971a) and for a critical study of the 'state of the art', Eliasson (1973).

In more recent years doubts have increasingly been voiced about the status and applicability of contrastive linguistic studies to language teaching (Ritchie, 1967; Nemser, 1971; Slama-Cazacu, 1971; Dulay & Burt, 1974d), firstly because not all difficulties and errors can be traced back to the influence of the mother tongue (Richards, 1971a; Dulay & Burt, 1973; Dušková, 1969) and consequently other explanations must be sought; secondly, what contrastive analysis predicted as a difficulty did not always in practice turn out to be so (Nickel, 1971b); and thirdly, the purely theoretical problems of making adequate comparisons of languages made the whole operation of doubtful validity (Hamp, 1968; Van Buren, 1974; Krzeszowski, 1974). As a result the theoretical basis for such studies has been questioned and its value for language teaching reappraised. Wardhaugh (1970) makes a clear distinction between the strong and weak hypothesis of contrastive linguistics. The strong hypothesis states that the difficulties of the learner can be *predicted* by a systematic contrastive analysis and teaching materials can then be devised to meet these difficulties. The weak hypothesis claims no more than an *explanatory* role for contrastive linguistics: where difficulties are evident from the errors made by learners, then comparison between the mother tongue and the second language may help to explain them. A reasoned reply to all these criticisms has been made by Nehls (1974) and notably by James (1971a) in which he argues that analysts have never explicitly made many of the claims for which they are attacked. Nevertheless there has been a gradual abandonment by contrastive analysts since 1968 of the stronger claims and, increasingly, research projects in this area have broadened their scope in two directions: firstly towards more theoretical objectives in language typology and the search for universals (always a preoccupation of one branch of linguistic enquiry); and secondly towards psycholinguistic orientation concerned with the explanation of second language acquisition. Here it merged significantly with *error analysis* as we shall see. This new development of contrastive analysis has been called 'contact analysis' (Nemser & Slama-Cazacu, 1970; Slama-Cazacu, 1971). These authors suggest that the task of contact analysis is to 'explain and predict language learner behaviour, with the concrete aim of developing a more scientific approach to the processes of foreign language teaching'.

2. *Error analysis*

There are now a number of general statements of the 'state of the art' which give a general comprehensive account of what error analysis is concerned with: Nickel (1972) in German; Lange (1974) in French; and Corder (1973), Svartvik (1973), Richards and Sampson (1974), and Schumann and Stenson (1975) in English.

Contrastive analysis developed in a climate in linguistics and psychology which can be broadly characterised as 'structural' and 'behaviourist'. 'Structuralism' in linguistics took the view that the structure of every language was *sui generis* and therefore to be described in its own terms. Consequently it followed logically that languages could not be compared. It was therefore somewhat paradoxical to attempt to account for learners' difficulties, which were clearly related to features of their mother tongue and explained psychologically as the transfer of their mother-tongue habits by undertaking a theoretically impossible task. With post-structuralist developments in linguistics, associated with the name of Chomsky, a willingness to seek common or even universal features in human languages became again a goal of linguistics, but now explicitly explained in psychological terms as inherent properties of the human mind. Language acquisition and second-language learning could now be approached as a problem of cognitive learning and the possession of a second language was seen as the possession of knowledge of a certain kind ('competence') rather than as a set of dispositions to respond in a certain way to external stimuli. A language user possesses a set of cognitive structures acquired by some process of data-processing and hypothesis formation in which the making of errors was evidence of the learning process itself and probably not only inevitable but necessary (Dulay & Burt, 1974*d*). It now became relevant to study a learner's linguistic performance in detail in order to infer from it the nature of that knowledge and the processes by which it was acquired. From the insights gained from such investigations one might be able to adapt the teaching methods and materials in order to facilitate the process of acquisition. Central to the investigations was the analysis of the errors made by learners since they represented the most significant data on which a reconstruction of his knowledge of the target language could be made. This is essentially the point of view presented by Corder (1967). He speculated that the processes of first- and second-language acquisition were fundamentally the same and suggested that when the utterances of first- and second-language learners differed, as clearly they did, these differences could be accounted for by differences in maturational development, motivation for learning and the circumstances of learning. The learner was seen as constructing for himself a grammar of the target language on the basis of the linguistic data in the language to which he was exposed and the help he received from teaching. This process has been called the 'creative construction hypothesis' by Dulay and Burt (1974*b*) following Roger Brown (1973). The grammar he created for himself is referred to by Nemser (1971) as an 'approximative system'. These systems are evidently 'transient' and the systematic nature of these systems is proved by 'the regularity of patterning of errors in perception and production of a given target language by learners sharing the same mother tongue'. James (1974) finds this proposal paradoxical. 'How can a system remain a system if it is in flux?' He speaks of a fictitious 'homeostasis'. To adopt this point of view, however, is to deny the possibility of all language description with available theoretical models. All languages are in a state of flux. The notion of *état de langue* is a necessary idealisation upon which all linguistics is founded.

Nemser does, however, allow that stable varieties of 'approximative systems' are found, for example in immigrant speech where the learners have 'reached a plateau' in their learning. Selinker (1972) devotes considerable space to this phenomenon of 'fossilization' as he calls it. These approximative systems are referred to by Corder (1971 a) as 'idiosyncratic dialects' of the target language, a point taken up by James (1971 b) when he refers to language learning as a process of dialect expansion and points out that he has referred to what Nemser calls approximative systems as the phenomenon of 'interlingua'.

Selinker (1972) in an influential paper refers to this same phenomenon as 'interlanguage'. This term emphasises the structurally intermediate status of the learner's language system between mother tongue and target language, whilst Nemser's term, 'approximative system', emphasises the transitional and dynamic nature of the system. Both terms have now received wide acceptance in the literature of error analysis and second-language learning.

3. *Lapses and mistakes*

Chomsky makes a distinction between what a speaker knows of his language (competence) and how he uses it for communicative purposes (performance). Native speakers are assumed to have a perfect knowledge of the systems of their mother tongue, but they nevertheless produce utterances which are judged 'ungrammatical' by other native speakers. It is necessary, therefore, to make an equivalent systematic distinction between errors, typically produced by people who do not yet fully command some institutionalised language system (e.g. learners or dialect speakers) and mistakes or lapses, which are failures to utilise a known system correctly (Corder, 1971 a). The native speaker is normally capable of recognising and correcting such lapses or mistakes, which are not the result of a deficiency in 'competence' but the result of some neurophysiological breakdown or imperfection in the process of encoding and articulating speech. These phenomena have been studied by linguists and phoneticians interested in explaining the process of speech perception and production (Boomer & Laver, 1968; Fromkin, 1973; Bierwisch, 1970). These studies give us insights into the actual production and processing of speech but are not relevant to the explanation of language learning. It is, however, necessary when undertaking error analysis of learners utterances to be able to distinguish between lapses and errors, since language learners are subject to the same failures in their performance in the second language. Unfortunately the important terminological distinction drawn here is not always carefully observed by all writers.

4. *Methods in error analysis*

The significance of the study of learners' errors given so far has been seen in its relevance to reconstructing the learner's 'approximative system' at any particular stage in his learning career, rather than providing the practising teacher with information and insight of a practical sort in the developing of teaching materials and classroom practices, e.g. corrective or remedial procedures. At this point we must note that error analysis can be seen to serve two related but distinct functions (Zydatiss, 1974a; Strevens, 1969). The one, pedagogical and 'applied' in aim, and the other, theoretical, leading to a better understanding of second-language learning processes and strategies. More will be said of each of these functions, but common to both aims is the need for an adequate *linguistic* explanation of the nature of the errors found in any particular learning situation. We are here concerned with the methodology of description. Until we are able to give a linguistic account of the nature of learners' errors we can neither propose pedagogical measures to deal with them nor infer from them anything about the processes of learning. However, even here the divergent aims of error analysis have a relevance. To understand the learning process we must study the development of individual learners in relation to their particular learning settings, social and linguistic, whilst pedagogical objectives are served by the study of errors in the performance of learning groups, i.e. groups of learners, homogeneous in terms of age, sex, stage of learning or mother tongue (Corder, 1973). This difference of objective determines the data for analysis. It is at this point that a useful terminological distinction has been proposed by Svartvik (1973). He suggests that the term 'error analysis' should be reserved for the study of erroneous utterances produced by groups of learners at some stage of their learning career and 'performance analysis' for the study of the whole performance data (not just erroneous utterances) from individual learners in the longitudinal studies called for by Corder (1973) and Hammarberg (1973).

For pedagogical purposes we need to know what are the principal learning difficulties of groups of learners (their well-formed utterances are assumed to be evidence of an absence of difficulty). To achieve this we need a *qualitative* linguistic classification of errors, and a *quantitative* statement of the relative frequency of each type of error. We need further some *evaluation* of the gravity of each type of error from a communicative or pedagogical point of view, so that we may assign priorities to the treatment of each problem, and finally we need some *explanation* of the cause of each type of error so that we undertake appropriate remedial measures.

4.1. *Classification of errors*
The traditional classification into errors of omission, addition, substitution and word order is too superficial to be of benefit to the learner or to explain difficulties (Corder, 1972). Satisfactory classifications begin with an analysis which assigns errors to levels of language description, i.e. errors of orthography or phonology, of morphology or syntax, of vocabulary, and within each level

according to systems, e.g. vowel or consonant systems, tense, aspect, number, gender or case. More recent classifications attempt to explain errors linguistically within the framework of various generative and transformational models of description. In such cases errors are described in terms of breaches of the rules of the grammar or phonology. The more descriptively adequate the aims of the classification are the more difficult the task.

In order to make a classification one must first distinguish between mistakes and errors and determine that error is in fact present. Not all apparently well-formed utterances are error-free (Corder 1971*b*) nor is error-free performance any indication that the learning goal has been reached (Levelt, forthcoming). In order to identify the presence and nature of an error an interpretation of the learner's utterance is necessary, but it is not always easy to know what the learner was trying to say. Hence the central role of interpretation in the techniques of error analysis (Corder, 1972). Many formally erroneous utterances are potentially ambiguous even when taking the context into account. Often it is only possible to discover the learner's communicative intent by asking him what he means. But access to the learner is also necessary because learners do not necessarily provide sufficient evidence to build a picture of their approximative system from their spontaneous utterances alone (Dušková, 1969). Therefore techniques of *controlled* elicitation, i.e. tests which force the learner to reveal some specific aspect of his interlanguage, are necessary (Corder, 1974*a*; Zydatiss, 1974*c*). These controlled elicitation techniques are of various sorts: multiple choice tests, translation tests, imitation tests (Naiman, 1974; Swain, Dumas & Naiman, 1974). It may even be useful to get the learner to introspect about his knowledge (Kellerman, 1974). Techniques of controlled elicitation are however not easy to apply in the case of young children and consequently investigations of child second-language learning have resorted to techniques similar to those proposed by Brown (1973) for the study of first-language acquisition. Thus, Burt, Dulay and Hernandez (1973) use a technique they have called the bilingual syntax measure which is an instrument designed to elicit natural speech from children, not specific responses, so that the proficiency with which the child uses certain specific grammatical structures can be logged.

4.2. *Evaluation*

The need to make judgements on errors derives from two sources: firstly the need to assess a learner's knowledge for administrative purposes (the assignment of grades/marks) and secondly to determine priorities for remedial measures. For a general discussion of evaluation see Nickel (1972, 1973). Attempts have been made to use linguistic criteria for the establishment of error *gravity*. James (1974) proposes an assessment based upon the number and nature of the rules transgressed in order to measure the degree of deviance of an error from the correct target language form and Olsson (1972) distinguishes between syntactic and semantic errors. An alternative linguistic evaluation is to be found in Burt and Kiparsky (1975). They make a hierarchical distinction between *global errors* which involve deviance in the overall structure of sentences and *local errors* involving the structure of constituents of simple sentences or subordinate clauses. Another approach to evaluation is to measure the degree of disturbance an error may have on the efficiency of communication in terms of its frequency, generality or comprehensibility (Johanssen, 1973), or to measure its gravity by the degree of tolerance extended to it by native speakers or language teachers (Lindell, 1973; Johanssen, forthcoming; James, 1975; Olsson, 1973, 1974). The problem of the relationship between the degree of linguistic deviance of an error as determined by some sort of linguistic measure and its comprehensibility or intolerability to native-speaking judges is still far from being understood.

4.3. Explanation

Whereas identification and description of errors is a matter for linguistics, the explanation of errors is a matter for the psychology of second language learning: it bridges the gap between *error analysis* as a pedagogical exercise and *performance analysis* as part of the investigation into the processes of second-language learning. In order to deal with errors teachers must be able to account for why they occurred, but in the broader considerations of performance analysis, it is the learner's whole performance which is in focus. Here no distinction is made between 'erroneous' and 'correct' utterances. Both are evidence of the learners approximative system at a particular stage in his interlanguage development (Corder, 1971 *b*). What is of interest is how his approximative system as a whole came to be as it is.

It is usual in error analysis to identify three principal causes for error (Richards, 1971 *b*): *language transfer* (Selinker, 1969) gives rise to *interlingual* errors, in which the learner's errors are accounted for by interference from the mother tongue. George (1972) found that as many as one third of the deviant sentences of learners could be attributable to this cause. Other workers have found similar or greater proportion (Grauberg, 1971; Dušková, 1969). In the case of child learners, however, as low a proportion as 3 per cent could be ascribed to this cause (Dulay & Burt, 1973). It is clear that many factors play a part in causing transfer errors: age of learner being the principal one, but also the formality of the learning situation and the method of teaching.

A second class of error has been called 'intralingual' by Richards (1971 *b*). These errors do not reflect features of the mother tongue, but result from the learning process itself. Learners are seen to make inductive generalisations about the target language system on the basis of the data to which they are exposed. Since the data is necessarily restricted they will tend to overgeneralise and produce incorrect forms by analogy. This type of error has been well documented by Jain (1974). The result of this process is to reduce the target language system to an apparently 'simpler' form (Richards, 1974*b*) or more 'regular' system (Slama-Cazacu, 1974). These types of error may also be regarded as *developmental* (Dulay & Burt, 1973), since similar processes are regularly observed in child language acquisition studies. Since errors having this provenance are independent of the mother tongue of the learner, one will find that they are common to all learners of any given second language. This provides some theoretical validity to the collections of 'common errors' which have been made from time to time (Fitikides, 1967; French, 1949; Ballard, 1970).

A third source of error is assigned to faulty teaching techniques or materials. Richards (1971*a*) calls this process 'hypothesizing false concepts'. Little systematic study of this cause of error has been made and, clearly, errors not readily classed as inter- or intra-lingual cannot be confidently assigned for this reason to this third category. Only prolonged observation of sets of learners in the learning situation permits the identification of such a cause of error. A recent study by Stenson (1975) is the fullest account available so far of what she calls 'induced errors'. Corder (1973) regards this class of error as the only *redundant error* from a language learning point of view. This same source of error is accounted for, somewhat idiosyncratically, by Selinker (1972) under the rubric of 'transfer of training', not to be confused with *language transfer* as a source of error. A recent interesting analysis of error from a psychological 'skill theory' approach with pedagogical implications is that of Levelt (forthcoming).

The number of published and unpublished descriptions of errors found in corpuses drawn from different teaching situations is very large. The most recent comprehensive bibliography of works on error analysis and related topics (Valdman, 1975) lists no less than 246 separate case studies, the majority of these having been produced in the last ten years and carried out in the light of the sort of theoretical orientations already outlined. They cover principally errors made by learners of English, French, German and Spanish from varying linguistic backgrounds and tend to deal separately with errors of syntax, pronunciation, spelling and vocabulary.

5. *Performance analysis*

A distinction has been drawn between studies of errors with a pedagogical objective of pointing to the development of appropriate remedial techniques and materials, and performance analysis, the study of the learner's language system in order to discover the psychological processes of second language learning. Selinker (1972) postulates five central processes, as he calls them, which are effective in determining the nature of a learner's interlanguage: *language transfer*, already discussed, *transfer of training*, i.e. teaching induced (incorrect) hypotheses about the target language, *strategies of second language learning*, the learning strategies of the individual learner, which leads him to purely idiosyncratic hypotheses about the target language, such as a preference for holistic learning rather than an inductive analytic approach (cf. Cancino, Rosansky & Schumann, 1974). Hatch (1974) contrasts such learners as 'data-gatherers' or 'rule-formers'. The fifth process Selinker identifies is *strategies of second language communication*. Strictly speaking, this is not a process of second-language learning, but is invoked to account for the phenomenon of *fossilisation*. This is a state of affairs when the learner ceases to elaborate or 'complexify' his approximative system in some respect, however long he is exposed to new data or new teaching. Selinker notes the important fact that learners regularly *regress* to an earlier approximative system under particular circumstances of communicative need.

The study of strategies of communication has been taken further by other investigators. The notion is that second-language learners adopt certain identifiable strategies when faced with the need to communicate with a less than adequate interlanguage system. Levenston (1971) identifies such features as *over-formality* or *over-informality, verbosity, use of substandard forms, underdifferentiation, interchangeability, archaism* as the unintended stylistic results of this inadequacy. Váradi (1973) compares the same messages in the mother tongue and the interlanguage of the learner to investigate how the learner copes with his communication problem, whilst Richards (1972) points to *simplification* as the result of such communication strategies and draws attention to the important structural similarities between pidgins and interlanguage: Linnarud (1975) compares the lexical usages of learners and native speakers in similar communication tasks, whilst Zydatiss (1973) investigates the availability of various 'thematising processes' in the interlanguage of German learners of English. Widdowson (forthcoming) treats the learner's performance as evidence of the possession of idiosyncratic 'rules of expression' in his 'communicative competence' in the target language. There is still a great deal of work to be done in understanding how learners use their interlanguage to achieve their communicative purposes.

6. *Second-language acquisition studies*

In section 2 an account was given of the 'creative construction' hypothesis of second-language learning, which proposed that the learner created for himself a series of hypotheses about the grammar of the target language by some process of data-processing, hypothesis formation and testing. In this theory all utterances made by learners serve to test his hypothesis and his errors are evidence of false hypotheses. The making of errors is a necessary part of language learning. As Dulay and Burt (1974d) say, 'You can't learn without goofing.' In their important series of investigations into child second-language acquisition (Dulay & Burt, 1972, 1973, 1974 *a, b, c*) they classify the errors of child learners into four categories: interference goofs, mother-tongue developmental goofs, ambiguous goofs and unique goofs. This categorisation is readily relatable to the classifications already reported above, but what is significant is that they are able to show that the distribution and nature of these errors is substantially the same as that of children acquiring their mother tongue. The only difference is a very small proportion of interference phenomena. This leads them to postulate the L 1 = L 2 hypothesis, which states that the learning of a second language is fundamentally the same process, at least in children, as the learning of a first language and that sequential development of the approximative systems is substantially the same in both cases whatever the mother tongue of the learner. Such research has naturally led to a revival of interest in the relationship between first- and second-language learning and to its relevance for language pedagogy (Cook, 1969, 1973; Ervin-Tripp, 1970; Newmark & Reibel, 1969; Taylor, 1974). Ervin-Tripp (1974) suggests from her investigations that older children may regress to processing strategies similar to those in first-language acquisition when faced with data in a second language. Hence the occurrence of utterances bearing no superficial resemblance to either the first or the second language.

These studies suggest that there may be some universal processing strategies of language learning which lead to a similar natural sequence of approximative system in all child second-language learners. These hypotheses have been carefully examined by Hatch (1974) in the light of the now substantial body of longitudinal studies of child second-language learners, unfortunately mostly unpublished. For published accounts see Cancino *et al.* 1974; Ravem, 1971; Dato, 1972; Dulay and Burt, 1974*a*; Hakuta, 1974; Milon, 1974. For a critical discussion of the work of Dulay and Burt, see Tarone (1974).

These studies have largely been on children, and the circumstances in which they have learned the second language have generally been informal. The question which still has to be resolved is the influence of the learning setting, the nature of language data and the communication functions of the second language on the learning process. Does this influence the 'natural' sequence and nature of the approximative systems which are developed? It is clear that if there is any truth in the speculation (Corder, 1967) that second-language learners might have 'built-in syllabuses' for learning second languages, as infants appear to be 'programmed' to learn their mother tongue (Brown, 1973), such knowledge would be of immense value for the design and sequencing of instructional materials.

7. *Simplified linguistic systems*

The discussion of the learner's language system so far has been in the light of linguistic and psycholinguistic notions. Language is a means whereby human beings communicate with each other in a social setting. The nature of the learner's approximative system as he constructs it must be sensitive to the needs he feels to be able to use it for communicative purposes. As Schumann (1974) points out, the need to elaborate and develop his approximative system is a response to the learner's widening communicative needs. When these are restricted, as they are when the learner does not seek integration into the target language community, a simpler version of the target language system emerges (Richards, 1972). This interlanguage system is seen to be structurally simpler by comparison with the fully complex target model. It has now become evident that interlanguage systems may often bear considerable resemblances to other simple linguistic codes such as pidgins and creoles, which are now recognised to bear strong resemblances to each other whatever their linguistic provenance. This is particularly true when the interlanguage systems have developed in informal learning settings. Clyne (1968) noted, for example, the strong resemblances of the interlanguage of immigrant workers in German whatever their mother tongues, and the similarity of these to pidgins. It is now generally agreed that the structural simplicity of pidgins is a result of their limited communicative function; development into a creole is a result of the broadening functional needs of their speakers. Thus the process of elaboration (creolisation) occurs when the need to express social identity and affective functions is felt. The same needs may account for the development of the mother tongue in infants. For this reason the study of pidginization and creolisation may yield valuable insights into the second-language learning process. Valdman (forthcoming) points out that creolists have recently shifted their interest towards the social-psychological processes underlying the development of pidgins and creoles and that this has brought these studies closer to the interests of those concerned with second language learning processes. Richards (1974b) suggests that simplification is perhaps a 'universal learning strategy'. We have already noted the process of overgeneralisation in learning and seen that this results in approximative systems which are structurally simpler than those of the target language. Samarin (1971) has even posited that there may be 'universal rules of simplification'. However, as Corder (forthcoming) has pointed out, we cannot simplify what we do not possess and a language learner can scarcely be said to be simplifying the rules of the target language in any psychological sense. What results from his learning strategies may however result in a system which is linguistically simpler.

Interlanguages and pidgins are not the only simple codes which we meet. Ferguson (1971) draws attention to the fact that language communities regularly use institutionalised and stereotyped codes for special communicative functions which are also simple in the same sense, and that these codes resemble, structurally, interlanguage systems. Such reduced codes as foreigner-talk (Ferguson, 1975) or baby-talk (Ferguson, 1964) are found in many language communities. Corder (forthcoming) has speculated that we do not in fact learn these codes anew as separate systems in later life but that they represent part of every native speaker's competence and represent, as it were, fossilised stages in the progressive elaboration of his knowledge of his mother tongue, available to him for use on socially approved occasions. Thus, in a sense, the whole of a person's linguistic development remains available to him all his life, and is thus part of his knowledge of language when he comes to learn a second language. The starting point of learning a second language is thus not necessarily the fully complex adult code of his mother tongue but might be one of its simpler codes. Widdowson (forthcoming) makes a similar point when he says that 'simplification is a process whereby a language user adjusts his behaviour in the interests of communicative effectiveness'. If this is true of the fully mature native speaker, then it may well be true of learners and account for the apparent regressions to earlier (simpler) approximative systems under the pressure of communicative needs noted by Selinker (1972). As Valdman (forthcoming) has pointed out, this throws doubt on the whole validity of attempting to reconstruct a learner's approximative system on the basis of his recorded utterances and indeed on the usefulness of the systematic distinction between competence and performance insisted upon by Chomsky.

8. *Pedagogical implications of error and performance analysis*

Indications of the pedagogical relevance of the studies discussed above have been made throughout the text. They fall into three categories: the problem of correction; the design of syllabuses and remedial programmes; and the writing of pedagogical grammars. All these are related to those studies which I have called error analysis. It is too early to draw any conclusions of an immediate practical sort from the work proceeding in performance analysis and the study of second-language learning processes, though some hints of what these may be like have been made, cf. Widdowson (forthcoming). For a general discussion of the relevance of errors to language teaching see Gorbet (1974). The problem of correction is two-fold: what to correct and how to correct. The first question relates to the assessment of the gravity of the error in terms of its interference with comprehensibility or the degree of linguistic deviance. George (1972) considers that sheer frequency is no criterion for decisions about whether to correct, whilst Sternglass (1974) maintains that comprehensibility of an incorrect utterance is not a reason for not correcting it; the degree of linguistic deviance is also an important consideration. Holley and King (1975) stress the need to encourage learners to communicate and to devise correction techniques with this always in mind, for example by requesting rephrasing or amplifying the message, in the way that adults react to infants' utterances in their mother tongue. Burt and Kiparsky (1975) stress that it is the global mistakes, in their analysis, which are unique to second-language learners and cause maximum interference with communication and hence demand attention. Local errors will to a large extent look after themselves. A similar proposal is made by Burt (1975).

The relevance of performance analysis to the designing of syllabuses is based on the notion that there is some 'natural' sequence of elaboration of the approximative system of the second-language learner and that when/if this can be well established it would provide a psychological logic to the ordering of material in a syllabus (Corder, 1967). Nickel (1973) flies a controversial kite when he suggests that the language-teaching materials should reflect the sequence of approximative systems of the learner to the point of actually teaching 'incorrect forms': 'If intralingual steps in a system of *états de dialecte* are necessary steps within the process of language acquisition, then one would in theory even have to consider the problems of error being built into the language material of any kind whatsoever.' This is at least the principle which lies behind the teaching of ITA. Up till now little experimental work has been done in actually trying out teaching sequences in the light of error analyses. An exception is Valdman (1975 a), who reports on a pilot study of teaching a course in French interrogatives based upon error analysis. He too is sympathetic to Nickel's proposals and is prepared at least to teach forms which offend the prescriptive and linguistic purist.

As far as the design of pedagogical grammars is concerned, the effectiveness of the presentation and practising of linguistic materials must ultimately depend upon what is discovered about the actual processes and strategies of language learning, that is, on performance analysis. For further discussions of this problem, see Allen (1973). Meanwhile there do exist pedagogic grammars based upon error analysis. Probably the foremost amongst these is Burt and Kiparsky (1972) for English. This is designed for remedial teaching. Another excellent example of such a grammar is Zydatiss (1974 b).   *October 1975*

Addendum, July 1977

It is not possible to deal exhaustively with the considerable amount of research that has taken place since the publication of this review article. One can only point to certain important areas where work has fruitfully concentrated, for example, the study of the so-called *input* to the learner, i.e. the nature of the linguistic environment in which he discovers the formal properties of the target language – mother-talk and teacher-talk (Snow & Ferguson, 1977). One could also mention the continuing work on simplified registers and pidginisation (Ferguson & De Bose, 1977) or the beginning of a categorisation of *strategies of communication* in second-language users (Tarone, Cohen & Dumas, 1976) or the important problem of the relation between linguistic complexification and communicative pressures (Valdman, forthcoming). But the main development in interlanguage studies has been the theoretical and methodological problem of reconciling the notion of language learner's performance as systematic with the fact of continual change. This was the problem raised by James in Section 2 when he asked: how can a system remain a system, if it is in flux? A learner's performance as judged by his errors shows a degree of apparent inconsistency, i.e. lack of system. This phenomenon has now effectively been accounted for by treating interlanguage as a continuum (see Corder, 1977) and adopting the theories and methods of description used by sociolinguists and appropriate for dealing with dynamic processes, e.g. dialect variation, language change and creole systems. Bickerton (1975) proposes that all real, as opposed to idealised, linguistic systems are continua and can be described by means of variable rules (Labov, 1972) and implicationally scaled (De Camp, 1971). The wave-theory of change (Bailey, 1973) has been applied by the Dickersons (1975, 1976) to the development of the phonological system of learners' interlanguage using these techniques. They have shown that the progress of the learner, far from being inconsistent or unsystematic, is indeed highly rule-governed. They have thus shown that the hitherto apparent inconsistency of learners' performance was a result of inadequate descriptive techniques and that the phenomenon of *regression* can be accounted for by stylistic variation in the learners' performance. More recently, similar descriptive techniques have been applied to interlanguage syntax by Hyltenstam (1977), who shows that the acquisition of sentence negation by adult learners of Swedish as a second language shows identical developmental sequences whatever their mother tongues. It should be emphasised that these new techniques will yield a much more detailed description of interlanguage continua and thus a much richer body of facts upon which psycholinguistic theories of second-language acquisition may be based.

Bibliography

Allen, J. P. B. (1973). Applied grammatical models in a remedial English syllabus. In S. Pit Corder & E. Roulet (eds.), *Theoretical linguistic models in applied linguistics.* AIMAV, Brussels; Didier, Paris.

Bailey, C.-J. N. (1973). *Variation and linguistic theory.* Washington: Centre for Applied Linguistics.

Ballard, V. S. (1970). Frequent errors in French. *T.Bull*, **5**, 2, 1–6.

Bickerton, D. (1975). *Dynamics of a creole system.* London: Cambridge University Press.

Bierwisch, M. (1970). Fehlerlinguistik. *Linguistic Inquiry*, **1**, 397–414.

Boomer, D. S. & Laver, J. D. M. (1968). Slips of the tongue. *British Journal of Disorders of Communication*, **3**, 1–12.

Brown, R. W. (1973). Development of the first language in the human species. *American Psychologist*, Feb. 73, 97–106.

Burt, M. K. (1975). Error analysis in the adult EFL classroom. *TESOL Quarterly*, **9**, 1, 53–65.

Burt, M., Dulay, H. & Hernandez, E. (1973). *Bilingual syntax measure*. New York: Harcourt Brace Jovanovich.

Burt, M. & Kiparsky, C. (1972). *The gooficon*. Rowley: Newbury House.

Burt, M. & Kiparsky, C. (1975). Global and local mistakes. In Schumann & Stenson, *New frontiers*.

Cancino, H., Rosansky, E. J. & Schumann, J. (1974). Testing hypotheses about second language acquisition: the copula and negative in three subjects. *Working Papers on Bilingualism*, no. 3. Ontario Institute for Studies in Education.

Clyne, M. (1968). Zum Pidgin-Deutsch der Gastarbeiter. *Zeitschrift für Mundartforschung*, **35**, 130–9.

Cook, V. J. (1969). The analogy between first and second language learning. *IRAL*, **7**, 207–16.

Cook, V. J. (1973). The comparison of language development in native children and foreign adults. *IRAL*, **11**, 13–28.

Corder, S. P. (1967). The significance of learners' errors. *IRAL*, **5**, 161–70.

Corder, S. P. (1971*a*). Idiosyncratic dialects and error analysis. *IRAL*, **9**, 147–60.

Corder, S. P. (1971*b*). Describing the language learner's language. In *Interdisciplinary approaches to language. CILT Reports and Papers*, no. 6, 57–64.

Corder, S. P. (1972). Die Rolle der Interpretation bei der Untersuchung von Schulfehlern. In G. Nickel, *Fehlerkunde*. Berlin.

Corder, S. P. (1973). *Introducing applied linguistics*. Harmondsworth: Penguin Education.

Corder, S. P. (1974*a*). The elicitation of interlanguage. In G. Nickel (ed.), special issue of *IRAL* on the occasion of Bertil Malmberg's 60th birthday. Heidelberg: Groos, 51–63.

Corder, S. P. (1977). Language continua and the interlanguage hypothesis. *Papers from the Vth Neuchatel Colloquium in Applied Linguistics*. Geneva: Edition Broz.

Corder, S. P. (forthcoming). Simple codes and the source of the second language learner's initial heuristic hypothesis. In Corder & Roulet (eds.), *Linguistic approaches*.

Corder, S. P. & Roulet, E. (eds.) (forthcoming). *Linguistic approaches to applied linguistics*. Papers from the IVth Neuchatel Colloquium, 1975.

Dato, D. P. (1972). The development of the Spanish verb phrase in children's second language learning. In Pimsleur & Quinn (eds.), *The psychology of second language learning*. Cambridge University Press.

De Camp, D. (1971). Towards a generative analysis of a post-creole speech continuum. In D. Hymes (ed.), *Pidginization and Creolisation of languages*. Cambridge University Press.

Dickerson, L. (1975). The learner's interlanguage as a system of variable rules. *TESOL Quarterly*, **9**, 401–7.

Dickerson, W. B. (1976). The psycholinguistic unity of language learning and language change. *Language Learning*, **26**, 2, 215–31.

Dulay, H. C. & Burt, M. K. (1972). Goofing: an indicator of children's second language learning strategies. *Language Learning*, **22**, 235–51.

Dulay, H. C. & Burt, M. K. (1973). Should we teach children syntax? *Language Learning*, **23**, 2, 245–58.

Dulay, H. C. & Burt, M. K. (1974*a*). Natural sequences in child second language acquisition. *Language Learning*, **24**, 37–53.

Dulay, H. C. & Burt, M. K. (1974*b*). A new perspective on the creative construction hypothesis in child second language acquisition. *Working Papers on Bilingualism*, **4**, 71–98. Ontario Institute for Studies in Education.

Dulay, H. C. & Burt, M. K. (1974*c*). Errors and strategies in child language acquisition. *TESOL Quarterly*, **8**, 129–36.

Dulay, H. C. & Burt, M. K. (1974*d*). You can't learn without goofing: an analysis of children's second language errors. In J. C. Richards (ed.), *Error analysis*.

Dušková, L. (1969). On sources of errors in foreign languages. *IRAL*, **7**, 11–36.

Eliasson, S. (1973). Review of Filipović (ed.), Zagreb conference on English contrastive projects. *Studia Linguistica*, **27**.

Ervin-Tripp, S. (1970). Structure and process in language acquisition. *Georgetown Monograph Series on Languages and Linguistics*, no. 23, 313–53. 21st Annual Round Table.

Ervin-Tripp, S. (1974). Is second language learning like the first? *TESOL Quarterly*, **8**, 111–29.

Ferguson, C. A. (1964). Baby-talk in six languages. In Gumperz & Hymes (eds.), *The ethnography of communication*, 103–4. Special number of *American Anthropologist*, **66**, 6, Pt. 2. Washington, American Anthropological Assoc.

Ferguson, C. A. (1971). Absence of the copula and the notion simplicity. In D. Hymes (ed.), *Pidginization and creolisation of languages*. London: Cambridge University Press.

Ferguson, C. A. (1975). Towards a characterisation of English foreigner talk. *Anthropological Linguistics*, **17**, 1–14.

Ferguson, C. A. & De Bose, C. (1977). Simplified registers, broken language and pidginization. In A. Valdman (ed.), *Pidgin and Creole linguistics*. Bloomington: University of Indiana Press.

Fitikides, T. J. (1967). *Common mistakes in English*. London: Longman.

French, F. G. (1949). *Common errors in English: their cause, prevention and cure*. London: Oxford University Press.

Fromkin, V. A. (1973). Slips of the tongue. *Scientific American*, **229**, 110–17.

George, H. V. (1972). *Common errors in language learning*. Rowley: Newbury House.

Gorbet, F. (1974). Error analysis: what teachers can do. In R. Shiu (ed.), *Errors: a new perspective*. Toronto: Research Division, Directorate of Studies, Civil Service Commission.

Grauberg, W. (1971). An error analysis in German of first year university students. In G. Perren & J. Trim (eds.), *Applications of linguistics*. London: Cambridge University Press.

Hakuta, Kenji (1974). Preliminary report on the development of grammatical morphemes in a Japanese girl learning English as a second language. *Working Papers in Bilingualism*, **3**, 18–43. Toronto: Ontario Institute for Studies in Education.

Hammarberg, B. (1973). The insufficiency of error analysis. In J. Svartvik (ed.), *Errata*.

Hamp, E. P. (1965). What a contrastive grammar is not, if it is. *Georgetown Round Table Monograph*, no. 21.

Hatch, E. R. (1972). Some studies in language learning. *Working papers in TESL*, no. 6, 29–36. Los Angeles: University of Los Angeles.

Hatch, E. R. (1974). Second language learning – universals? *Working Papers in Bilingualism*, no. 3, June 1974. Toronto: Ontario Institute for Studies in Education.

Holley, F. & King, J. M. (1975). Imitation and correction in foreign language learning. In Schumann & Stenson, *New frontiers*.

Hyltenstam, K. (1977). Implicational patterns in interlanguage syntax variation. *Work in Progress No. 10*. Dept. of Linguistics, University of Edinburgh.

Jain, M. P. (1974). Error analysis: source, cause and significance. In J. C. Richards (ed.), *Error analysis.*

James, C. (1971 a). The exculpation of contrastive linguistics. In G. Nickel (ed.), *Papers in contrastive linguistics.* London: Cambridge University Press.

James, C. (1971 b). *Foreign language learning by dialect expansion.* Paper read to PAKS Symposium, Stuttgart, 1971.

James, C. (1974). Linguistic measures for error gravity. *Audio-Visual Language Journal,* **12,** 1, 3–9.

James, C. (1975). Judgements of error gravities. *ELS,* July 1975.

Johansson, S. (1973). The identification and evaluation of error in foreign languages; a functional approach. In J. Svartvik (ed.), *Errata.*

Johansson, S. (forthcoming). Problems in the study of the communicative effect of learner's errors. In Corder & Roulet (eds.) (forthcoming), *Linguistic approaches.*

Kellerman, E. (1974). Elicitation, lateralization and error analysis. *York Papers in Linguistics,* **4.** University of York.

Krzeszowski, T. P. (1974). *Contrastive generative grammar: theoretical foundatwis.* Lodz: University Press.

Labov, W. (1972). Some principles of linguistic methodology. *Language in Society,* **1,** 97–120.

Lado, R. (1957). *Linguistics across cultures.* Ann Arbor: University of Michigan.

Lange, M. (1974). L'analyse des erreurs: état actuel de la recherche. In R. Shiu (ed.), *Errors: a new perspective.* Toronto: Research Division, Directorate of Studies, Civil Service Commission.

Leisi, E. (1972). Theoretische Grundlagen der Fehlerbewertung. In G. Nickel (ed.), *Fehlerkunde.*

Levelt, W. S. M. (forthcoming). Skill theory and language teaching. In Corder & Roulet (eds.) (forthcoming), *Linguistic approaches.*

Levenston, E. A. (1971). Over-indulgence and under-representation – aspects of mother tongue interference. In G. Nickel (ed.), *Papers in contrastive linguistics.* London: Cambridge University Press.

Lindell, E. (1973). The four pillars: on the goals of foreign language teaching. In J. Svartvik (ed.), *Errata.*

Linnarud, M. (1975). Lexis in free production. An analysis of the lexical texture of Swedish students' written work. *Report No. 6.* Department of English, Lund University.

Milon, J. P. (1974). The development of negation in English by a second language learner. *TESOL Quarterly,* **8,** 137–45.

Naiman, Neil. (1974). The use of elicited imitation in second language acquisition research. *Working Papers in Bilingualism,* no. 2. Toronto: Ontario Institute for Studies in Education.

Nehls, Dietrich (1974). Fehleranalyse versus Kontrastive Analyse. In G. Nickel & A. Raasch (eds.), *Kongressbericht der 5. Jahrestagung der Gesellschaft für angewandte Linguistik* (IRAL Sonderband GAL '73). Heidelberg: Groos.

Nemser, W. (1971). Approximative systems of foreign language learners. *IRAL,* **9,** 115–23.

Nemser, W. & Slama-Cazacu, T. (1970). Contact analysis: a psycholinguistic approach. *Revue Romaine de Linguistique,* **15,** 2.

Newmark, L. & Reibel, D. (1967). Necessity and sufficiency in language learning. *IRAL,* **6,** 3.

Nickel, G. (1971 a). Contrastive linguistics and foreign language teaching. In G. Nickel (ed.), *Papers in contrastive linguistics.* London: CUP.

Nickel, G. (1971 b). Problems of learners' difficulties in foreign language acquisition. *IRAL,* **9,** 3, 219–27.

Nickel, G. (1972). Grundsätzliches zur Fehleranalyse und Fehlerbewertung. In G. Nickel (ed.), *Fehlerkunde.*

Nickel, G. (ed.) (1972). *Fehlerkunde.* Berlin: Cornelsen-Velhagen & Klasing.

Nickel, G. (1973). Aspects of error analysis and grading. In J. Svartvik (ed.), *Errata.*

Olsson, M. (1972). Intelligibility: a study of errors and their importance. *The GUME project.* Göteborg: Pedagogiska Institutionen Lärarhögskolan.

Olsson, M. (1973). The effects of different types of errors in the communication situation. In J. Svartvik (ed.), *Errata.*

Olsson, M. (1974). A study of errors: frequency, origins and effects. Göteborg: Pedagogiska Institutionen Lärarhögskolan.

Ravem, R. (1974). WH-questions in first and second language learners. In J. C. Richards (ed.), *Error analysis.*

Richards, J. C. (1971 a). A non-contrastive approach to error analysis. *ELT*, **25**, 204–19.

Richards, J. C. (1971 b). Error analysis and second language strategies. *Language Sciences*, **17**, 12–22.

Richards, J. C. (1972). Social factors, interlanguage and language learning. *Language Learning*, **22**, 2, 159–88.

Richards, J. C. (ed.) (1974 a). *Error analysis. Perspectives on second language acquisition.* London: Longman.

Richards, J. C. (1974 b). Simplification: a strategy in the adult acquisition of a foreign language: an example from Indonesian/Malay. Paper given at the Second Conference on the Standardisation of Asian Languages. Manila, 1974.

Richards, J. C. & Sampson, G. P. (1974). The study of learner English. In J. C. Richards (ed.), *Error analysis.*

Ritchie, W. (1967). Some implication of generative grammar for the construction of courses in English as a foreign language. *Language Learning*, **17**, 45–68, 111–32.

Samarin, W. J. (1971). Salient and substantive pidginization. In D. Hymes (ed.), *Pidginization and creolisation of languages.* London: Cambridge University Press.

Schumann, John (1974). The implications of interlanguage, pidginization and creolization for the study of adult second language acquisition. *TESOL Quarterly*, **8**, 2.

Schumann, J. & Stenson, N. (1975). *New frontiers in second language learning.* Rowley: Newbury House.

Selinker, Larry (1969). Language transfer. *General Linguistics*, **9**, 67–92.

Selinker, Larry (1972). Interlanguage. *IRAL*, **10**, 3, 219–31.

Slama-Cazacu, T. (1971). Psycholinguistics and contrastive studies. Zagreb Conference on English Contrastive Projects. Zagreb: Institute of Linguistics.

Slama-Cazacu, T. (1974). Theoretical interpretation and methodological consequences of 'regularisation'. In *Further developments in contrastive studies. Romanian–English Contrastive Analysis Project.* Bucharest University Press.

Snow, C. & Ferguson, C. A. (1977). *Talking to children: language input and acquisition.* Cambridge University Press.

Stenson, Nancy (1975). Induced errors. In Schumann & Stenson (eds.), *New frontiers in second language learning.*

Sternglass, M. S. (1974). Close similarities in dialect features of black and white college students in remedial composition classes. *TESOL Quarterly*, **8**, 3, 271–83.

Strevens, Peter, (1969). Two ways of looking at error analysis. Paper given at GAL meeting, Stuttgart (1969). *Zielsprache Deutsch*, **1** (1971), 1–6.

Svartvik, J. (1973). Introduction to Svartvik, J. (ed.), *Errata: papers in error analysis.*

Svartvik, J. (1973). *Errata: papers in error analysis.* Lund: Gleerup.

Swain, M., Dumas, G. & Naiman, N. (1974). Alternatives to spontaneous speech: elicited translation and imitation as indicators of second language competence. *Working Papers in Bilingualism*, no. 3. Toronto: Ontario Institute for Studies in Education.

77

Tarone, Elaine (1974). A discussion on the Dulay and Burt studies. *Working Papers on Bilingualism*, no. 4. Toronto: Ontario Institute for Studies in Education.

Tarone, E., Cohen A. D. & Dumas, G. (1976). A closer look at some interlanguage terminology: a framework for communication strategies. *Working Papers in Bilingualism*, **9**, 76–90.

Taylor, B. P. (1974). Toward a theory of language acquisitior *Language Learning*, **24**, 1, 23–35.

Thiem, R. (1969). Bibliography of contrastive linguistics. *PAKS – Arbeitsbericht*, **2**, 79–96; **3/4**, 93–120.

Valdman, Albert & Phillips, J. S. (forthcoming). Pidginization, creolisation and the elaboration of learner systems. In Corder & Roulet (eds.) (forthcoming), *Linguistic approaches*.

Valdman, Albert (1975 a). Error analysis and pedagogical ordering. In Corder & Roulet (eds.), *Linguistic insights in applied linguistics*. Brussels, AIMAV; Paris, Didier.

Valdman, Albert (1975 b). *Bibliography of language learners' approximative systems and error analysis*. Washington: Centre for Applied Linguistics.

Valdman, Albert (forthcoming). On the relevance of the pidginization–Creolization model for second language learning. Papers from the IVth Neuchatel Colloquium. *Studies in Second Language Acquisition*. Indiana University Linguistics Club.

Van Buren, P. (1974). Contrastive analysis. In J. P. B. Allen & S. P. Corder, *Techniques in applied linguistics*. London: Oxford University Press.

Váradi, Tamás (1973). Strategies of target language learner communications: message adjustment. Paper given at the 6th Conference of the Rumanian–English Linguistic Project, Timisoara, 1973.

Wardhaugh, G. (1970). The contrastive analysis hypothesis. *TESOL Quarterly*, **4**, 2. Reprinted in Schumann & Stenson (eds.), *New frontiers*.

Widdowson, H. W. (forthcoming). The significance of simplification. In Corder & Roulet (eds.) (forthcoming), *Linguistic approaches*.

Zydatiss, W. (1973). Fehler in der Englischen Satzgliedfolge. *IRAL*, **11**, 4, 319–55.

Zydatiss, W. (1974 a). A 'kiss of life' for the notion of error. *IRAL*, **12**, 3, 234–7.

Zydatiss, W. (1974 b). Lernprobleme im Englischen und ihre Behandlung in einer didaktischen Grammatik. *Linguistik und Didaktic*, **20**, 5.

Zydatiss, W. (1974 c). Some test formats for elicitation procedures. *IRAL*, **12**, 281–7.

THE THEORY AND THE CRAFT OF TRANSLATION

Peter Newmark

Polytechnic of Central London

1. *Historical introduction*

The first traces of translation date from 3000 BC, during the Egyptian Old Kingdom, in the area of the First Cataract, Elephantine, where inscriptions in two languages have been found. It became a significant factor in the West from 300 BC, when the Romans took over wholesale many elements of Greek culture, including the whole religious apparatus. In the twelfth century the West came into contact with Islam in Moorish Spain. The situation favoured the two essential conditions for large-scale translation (Störig, 1963): a qualitative difference in culture (the West was inferior but scientifically acquisitive and receptive to new ideas) and continuous contact between two languages. When the Moorish supremacy collapsed in Spain, the Toledo School of Translators translated Arabic versions of Greek scientific and philosophical classics. Luther's Bible translation in 1522 laid the foundations of modern German, and King James' Bible (1611) had a seminal influence on English language and literature. Significant periods of translation preceded Shakespeare and his contemporaries, French classicism, and the Romantic Movements.

2. *Translation today*

The twentieth century has been called the 'age of translation' (Jumpelt, 1961) or 'reproduction' (Benjamin, 1923). Whereas in the nineteenth century it was mainly a one-way means of communication between prominent men of letters and to a lesser degree philosophers and scientists and their educated readers abroad, whilst trade was conducted in the language of the dominant nation, and diplomacy, previously Latin, was in French, now international agreements between state, public and private organisations are translated for all interested parties, whether or not the signatories understand each other's languages. The setting up of a new international body, the constitution of an independent state, the formation of a multinational company or state, gives translation enhanced political importance. The exponential increase in technology (patents, specifications, documentation), the attempt to bring it to developing countries, the simultaneous publication of the same book in various languages, the increase in world communication, has correspondingly increased requirements. UNESCO, which up to 1970 published an *Index Translationum*, recorded a 4½-fold increase since 1948, with translations into German nearly twice as many as into Russian, the second most numerous. (Correspondingly, most theoretical literature is in German.) Scientific, technical and medical journals are translated wholesale in the USA and USSR. EEC now employs 1,300 translators. In 1967 80,000 scientific journals were being translated annually (Spitzbart, 1972). Some 'international' writers (in the age of 'international' culture) immediately sell more widely in translation than in the original, whilst others in Italy and the smaller European countries depend for a living on the translation of their works as well as their own translations. The translation of literature in the 'minor' languages, particularly in the developing countries, is much neglected.

3. *Writing on translation*

In relation to the volume of translation, little was written about it. The wider aspects were ignored: translation's contribution to the development of national languages, its relation to meaning, thought and the language universals. It was mainly discussed in terms of (*a*) the conflict between free and literal translation, and (*b*) the contradiction between its inherent impossibility and its absolute necessity (Goethe, 1826). The classical essays are those of St Jerome (1400), Luther (1530), Dryden (1684) – all favouring colloquial and natural renderings. Tytler wrote the first significant book on translation in 1790, stating that 'a good translation is one in which the merit of the original work is so completely transfused into another language as to be as distinctly apprehended and as strongly felt by a native of the country to which that language belongs as it is by those who speak the language of the original work'. In the nineteenth century the important essays and references by Goethe (1813, 1814), Humboldt (1816), Novalis (1798), Schleiermacher (1813), Schopenhauer (1851) and Nietzsche (1882) inclined towards more literal translation methods, while Matthew Arnold (1861) favoured a simple, direct and noble style for translating Homer. In the twentieth century, Croce (1922), Ortega y Gasset (1937) and Valéry (1941) questioned the possibility of adequate translation, particularly of poetry. Benjamin (1923) saw translation filling in the gaps in meaning in a universal language. He recommended literal translation of syntax as well as words: 'The sentence is a wall blocking out the language of the original, whilst word for word translation is the arcade.'

The above is a brief conspectus of views in the pre-linguistics period of translation. On the whole they make no attempt to distinguish types or quality of texts (which are mainly Biblical or literary), and while they are strong on theory, they are short on method and practical examples. They show a gradual transition from a natural or free treatment towards a literal analysis, if not translation, of the original, but there is no development of a theory, and many of the writers were not aware of each other's work.

4. *Present requirement for translation theory*

With the increasing number of translator and revisor teams for documents and glossaries, the formulation of some translation theory, if only as a frame of reference, becomes necessary. The need is reinforced by the proliferation of terms of art, in particular of technological terms – in chemistry, for instance, a hundred internationalisms a month, in electronics, a few thousand a year (Spitzbart, 1972) – and for standardising the terminology, intra- and inter-lingually. But the main reason for formulating a translation theory, for proposing methods of translation related to and derived from it, for teaching translation and for translation courses, is the appalling badness of so many published translations (Widmer, 1959). Literary or non-literary translations without mistakes are rare. Already in 1911, the *Encyclopaedia Britannica* stated in a good article absurdly restricted to literary translation: 'Most versions of modern foreign writers are mere hackwork carelessly executed by incompetent hands.' Now that accurate translation has become generally important politically, the need to investigate the subject is urgent, if only to agree on general principles.

5. *Relationship between translation and other disciplines*

Translation theory derives from comparative linguistics, and within linguistics it is mainly an aspect of semantics; all questions of semantics relate to translation theory. Sociolinguistics, which investigates the social registers of language and the problems of languages in contact in the same or neighbouring countries, has a continuous bearing on translation theory. Sociosemantics, the theoretical study of *parole*, language in context, as opposed to *langue*, the code or system of a language, indicates the relevance of 'real' examples – spoken, taped, written, printed. Since semantics is often presented as a cognitive subject without connotations, rather than as an exercise in communication, semiotics, the science of signs, is an essential factor in translation theory. The American philosopher Charles Peirce (1897) is usually regarded as its founder. He stressed the communicative factor of any sign: 'The meaning of a sign consists of all the effects that may conceivably have practical bearings on a particular interpretant, and which will vary in accordance with the interpretant' – no sign therefore has a self-contained meaning. Typically, an iced lolly may mean a flavoured frozen confection on a stick to the reader (as a non-participant, the purpose of the object is not important to him), but to the manufacturer it means a profitable source of income, to a housewife a messy nuisance for which she gets a demand all the year round, to a child a satisfying cold drink on a stick which lasts a long time. If one puts oneself as reader of a translated text in the place of the manufacturer, the housewife or the child, the importance of Pierce's theory of meaning for translation theory is clear. Charles Morris's division of semiotics into syntactics (the relation of signs to each other), semantics (the allocation of signs to their real objects), and pragmatics (the relation between signs and their interpreters) has been taken as a model by the Leipzig translation theorists (Neubert, 1968, 1972; Kade, 1965, 1968), who have been particularly sensitive to the pragmatics of political statements. Thus what is approvingly translated as 'profit' in the Federal Republic might be rendered pejoratively as 'profit' in the GDR.

A translator requires a knowledge of literary and non-literary textual criticism, since he has to assess the quality of a text before he decides how to interpret and then translate it. All kinds of false distinctions have been made between literary and technical translation. Both Savory (1957) and Reiss (1971) have written that the technical translator is concerned with content, the literary translator with form. Other writers have stated that a technical translation must be literal, a literary translation must be free – and again, others have said the opposite. A traditional English snobbery puts literary translation on a pedestal and regards other translation as hackwork, or less important, or easier. But the distinction between careful, sensitive and elegant writing – proper words in proper places, as Swift put it – on the one hand, and predictable, hackneyed and modish phrases – in fact bad writing – on the other, cuts across all this. A translator must respect good writing scrupulously by accounting for its language, structures and content, whether the piece is scientific or poetic, philosophical or fictional. If the writing is poor, it is normally his duty to improve it, whether it is technical or a routine, commercialised best-seller. The basic difference between the artistic and the non-literary is that the first is symbolical or allegorical and the second representational in intention; the difference in translation is that more attention is paid to connotation and emotion in imaginative literature. The translator has to be a good judge of writing; he must assess not only the literary quality but the moral seriousness of a text, in the sense of Arnold and Leavis. Moreover, any reading in stylistics, which is at the intersection between linguistics and literary criticism, such as a study of Jakobson (1960, 1966) and Spitzer (1948), both of whom discuss translation as well as comparative literature, will help him.

Logic and philosophy, in particular ordinary language philosophy, have a bearing on the grammatical and lexical aspects of translation respectively. A study of logic will assist the translator to assess the truth-values underlying the passage he is translating; all sentences depend on presuppositions and where the sentences are obscure or ambiguous, the translator has to determine the presuppositions. Moreover a translation-rule such as the following on negations (my own) derives from logic: 'A word translated by a negative and its noun or object complementary term may be a satisfactory equivalent.' (Thus a 'female' is 'not a male'.) A word translated by a negative and its verb or process converse term is not a satisfactory equivalent, although the equivalent meaning may be ironically implied. (Compare 'we advanced' and 'we didn't retreat'.) A word translated by a negative and its contrary term is not a satisfactory equivalent unless it is ironically used. (Compare 'spendthrift' and 'not stingy'.) A word translated by a negative and its contradictory term is a weakened equivalent, but the force of the understatement may convey equivalence (e.g. 'false' is almost 'not true'; 'he agreed with that' is almost 'he didn't dissent from that'). Lastly, a word translated by a double negative and the same word or its synonym is occasionally an effective translation, but normally in a weakened form (e.g. 'grateful' may be 'not ungrateful', 'not unappreciative'). A translator has to bear all the above options in mind, in particular where the contrary, contradictory or converse term is plainly or approximately missing in the target language, which should be his own.

Philosophy is a fundamental issue in translation theory. When Wittgenstein 'abandoned the idea that the structure of reality determines the structure of language, and suggested that it is really the other way round' (Pears, 1971) he implied that translation was that much harder. His most often quoted remark: 'For a large number of cases – though not for all – in which we employ the word "meaning", it can be defined or explained thus: "the meaning of a word is its use in the language"' (Wittgenstein, 1953), is more pertinent to translation, which is only concerned with contextual use, than to language as a system. Again, when Austin (1963) made his revolutionary distinction between descriptive and performative sentences, he illustrated a valuable contrast between non-standardised and standardised language which always interests a translator: for a formulaic sentence such as *I name this ship 'Liberté'* there is normally only one equivalent in, say, French, and the translator has no options such as would be available if the sentence had read: *I wish the 'Liberté' all success.* Further, Kant's distinction between analytical propositions which are linguistic, e.g. *All spinsters are unmarried*, gives the translator more licence than a synthetic referential proposition such as *The spinster hid in the cupboard*, provided the rest of the passage clarifies the type of cupboard she hid in. Lastly, Grice's 'meaning means intention' helps the translator to see that *Would you mind doing it?* and *I refuse to believe it* have nothing to do with minding or refusing. Usually, a text's or a proposition's intention can only be ascertained *outside* the utterances, by examining the reason and the occasion for the utterance. *I'll murder you if you do that again* may be a mother exercising discipline.

Translation theory is not only an inter-disciplinary study, it is even a function of the disciplines I have briefly alluded to.

6. *Translation and losses of meaning*

Translation is a craft consisting in the attempt to replace a written message in one language by the same message in another language. Each exercise involves some loss of meaning, due to a number of factors. It provokes a continuous tension, a dialectic, an argument based on the claims of each language. The basic loss is on a continuum between overtranslation (increased detail) and undertranslation (increased generalisation).

In the first place, if the text describes a situation which has elements peculiar to the natural environment, institutions and culture of its language area, there is an inevitable loss of meaning, since the transference (or rather the substitution or replacement (Haas, 1970) – the word 'translation' like so many others is misleading, due to its etymology) to the translator's language can only be approximate. Unless there is already a recognised translation equivalent – but will the reader be familiar with it, and will he accept it? – here we must bear Peirce's pragmatics in mind – the translator has to choose from transliterating the foreign word (say *directeur du cabinet*), translating it ('head of the minister's office'), substituting a similar word in his own culture ('Permanent Under-Secretary of State'), naturalising the word with a loan translation ('director of the cabinet'), sometimes adding or substituting a suffix from his own language (for example, *apparatchik*, Prague, *footballeur*), defining it, or paraphrasing, the last resort ('head of the Minister's departmental staff'), which is sometimes added in parenthesis or as a footnote to a transliteration. However, there is no 'referential' loss if the situation is on neutral, non-national ground with participants without specifically local features (e.g. a mathematical study, a medical experiment using standard equipment).

The second and inevitable source of loss is the fact that the two languages, both in their basic character (*langue*) and their social varieties (*parole*) (bearing in mind Jakobson's (1971) gloss on Saussure) in context have different lexical, grammatical and sound systems, and segment many physical objects and virtually all intellectual concepts differently. (Usually, the closer the language and the culture, the closer the translation and the original.) Few words, phrases or sentences correspond precisely on the four lexical scales (Newmark, 1969): (1) formality (from frozen to uninhibited) (cf. Joos, 1967), (2) feeling or affectivity (from overheated to dead pan), (3) generality or abstraction (from categorical to subspecific), and (4) evaluation – four subscales: morality (good to bad), pleasure (nice to nasty), intensity (strong to weak), dimension (e.g. wide to narrow) – which interest the translator. I have proposed (Newmark, 1973) a translation rule that corresponding words, idioms, metaphors, proverbs, sayings, syntactic units and word-order must be equally frequent (in the type of text) in the source and the target language, but the translator can never follow this rule to the letter, since it even has inherent contradictions.

Thirdly, the individual use of language of the text-writer and the translator do not coincide. Everybody has lexical if not grammatical idiosyncrasies, and attaches 'private' meanings to a few words. The translator normally writes in a style that comes naturally to him, desirably with a certain elegance and sensitivity unless the text precludes it. Moreover, as Weightman (1947) has pointed out, a good writer's use of language is often remote from, if not at cross-purposes with, some of the conventional canons of good writing, and it is the writer not the canons that the translator must respect.

Lastly, the translator and the text-writer have different theories of meaning and different values. The translator's theory colours his interpretation of the text. He may set greater value than the text-writer on connotation, and correspondingly less on denotation. He may look for symbolism where realism was intended; for several meanings where only one was intended; for different emphasis, based on his own philosophy or even his reading of the syntax. The different values of writer and translator may be parodied through a school-report, where words like competent, fair, average, above average, satisfactory, passable, middling, may mean all things to all men (cf. Trier, 1973). Thus diagrammatically one may see a target language text as an object in a magnetic field which has seven or eight conflicting forces exerted upon it. The resulting loss of meaning is inevitable and is unrelated to, say, the obscurity or the deficiencies of the text and the incompetence of the translator, which are additional possible sources of this loss of meaning, sometimes referred to as entropy (Vinay, 1968).

7. *Translation theory literature*

This then is the problem, and in the last thirty years a considerable theoretical literature has been devoted to it. A few professional linguists as well as translators began to turn their attention to translation theory at a time when philosophy was substantially concerned with language, and later when with the decline of Bloomfieldian or behaviourist (rather than structuralist) linguistics and rapid progress in applied linguistics, semantics was being (grotesquely) 'reinstated' within linguistics. Prior to this period, translation theory was almost exclusively the concern of men of letters, with the notable exception of Humboldt.

The literature is dominated by Nida, whose work is informed by his experience as a linguist and as a bible-translator. In Nida (1964, 1969) almost every translation problem is discussed. He adapts transformational grammar by proposing eight model kernel sentences as transitional stages between source and target language structures. He applies componential analysis by using common, diagnostic and supplementary components as tools for comparing and contrasting items within a semantic field. He discusses the logical relations of words with each other, the difference between cultural and linguistic translation, the relevance of discourse analysis, the difficulties of translating between remote cultures, levels of usage, the psychological connotations of words, and practical problems of translation. His reduction of propositions to objects, events, relationals and abstracts may be more fruitful to translators as a comprehension

85

procedure than the kernel sentences. His distinction between dynamic and formal equivalence is too heavily weighted against the formal properties of language. Nida's recent books (1974 *a*, 1975) are specifically concerned with componential analysis, but they can be profitably applied to the first stages of translation procedure. He has notably summarised the present state of translation theory (1974 *b*).

Fedorov (1958, 1968) stresses that translation theory is an independent linguistic discipline, deriving from observations and providing the basis for practice. Like the Leipzig school, he believes that all experience is translatable, and rejects the view that language expresses a peculiar mental word-picture. However, the lack of a common outlook or ideology at present impairs the effectiveness of translation. Komissarov (1973) sees translation theory moving in three directions: the denotative (information translation), the semantic (precise equivalence) and the transformational (transposition of relevant structures). His theory of equivalence distinguishes five levels: (1) lexical units, (2) collocations, (3) information, (4) the situation, and (5) the communication aim. Jumpelt (1961) applies the Trier–Weisgerber field theory to technological texts, and effectively distinguishes superordinate and subordinate terms in the technical literature. The Leipzig school (Neubert, Kade, Wotjak, Jäger, Agricola, Ruzička), much of whose work has been published in the periodical *Fremdsprachen* and its six *Beihefte*, distinguishes sharply between the invariant (cognitive) and the variant (pragmatic) elements in translation, and turns transformational grammar and semiotics to account. It is sometimes short on procedures and examples, and restricts itself to non-literary texts. Neubert's and Agricola's writing has been imaginative. Koller (1972) is particularly useful in distinguishing information from communication, and Reiss (1971) has categorised and illustrated the variety of text-types. Catford (1965) has applied Halliday's systemic grammar to translation theory, and has fruitfully categorised translation shifts between levels, structures, word-classes, units ('rank-shifts') and systems. He distinguishes between 'context' (of situation) and 'co-text' (of language). He sets greater limits to the possibilities of translation than other theorists. Firth (1968) points to contextual meaning as the basis of a translation theory. Mounin (1955, 1963, 1967) discusses translation theories and their relation to semantics and supports the 'linguistic' against the literary theory of translation. Levy (1969) and Winter (1969) apply linguistics to the translation of literary texts, including the phonological aspects of poetry. Wuthenow (1969), Kloepfer (1967) and Cary (1956) reject all but a literary approach to translation theory.

The above-mentioned literature is basically theoretical. Of the literature which applies linguistics to translation procedures, Vinay and Darbelnet (1969) is outstanding. They enumerate seven procedures: transliteration, loan translation, literal translation, transposition, modulation, equivalence and adaptation, and make perceptive distinctions between French and English. Friederich's work on English and German (1969) is also invaluable, whilst German and French have been compared by Truffaut (1968) and Malblanc (1961). Mention should also be made of Wandruszka's (1969) multilingual comparisons and Fuller's (1973) distinctions between French and English. Valuable essays are collected in Störig (1963), Brower (1966), Smith (1958) and Kapp (1974), whilst Garvin (1955) includes the Prague School's contributions to translation theory.

There is a considerable literature on Machine Translation (e.g. Booth, 1967) but at least since Bar-Hillel (1964) there is fairly general agreement that computers will not be much used for translation in the foreseeable future; they are already of incalculable assistance to terminologists in compiling glossaries and bilingual dictionaries. Melčuk's work on MT (e.g. in Booth, 1967) has thrown light on translation procedures.

Steiner (1975) contains a variety of outstanding literary translations and summaries of translation theories, and emphasises the importance of translation as a key to the understanding of thought, meaning, language, communication and comparative linguistics. He puts the case for 'poem to poem' against 'plain prose' translations (1966).

8. The 'equivalent effect' and the 'literal' principles and other methods of translation.

There is wide but not universal agreement that the main aim of the translator is to produce as nearly as possible the same effect on his readers as was produced on the readers of the original (see Rieu, 1953). The principle is variously referred to as the principle of similar or equivalent response or effect, or of functional or dynamic (Nida) equivalence. It bypasses and supersedes the nineteenth-century controversy about whether a translation should incline towards the source or the target language, and the consequent faithful versus beautiful, literal versus free, form versus content disputes. The principle demands a considerable imaginative or intuitive effort from the translator, since he must not identify himself with the reader of the original, but must empathise with him, recognising that he may have reactions and sympathies alien to his own. The emphasis of this principle is rightly on communication, on the third term in the translation relationship, on the reader ('Who is the reader?' is the teacher's first question), who had been ignored previously, except in Bible translation. The translator should produce a different type of translation of the same text for a different type of audience. The principle emphasises the importance of the psychological factor – it is mentalistic – its success can hardly be verified. One would want to know how each reader reacts – how he thinks, feels and behaves. The principle allows for a wide range of translation styles – if the writer of the original has deviated from the language norms of the type of text he has written, whether it is an advertisement, a report or a literary work, one would expect the translation to do likewise. A poem or a story in such a case would retain the flavour of the original, and might perhaps read like a translation.

Whilst the successful practitioner of equivalent effect appears to me to be achieving something like the crystallisation stated by Stendhal to be the essence of love, there are some cases where the effect cannot be realised. If a non-literary text describes, qualifies or makes use of a peculiarity of the language it is written in, the reader of the translation will have to have it explained to him, unless it is so trivial that it can be omitted. This applies say to Freud's slips of the tongue and 'jokes', where a similar communicative effect might be obtained by fresh examples, but where the source language examples would still have to be retained. In fact, the sentence *Er behandelte mich wie seinesgleichen, ganz famillionär* (Freud, 1905) could be translated as 'He treated me as an equal, quite like a famillionaire', but it has not the naturalness of the German; similarly with Freud's puns on anec-dotage, alco-holidays, monument-arily – the German must be retained.

Secondly, a non-literary text relating to an aspect of the culture familiar to the first reader but not to the target-language reader is unlikely to produce equivalent effect, particularly if originally only intended for the first reader. The translator therefore, say in translating the laws of a source-language country, cannot 'bend' the text towards the second reader.

Thirdly, there is the artistic work with a strong local flavour which may also be rooted in a particular historical period. The themes will consist of comments on human character and behaviour – universals, applicable to the reader of the translation, and therefore subject to the equivalent effect principle. On the other hand, the work may describe a culture remote from the second reader's experience which the translator wants to introduce to him not as the original reader, who took or takes it for granted, but as something strange with its own special interest. In the case of the Bible, the translator decides on equivalent effect – the nearer he can bring the human truth and the connotations to the reader, the more immediately he is likely to transmit its religious and moral message. But if the culture is as important as the message – the translator has to decide – he reproduces the form and content of the original as literally as possible (with some transliterations), without regard for equivalent effect. If Homer's οἶνοψ πόντος, 'the wine-dark sea', were to be translated as the '(sky) blue sea' merely to achieve equivalent effect, much would be lost. As Matthew Arnold (1928) pointed out, one cannot achieve equivalent effect in translating Homer, as one knows nothing about his audiences.

In fact, if the creative artist writes to relieve himself – in Benjamin's words: 'No poem is written for its reader, nor is regard for those who receive a work of art useful for the purpose of understanding it' (1923) – then the equivalent effect principle is irrelevant in the translation of a work of art; the translator's loyalty is to the artist, and he must concentrate on recreating as much of the work as he can. This is literal or maximal translation in Nabokov's sense (1964): 'rendering as closely as the associative and syntactical capacities of another language allows the exact contextual meaning of the original'. Syntax, word-order, rhythm, sound, all have semantic values. The priorities differ for each work, but there are three rules of thumb: (*a*) the translation should be as literal as possible and as free as is necessary (Cauer, 1896), i.e. the unit of translation should be as small as possible (Haas, 1970); (*b*) a source-language word should not be translated into a target-language word which has another primary one-to-one equivalent in the source language (*schwarz* should not be translated as 'dark' because 'dark' is *finster* or *dunkel* (back translation test) (established collocations like *schwarze Augen* 'dark eyes' are the exception); (*c*) a translation is impermeable to interference – it never takes over a peculiar source-language collocation, structure or word-order. This rule applies to 'literal' as to the much more common 'equivalent effect' translation. Interference, however plausible, is always mistranslation. *The European Communities Glossary* (1974) reads like a guide on how to avoid it. Paradoxically, the 'literal' principle of translating works of art is 'scientific' and verifiable, whilst the equivalent effect principle is intuitive. If the emphasis is on human nature rather than a local culture, a masterly translation, such as Stefan George's of Shakespeare or Baudelaire, may conform to both principles.

There are also other restricted methods of translation: information translation, ranging from brief abstracts through summaries to complete reproduction of content without form; plain prose translation (as in Penguin books) to guide one to the original, whose language should already be a little familiar; interlinear translation, which shows the mechanics of the original; formal translation, for nonsense poetry (Morgenstern) and nursery rhymes where the meaning and the scenario, but not the tone, can be ignored; academic translation, for converting a text to a standard literary style; and a combination of transliteration, translation and paraphrase for texts concerned with the source language, where the metalingual (Jakobson, 1960) function predominates. Translation theory, however, is not concerned with restricted translation. Whilst principles have been and will be proposed for dealing with recurrent problems ('translation rules'), a general theory cannot propose a single method (e.g. dynamic equivalence) but must be concerned with the full range of text-types and their corresponding translation criteria, as well as the major variables involved (see Newmark, 1974*a*, *b*).

9. *Translation theory related to functions of language*

Many theorists have divided texts according to subject-matter (literature, institutions, technology, etc.) but it is perhaps more profitable to begin with

Bühler's statement (1934) of the functions of language, which had a wide influence on the Prague School and has been used by some translation theorists (Reiss, 1971; Hartmann & Vernay, 1968) (Fig. 1 is an extended version). In this scheme, the expressive function A is author-centred, the personal use the writer makes of his language; function B is the 'extra-linguistic' information content of the text; function C is reader-centred (for this Bühler used the inadequate word *Appell* (he also used 'signal', a better term). In calling it the communicative function, I include all the resources with which the writer affects the reader, in particular the emotive, so that he 'gets the message'.

Looking at the text from the translator's angle, I adapt Frege's (1970) distinctions (Fig. 2). The translator works on level Y, which is the language of the text. He has two parallel sources of reference and comparison: X_1 is the situation in the real world, or its reflection in the text-writer's mind, when he (the translator) steps aside from the text, and asks himself: 'Now what is actually happening? Who is this? Where is this? Can I name it? Is this true?', etc. X_2 is the logical structure of the underlying clauses, the clauses in their simple uncluttered form, desirably with an animate subject and an inanimate object, and which may later have to be converted to corresponding syntactic structures in the target language. Level Z is the 'internal image...properly, differences in translation should only be at this level '(Frege). Thus, for a part of a text Y, *le Président de la République*, X_1 may be Valéry Giscard d'Estaing, while X_2 is perhaps 'The man presides over the Republic'. Level Z may suggest any subjectively coloured figure of authority, but as this is standardised language (see § 10), it does not obtrude upon the translation ('the French President').

In Fig. 3 the scheme is simplified. The translator has an instrument consisting of three levels XYZ – compare the tubes of a jointed telescope. With it he observes a text which exhibits the three functions of language ABC in varying degrees. He may have to deflect his instrument, which may be focused mainly at A for a poem, or B for a technical report, or C for an advertisement, but sometimes rests between A and B for a description of nature in the poem, or between B and C for the final recommendations of a report, as no text and few sentences are undiluted A or B or C. Even names like 'Johnny' or 'Petrushka' may be C as well as B. Whilst the translator always works from X, he continuously checks Y against X. Level Z, the partly conscious and partly unconscious element corresponding to the text writer's A, is always present, but the translator has to reduce its influence to a minimum, until he is left with what appears to him to be an almost gratuitous choice between equally valid units of language, which may be lexical or grammatical; this then becomes a question of stylistics, and his version on this level of *quot homines, tot sententiae* may be as good as ten others. A difference between literary and non-literary translation is also clarified by the diagram. In non-literary translation, the

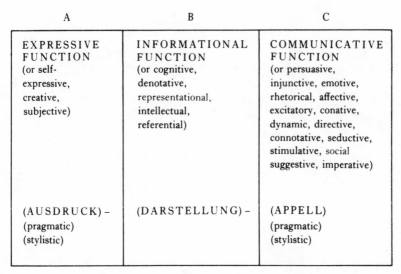

Fig. 1. Text continuum (adapted from Bühler).

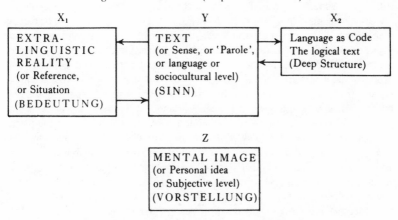

Fig. 2. Translator's continuum (adapted from Frege).

informational function B, which is identical with the translator's referential X, is real; in the case of a realistic literary text, the function B is also treated factually but even the details have typical and general implications. In any work of art of moral seriousness, the referential function is a comment on human behaviour and character and all passages are implicitly metaphorical and allegorical; whatever the content – abstract, symbolical, naturalistic – the ex-

91

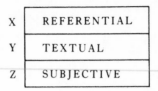

TEXT FUNCTION

A	B	C
EXPRESSIVE	INFORMATIONAL	COMMUNICATIVE

TRANSLATION LEVEL

X	REFERENTIAL
Y	TEXTUAL
Z	SUBJECTIVE

Fig. 3.

pressive function A is most important in the text, and inevitably the translator's level Z is more influential than in other types of text.

Fig. 4 shows tentatively how the three functions may affect the work of the translator. All texts have an informational function, and the examples (1) merely illustrate the main emphasis. Style (2) for A is assessed by the translator according to its grammatical and lexical deviations from ordinary language; for B one would expect the appropriate register, whilst for C, where examples are sharply divided between official writing (laws and notices) and publicity and propaganda, styles are correspondingly formulaic or persuasive. In a scientific report, there would be considerable use of the third person, past tenses and multi-noun compounds. For notices, grammatical divergencies in each language: *Wet paint* becomes 'Freshly painted' in German and 'Mind the paint' in French; *Beware of the dog* is 'Biting dog' in German and 'Wicked dog' in French. The unit of translation (6) is always as small as possible and as large as is necessary (grammatically, it is usually the group or phrase), but an advertiser is likely to ignore it, whilst a literary translator may try to bring it down to the word. The more the text uses the resources of language, and therefore the more important its form, the greater the losses of meaning (8); the greatest loss is in poetry since it uses all resources of language. (The poetry is the untranslatable element, Robert Frost said.) A technical translator has no right to create neologisms (9), unless he is a member of an interlingual glossary team, whilst an advertiser or propaganda writer can use any linguistic resources he requires. Conventional metaphors and sayings (10) should always be conventionally translated (the convention is shown in the dictionary) but unusual metaphors and comparisons should be reduced to their sense if the text has a mainly informational function. The appropriate equivalents for keywords

	(A) EXPRESSIVE	(B) INFORMATIONAL	(C) COMMUNICATIVE
1. Typical Examples	Romantic Writing Intimate Letters	Scientific and technical reports and textbooks	Advertisements Notices Propaganda
2. 'Ideal' style	Artistic and individual	Logical (standard register)	Persuasive (innovatory in register except in official notices and statutes)
3. Text emphasis	Source Language	Target Language	Target Language
4. Focus	Writer (1st person)	Situation (3rd person)	Reader (2nd person)
5. Method	'Literal' translation	Equivalent effect translation	Equivalent effect recreation
6. Unit of translation	Small	Medium	Large
maximum	Collocation	Sentence	Text
minimum	Word	Collocation	Paragraph
7. Type of language	Figurative, exclamatory	Factual	Compelling
8. Loss of meaning	Considerable	Small	Dependent on cultural differences
9. New words and meanings	Mandatory if in text (not otherwise)	Not permitted unless reason given	Yes, except in formal texts
10. Keywords	Leit-motivs Stylistic markers	Main concepts	Token words
11. Unusual metaphors	Reproduce	Give sense (tenor)	Recreate
12. Length in relation to original	Approximately the same	Slightly longer	No norm

Fig. 4

(11) should be scrupulously repeated throughout a text: in a philosophical text, these are the writer's main concepts and terms of art; in literary works, they are likely to be an author's characteristic words (Thomas Mann's *verworfen, mürbe, abnutzbar, überreizt* in *Death in Venice*, or his leit-motivs 'the gypsy in the green wagon' and 'the fair and blue-eyed ones' in *Tonio Kröger*); in an advertisement for wine they may be the token-words, i.e. *mots-témoins* (Matoré, 1953), that are transferred to evoke a fact of civilisation too snobbish to be translated: *cuvée, château, grand cru*. In a non-literary text, there is a case for transliterating as well as translating any key-word of linguistic significance, e.g. Hitler's favourite political words in Maser's biography. Jakobson (1960) has added the metalingual, the phatic and the aesthetic to Bühler's language functions, and Fig. 4 could be expanded to include them.

10. *Standardised language*

All texts may be regarded by the translator as an amalgam of standardised and non-standardised language. The distinction between them is that for standardised language, when it is used as such (but technical terms often melt into ordinary language – e.g. *fail-safe, parameter*), there should be only one correct equivalent, provided one exists, provided it is used in the same situations by the same kind of person, and that is the 'science' of translation. Whilst for non-standardised language, of whatever length, there is rarely only one correct equivalent, and that is the art or craft of translation.

Standardised language consists partly of terminology, and as Bachrach (1974) has stated, increased research and teaching is required here. The terms need attaching to pictures and diagrams (the Duden principle – processes as well as objects), collecting in lexical fields, as in a thesaurus, cognate groups, with frequency, formality, etc., indicated. Whilst many terms are internationalisms others, as Maillot (1970) has pointed out, are polysemous. *Résistance* means 'resistor' as well as 'resistance', *réacteur* 'resistance' and 'reactor', *capacité* 'capacitance' and 'capacity'. Larbaud (1946) stated that a translator must look up every word, especially the ones he knows best. Preferably, words should only be looked up to confirm knowledge, and every time one consults a bilingual dictionary the word should be checked in half a dozen source and target language monolingual dictionaries and reference books. Any target-language word found in a bilingual but not in a monolingual dictionary must be rejected. Bilingual dictionaries often have obsolete, rare or one-off words invented through interference.

However, standardised language goes beyond technical terms. It includes any commonly used metaphor, idiom, proverb, public notice, social phrase, expletive, the usual ways of stating the date or time of day, giving dimensions, and performatives expressed in accepted formulae. Thus one would expect only one valid translation for *Keep Britain tidy, One man's meat is another's poison, c'est un con* and for phatic phrases such as *Nice weather we're having*. There should be little choice in translating the restricted patter in the specialised uses of language mentioned in Halliday (1973) – weather reports, recipes, the language of games, as well as company reports and accounts, the format of agenda and minutes, and medical reports. The stale language within each peer-group, the modish words instantly internationalised by the media, the predictable patter, the fill-ins between stimulus and response – all often have their equally predictable equivalents in the detritus of the target language. The translator's invariant terms include not only the technical and scientific which may be supranational, and the institutional, cultured and ecological which may be national, but also the characteristic expressions within a register, e.g. a patient's 'admission' (*accettazione*) or 'discharge' (*dimissione*) from hospital; the referring terms noted by Strawson (1970) as 'quaint names, substantial phrases which grow capital letters' such as the 'Great War', 'The Annunciation', names of organisations and companies, titles of books, pictures, etc., which are transliterated unless there is already a generally accepted translation, which must then be used; quotations from authorised translations, which must be used and acknowledged; the jargon and 'in' words that cluster round social groups and occupations ('We call it "stint" and "snap" – what do you call it?'). Inevitably organisation, bureaucracy, technology and the media continuously increase and congeal the area and extent of standardised language.

11. *The craft of translation*

Which leaves non-standardised language, language creatively used, which is how language is daily used by everyone. Here translation becomes a craft and an art – or simply art – where there are limited choices. Here too the scientific method operates, since the sense of the translation must be tested for each unit and stretch of language against the original, and vice versa, as well as against the reference, so that clear errors of language and fact are eliminated. Further, the translation has to be seen as natural language acceptably used in the context, if it is so in the original. The translator's craft lies first in his command of an exceptionally large vocabulary as well as all syntactic resources – his ability to use them elegantly, flexibly, succinctly. All translation problems finally resolve themselves into problems of how to write well in the target language. Benjamin (1923) stated that in a good work, language surrounds the content as a shell surrounds its fruit, whilst a translation is a coat hanging loosely round the content of the original in large folds. A translation is never finished, and one has to keep paring away at it, reducing the element of paraphrase, tightening the language. The shorter the translation, the better it is likely to be.

Secondly, the translator as craftsman has to know the foreign language so well

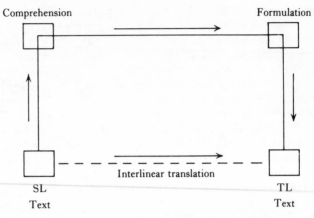

Fig. 5.

that he can determine to what extent the text deviates from the language norms usually used in that topic on that occasion. He has to determine with an intuition backed by empirical knowledge the extent of the text's grammatical and semantic oddness, which he must account for in a well written 'expressive' text, and may decide to normalise in a badly written 'informational' or 'communicative' text. Moreover, he requires a degree of creative tension between fantasy and common sense. He has the fantasy for making hypotheses about apparently unintelligible passages, and the common sense for dismissing any unrealistic hypothesis – it is pointless to pursue an idea (unlike an ideal) that cannot be real or realised. More practically, he needs the common sense for eliminating interference and spotting strange acronyms (what are *K opéra-toires* but *cas opératoires?*).

The translator has to acquire the technique of transferring smoothly between the two basic translation processes: comprehension, which may involve interpretation, and formulation, which may involve recreation (Fig. 5). He has to have a sharp eye for oppositions, contrasts and emphases (foregrounding, see Garvin, 1955) in the original, and if it is a non-literary text he has to know how to accentuate these in his own version. He has to distinguish synonyms used to give additional or complementary information from synonyms used simply to refer to a previously mentioned object or concept. In literary translation (see Nietzsche, 1962 *b*) his hardest task is to catch the pace of the original.

Translation shares with the arts and other crafts the feature that its standards of excellence can only be determined through the informed discussion of experts or exceptionally intelligent laymen; no popular acclaim can stamp the value of a translation any more than of a vase or a new piece of music. After mistakes have been 'proved' by reference to encyclopaedias and dictionaries, experts have to rely on their intuition and taste in preferring one of two or three good translations of a sentence or paragraph. Their final choice at this level is as subjective as the translator's choice of words, but they must be ready to give reasons for their choice. The main matters under dispute may be whether the translator has understood the tone, the writer's attitude towards the information presented, which is often indicated in the syntax, say the use of modals and subjunctives, rather than the words. Further, the experts, the third readers, have intuitively to decide whether the text is natural – would one actually see that on the printed page? – with the proviso that they first agree what kind of printed page they are talking about. In the case of 'expressive' writing the criterion is: would *he* write that?

12. *Beyond translation*

Goethe (1826) stated that translation is impossible, essential and important. The words of all languages overlap and leave gaps of meaning: there are unnamed and perhaps unnameable parts of a hand or a cloud. Benjamin (1923) stated that translation goes beyond enriching the language and culture of a country which it contributes to, beyond renewing and maturing the life of the original text, beyond expressing and analysing the most intimate relationships of languages with each other, and becomes a way of entry into a universal language. Words that according to the conventional wisdom are peculiar to national character, say *nichevo* for Russian, *magari* for Italian, *hinnehmen* for German, *sympathique* for French, *schlampig* for the Austrian dialect (many more come to mind) may perhaps fill in the gaps of general and universal experience.

This article is partly based on a lecture delivered at the Polytechnic of Central London on 24 October 1974. I am grateful to Pauline Newmark, Anthony Crane, Ralph Pemberton, John Trim and Alex Auswaks for suggestions and advice.

January 1976

References

Albrecht, J. (1973). *Linguistik und Übersetzung*. Tübingen: Niemeyer.
Arnold, M. (1861). On translating Homer *and* Last words on translating Homer. In *Essays Literary and Critical*. London: Everyman; Dent, 1928.
Arrowsmith, W. & Shattuck, R. (1971). *The craft and context of translation*. Austin: University of Texas Press.
Austin, J. L. (1963). Performative-constative. In C. E. Caton (ed.), *Philosophy and ordinary language*. London: Oxford University Press.
Bachrach, J. A. (1974). An experiment in automatic dictionary look-up. *Incorporated Linguist*, **13**, 2, 47–9.
Benjamin, W. (1923). The translator's task: In H. Arendt (ed.), *Illuminations*. London: Cape, 1970.

Peter Newmark

Booth, A. D. (1967). *Machine translation.* Amsterdam: North-Holland.
Brislin, R. W. (ed.) (1976). *Translation: application and research.* New York: Gardner Press.
Brower, R. A. (ed.) (1966). *On translation.* New York: Oxford University Press.
Bühler, K. (1934). *Die Sprachtheorie.* Jena: Fischer.
Cary, E. (1956). *La traduction dans le monde moderne.* Geneva: Georg and Cie.
Catford, J. C. (1965). *A linguistic theory of translation.* London: Oxford University Press.
Cauer, P. (1896). *Die Kunst des Übersetzens.* Berlin: Weidmann.
Chomsky, N. (1972). *Studies on semantics in generative grammar.* The Hague: Mouton.
Cobb, R. (1969). When to translate. In *A second identity.* London: Oxford University Press.
Croce, B. (1922). *Aesthetics.* London: P. Owen.
Dagut, M. B. (1976). Can metaphor be translated? *Babel,* **20,** 1, 21–33.
Davie, D. (1975). *Poetry in translation.* Milton Keynes: Open University Press.
Dryden, J. (1684). Preface to Ovid's *Epistles.* In Ker (ed.), *Essays.* London: Oxford University Press, 1900.
Études de Linguistique Appliquée (1976). Traduire: les idées et les mots. Special number, **24** (1976).
European Communities Glossary (1974). (F-E) 5th Edition. Council of the European Communities.
Fedorov, A. V. (1958). *Vvedenji v teoriju perevoda.* Moscow.
Fedorov, A. V. (1968). *Osnovy obščej teorii perevoda.* Moscow.
Firth, J. R. (1968). Linguistic analysis and translation. In F. R. Palmer (ed.), *Selected papers 1952–9.* London: Longman.
Frege, G. (1892). Sense and reference. In P. Geach and M. Black (eds.), *Translations from the philosophical writings of Gottlieb Frege.* Oxford: Blackwell, 1952.
Freud, S. (1905). *Der Witz.* Frankfurt: Fischer, 1958.
Freud, S. (1917). *Vorlesungen zur Einführung in die Psychoanalyse.* Vienna: Fischer.
Friederich, W. (1969). *Technik des Übersetzens.* Munich: Hueber.
Fuller, F. (1973). *A handbook for translators.* Gerrards Cross: C. Smythe.
Garvin, P. (1955). *Prague School reader on aesthetics, literary structure and style.* Georgetown University Press.
Gasset, Ortega y. (1937). Miseria y esplendor de la traduccion. See Störig, 1963.
Geckeler, H. (1971). *Zur Wortfelddiskussion.* Munich: Fink.
Goethe, J. W. v. (1813). *Sämtliche Werke* Zu brüderlichem Andenken Wielands. Propyläen edition. Vol. 20, p. 94. Munich, 1909.
Goethe, J. W. v. (1814). *Sämtliche Werke* Besserem Verständnis. Vol. 21, p. 136.
Goethe, J. W. v. (1826). *Sämtliche Werke,* vol. 39. (Letter to Thomas Carlyle.)
Graves, R. (1963). Moral principles in translating. *Incorporated Linguist,* **2,** 2.
Güttinger, F. (1963). *Zielsprache.* Zurich: Manesse.
Haas, W. (1970). The theory of translation. G. H. R. Parkinson (ed.), *The theory of meaning.* London: Oxford University Press.
Halliday, M. A. K.(1973). *Explorations in the functions of language.* London: Edward Arnold.
Harris, B. (1975). Importance of natural translation. *University of Ottawa Papers in Translatology.*
Hartmann, P. & Vernay, H. (1970). *Sprachwissenschaft und Übersetzen.* Munich: Hueber.
Humboldt, W. v. (1816). Einleitung zu Agamemnon. See Störig, 1963.
Jakobson, R. (1960). Linguistics and poetics. In T. Sebeok (ed.), *Style in language.* Technology Press of Massachusetts Institute of Technology, and Wiley.
Jakobson, R. (1966). 'On linguistic aspects of translation'. See Brower, 1966.

Jakobson, R. (1973). *Main trends in the science of language.* London: Allen & Unwin.

Jerome, St. (1400). Letter to Pammachius. See Störig, 1963, 1–13.

Joos, M. (1967). *The five clocks.* New York: Harcourt.

Jumpelt, R. J. (1961). *Die Übersetzung naturwissenschaftlicher und technischer Literatur.* Berlin: Langenscheidt.

Kade, O. (1965). *Fremdsprachen,* Beiheft 1. Leipzig.

Kade, O. (1968). Zufall und Gesetzmässigkeit in der Übersetzung. Leipzig: VEB Verlag. Enzyklopädie.

Kapp, V. (1974). *Übersetzer und Dolmetscher.* Heidelberg: Quelle & Meyer.

Kloepfer, W. (1967). *Die Theorie der literarischen Übersetzung.* Munich: Fink.

Knox, R. A. (1949). *On Englishing the Bible.* London: Burns, Oates.

Knox, R. A. (1958). On English translation. In *Literary diversions.* London: Sheed & Ward.

Koller, W. (1972). *Grundprobleme der Übersetzungstheorie.* Berne: Franke.

Komissarov, V. H. (1973). *Slovo o perevode.* Moscow.

Levy, J. (1969). *Die literarische Übersetzung.* Frankfurt: Athenaeum.

Larbaud, V. (1946). *Sous l'invocation de S. Jérôme.* Paris: Gallimard.

Lefevère, A. (1975). *Translating poetry.* Amsterdam: Van Gorcum, Assen.

Ljudaskanov, A. (1972). *Mensch und Maschine als Übersetzer.* Tr. G. Jäger H. Walter. Munich: Hueber.

Luther, M. (1530). Sendbrief vom Dolmetschen. See Störig, 1963, 1–14.

Maillot, J. (1969). *La traduction scientifique et technique.* Paris: Eyrolles.

Malblanc, A. (1961). *Stylistique comparée du français et de l'allemand.* Paris: Didier.

Matoré, G. (1953). *La méthode en lexicologie.* Paris: Didier.

Mounin, G. (1935). *Les belles infidèles.* Paris: Cahiers du Sud.

Mounin, G. (1963). *Les problèmes théoriques de la traduction.* Paris: NRF.

Mounin, G. (1967). *Die Übersetzung.* Munich: Nymphenburger Verlag.

Nabokov, A. (1964). *Eugene Onegin* (Pushkin), VII. Bollingen, N.Y.

Neubert, A. (1968). Pragmatische Aspekte der Übersetzung in *Grundfragen der Übersetzungswissenschaft.* Leipzig: VEB Verlag Enzyklopädie.

Neubert, A. (1972). Theorie und Praxis für die Übersetzungswissenschaft. 3rd A.I.L.A. Congress, Copenhagen.

Newmark, P. P. (1969). Some notes on translation and translators. *Incorporated Linguist,* **8** (4), 79–85.

Newmark, P. P. (1974). Further propositions on translation. Parts I and II. *Incorporated Linguist,* **13** (2), 34–42; **13** (3), 62–72.

Newmark, P. P. (1976). A tentative preface to translation: methods, principles, procedures. *Audio-Visual Language Journal,* **14**, 3, 161–9.

Newmark, P. P. (1977). The translation of proper names and cultural terms. *Incorporated Linguist,* **16**, 3.

Nida, E. A. (1964). *Towards a science of translating.* Leiden: Brill.

Nida, E. A. & Tabor, C. (1969). *The theory and practice of translating.* Leiden: Brill.

Nida, E. A. (1974 a). *Exploring semantic structures.* Munich: Fink.

Nida, E. A. (1974 b). Translation. In T. Sebeok (ed.), *Current trends in linguistics,* vol. 12. The Hague: Mouton.

Nida, E. A. (1975). *Componential analysis of meaning.* The Hague: Mouton.

Nida, E. A. (1977). *Good news for everyone: how to use the Good News Bible.* Waco, Texas: Word Books.

Nida, E. A. (forthcoming). Translating means communicating: a sociological theory of translation.

Nietzsche, F. (1882). Complete Works, vol. 2. Hauser, 1962.

Nietzsche, F. (1886). Complete Works, vol. 2. Hauser, 1962.

Novalis (1798). Blüthenstaub. See Störig, 1963, 33.

Paepcke, F. (1968). Verstehen und Übersetzen. *Linguistica Antverpensia,* 1, 2, 329–36.

Pears, D. (1972). *Wittgenstein.* London: Fontana.

Peirce, C. (1897). *Collected Papers.* Cambridge: Harvard University Press, 1934.

Reiss, K. (1971). *Möglichkeiten und Grenzen der Übersetzungskritik.* Munich: Hueber.

Revzin, I. I. & Rozencvejg, V. U. (1964). *Osnovi obshchevo i mashinnovo perevoda.* Moscow.

Rieu, E. V. (1953). Translation. In Cassell's *Encyclopaedia of literature,* vol. I. London: Cassell.

Savory, T. H. (1957). *The art of translation.* London: Cape.

Schleiermacher, F. (1813). Methoden des Übersetzens. See Störig, 1963.

Schopenhauer, A. (1851). Über Sprache und Worte. See Störig, 1963, 101–7.

Seleskovitch, D. (1977). Why interpreting is not tantamount to translating. *Incorporated Linguist,* 16, 2, 27–33.

Smith, A. G. (pref) (1958). *Aspects of translation.* London: Secker & Warburg.

Spitzbart, H. (1972). *Spezialprobleme der wissenschaftlichen und technischen Übersetzung.* Munich: Hueber.

Spitzer, L. (1948). *Linguistic and literary history: essays in stylistics.* Princeton.

Steiner, G. (1966). Introduction to *Penguin book of modern verse translation.* Harmondsworth: Penguin.

Steiner, G. (1975). *After Babel. Aspects of language and translation.* London: Oxford University Press.

Störig, H. J. (1963). *Das Problem des Übersetzens.* Darmstadt: Wissenschaftliche Buchgesellschaft.

Strawson, P. F. (1970). On referring. In G. R. H. Parkinson (ed.), *Theory of meaning.* London: Oxford University Press.

Svejtser, A. D. (1973). *Perevod i lingvistika.* Moscow.

Tesniere, L. (1966). Metataxe. In *Elements de Syntaxe Structurale* (283–323). Paris: Klincksieck.

Trier, J. (1973). *Aufsätze und Vorträge zur Wortfeldtheorie.* The Hague: Mouton.

Truffaut, L. (1968). *Grundprobleme der deutsch-französischen Übersetzung.* Munich: Hueber.

Tytler, A. (1790). *Essay on the principles of translation.* London: Dent, 1912.

Valery, P. (1941). Cantiques spirituels. In *Variétes, V.* Paris: NRF.

Vinay, J. P. (1968). La traduction humaine. In A. Martinet (ed.), *Langage.* Paris: Gallimard.

Vinay, J. P. & Darbelnet, J. (1969). *Stylistique comparée du français et de l'anglais.* Paris: Didier.

Wandruszka, M. (1969). *Sprachen, vergleichbar und unvergleichlich.* Munich: Piper.

Weightman, J. G. (1947). *On language and writing.* London: Sylvan Press.

Widmer, F. (1959). *Fug und Unfug des Übersetzens.* Cologne and Berlin: Kiepenheuer & Witsch.

Wilss, W. (1977). *Probleme und Methoden des Übersetzens.* Stuttgart: Klett.

Winter, W. (1969). Impossibilities of translation. In T. M. Olshevsky (ed.), *Problems in the philosophy of language.* New York: Holt, Rinehart & Winston.

Wittgenstein, L. (1953). *Philosophical investigations.* Oxford: Blackwell.

Wuthenow, R. R. (1969). *Das fremde Kunstwerk.* Göttingen: Vandenhoeck & Ruprecht.

LANGUAGES FOR ADULT LEARNERS

J. L. M. Trim

Fellow of Selwyn College and Director of the Department of Linguistics, University of Cambridge

1. *The language needs of society*

In recent years, increasing attention has been paid to the teaching of languages to adults, previously a neglected aspect of educational provision. The reasons for this change have been manifold. Improvements in communications of all kinds have brought contact with speakers of other languages within the everyday experience of larger and larger numbers of people. The contact may be simply a question of exposure to information and entertainment media: books, newspapers, films, radio and television. The opportunities for physical mobility have also increased. International tourism has become a substantial industry, a major factor in the balance of trade. The total number of visitors to Spain in 1974 was greater than the total population of that country. With the increasing affluence and democratisation of Western societies, foreign travel has ceased to be the prerogative of a leisured, cultured élite. 'Seasonal migration' has become an accepted part of normal living, with the working class taking an increasing part.

Beyond tourism, vocational mobility is also rapidly increasing. The day-to-day conduct of industrial, commercial and professional affairs are all increasingly internationalised. Temporary and permanent immigration of workers at all social and professional levels is becoming increasingly common, partly in consequence of differential living standards and employment prospects, but also, at a higher level, in the course of careers in multi-national firms and organisations.

As a result of all these changes, language contact has moved far beyond the stage where a small professional class of translators and interpreters could mediate between societies which were essentially monolingual, living self-contained lives within their own borders. The need for translators and interpreters, trained to the highest professional standards, remains, of course, and increases. Since, however, every personal encounter between speakers of different mother tongues requires one if not both of them to have acquired an ability to communicate in the language of the partner, or both to have acquired a common lingua franca distinct from the mother tongue of either, it is self-evident that as intercommunication on a mass-scale develops internationally, it is creating a demand for language learning on a vast scale. The problem arises in many parts of the world. Emergent states face the problem of establishing a national identity and a common means of internal communication against the background of a plethora of small-scale tribal communities with distinct, often mutually incomprehensible languages (Prator, 70; Harries, 70; Gage, 72; Wong, 72; Sharma, 73).[1] The former colonial language may retain its function as a supra-regional language. This is particularly likely when the ex-colonial language is a major world language, and no more regionally based language of international communication has emerged. This is the case in Africa, where Gage lists 16 languages of more than local importance. Trilingualism between a local verna-cular, a regional lingua franca and a language of culture may then be imposed (Mkilifi, 74). Furthermore, where anglophone and francophone Africa are in contact a second European language may be demanded (Haggis, 74; Treffgarne, 1975). There are, however, many tensions. MacMillan (74), defending the international role of English, acknowledges the resentment caused by fears of infiltration and neocolonialism. English as an exogenic language of culture, while providing access to a means of communication dominant in international travel, media, trade, industry and research (Girard, 71; King, 71) may distort or inhibit the development of the mother tongue. Kerr (73) illustrates this principle from Yoruba-English diglossia in Nigeria. Shukla (71) points out that barely two per cent of Indians speak English, yet a knowledge of the language is essential for posts in government, as well as senior posts in trade, commerce and education. Lewis (72), examining bilingualism in Canada and Papua, points out the serious psychological and intellectual handicap faced by individuals in bilingual societies where there are great economic and cultural disparities between two languages and cultures, making a native-like competence in the foreign language essential for their cultural development and social advance. In these circum-stances the underprivileged adult faces a formidable multiple task. The inherent instability of language roles in emergent states is underlined by Liem (69). Writing of Vietnam in 1967 he speaks of the rising demand for English and the decline of French. What is the position today?

Europe faces different linguistic problems. Dense populations, high standards of education, high income, high mobility of populations, a cultural and political polycentrism with strong national cultural and literary traditions, make for an extremely complex pattern of attitudes and interactions. In some areas, as Scandinavia (Lind, 73), similarity of language and frequent contact have pro-duced 'semi-communication', where speakers use their mother tongue freely and understand that of their partner. Ross (73), basing himself on a principle of parity of esteem, expects every European to acquire two foreign languages, one chosen on the criterion of propinquity, the other on international currency, the

[1] Numbers such as 70 refer to year of publication in *Language Teaching Abstracts*; full reference (1975) refers to year of original publication of book or article.

priority being determined by the political, economic and cultural importance of the language concerned. Châlon (73) expects 10% of the French to need to be professionally bilingual by 1985. He expects to see the emergence of a culture-free world lingua franca, with receptive skills nevertheless required in further languages. Girard's reason for expecting this lingua franca to be English corresponds to experience and the increasing dominance of English as the first foreign language in nearly all Western European countries – as indeed on a world scale. Denison (71) does well however to remind the English of the established position of French within the E.E.C. Bormann (74) characterises German as one of a group of languages holding second place in the flow of culture in the world, but points to its increasing use in international organisations and under the influence of foreign workers, following a long decline, accelerated during and after the Nazi period, from its nineteenth-century peak.

To meet the demands of such diverse, complex and rapidly changing situations more conscious appraisal of national language use, needs and demands is called for, so that a sensible language policy can be devised. Language planning of this sort has to cover both internal and external language relations. It is in the light of this appraisal that the allocation of resources for the encouragement and organisation of language learning has to be made.

A number of studies (cf. bibliography, section 4) have been made to ascertain language needs in various European countries. 'Needs' are as such notoriously difficult to ascertain. Where the actual language situations arising in particular employments or other activities can be directly investigated (cf. Evans & Pastor, 1972; Bung, 1973; Candlin *et al.*, 1974) it seems reasonable to assume that the language use as observed will be that needed by a recruit. The results of such field studies may be taken as predictive of the whole class of learners with similar occupations. Where the scale of operation is too great for field studies, other methods must be used in addition or in substitution. Larsson (1969), Alquist (1968) and the London Chamber of Commerce (1972) employed a postal questionnaire, with results clearly dependent for their validity upon how reliable and representative the informants are. The pilot study of Emmans *et al.* (1974) was wider in its approach, combining the analysis of advertisements in selected newspapers with a postal questionnaire to selected foreign-language graduates in employment, a questionnaire plus follow-up visits to personnel officers of 40 major firms and a questionnaire to their employees. Alquist's replies were indicative of the advance in the position of English in Sweden in recent years. Fifty per cent of the population had studied English. But while no significance by sex was found, the differences by age-group were sharp. Ninety-two per cent of the under-30s had studied English, but only 23% of the over 50s. Over 90% of those who had studied English felt a need to understand and produce spoken English, as did over half of those who had not. Fewer acknowledged a need to read English, but the 70% who did so read more than they spoke or listened.

Under half felt any need to write English. Those who did were for the most part in formal education or had private connections. Larsson found a similar rank-order for German in Swedish industry, but a lower demand – one-fifth of the employees of 84 % of firms had some requirement for German. The Emmans enquiry dealt only with the private sector of industry and commerce. While casting further doubt on the adequacy of full-time initial education to meet language needs (less than 10 % of language graduates were found to use a foreign language in employment other than teaching), it revealed a similar rank order for the use of skills. The order of languages required was French, German, Spanish, Italian and Russian. In general, however, the enquiry revealed a very low level of awareness of the extent of language use and needs. This low level is further demonstrated by the drop in demand for language courses organised under the aegis of the CBI and the refusal of the government to make grants under the export aid scheme available for language training, as well as the low (22·8 %) proportion of questionnaires returned in the London Chamber of Commerce market survey. The decisive priority given to 'listening and speaking' (62 % of selective responses) over reading (14 %) and writing (15 %), may therefore not be representative. For the same reason some doubt must also attach to the statistical validity of the very detailed breakdown of specific activities and areas of skill for particular categories of employee. Nevertheless, the 'profiles' arrived at form, together with the analytical classifications of Richterich (1971) and OUP (1975), the most detailed specifications of the language needs of specific groups of foreign language users.

The results of these enquiries, fragmentary and unreliable though they may be, seem to confirm what common sense might suggest: that the need for foreign languages is extremely diversified according to country, age, class and occupation, and as concerns the language required, as well as the situations and conditions of use and thus the kind of knowledge of the language and the balance of skills in bringing it into action.

2. *The role of adult education*

What is the part to be played by adult language learning in this context? Traditionally, public educational provision has concentrated heavily on the period of full-time education. The first responsibility of the state has been to provide universal compulsory full-time institutionalised education for its children, with adequate opportunities for a limited but increasing proportion of gifted and motivated children to go on into higher secondary, further and higher education. As it has been possible to increase the resources devoted to education, priority has been given to improving the quality, and particularly the material basis, of full-time compulsory education, to extend its duration, to raise the length and quality of teacher training, to increase the proportion of adolescents and young adults to pursue their studies, either academically as far as a degree and beyond, or vocationally in full or part-time study to reach proficiency in crafts, trades and professions. But what share of always scarce educational resources may languages claim in competition with other established studies, not to mention the vigorous new ones generated by modern life? The debate on the proper place of languages has centred on their educational value in the guided development of the individual intellect and personality as much as on a future utility, which in early years can only be guessed at and which may be severely eroded by disuse once schooldays are over. For what proportion of children can the learning of languages in the artificial and alien environment of the school-room be a worthwhile, effective undertaking? How widespread is under-achievement? Can it be cured by the setting of more appropriate objectives, the employment of more effective methods and better teachers, or at a different age? Although language teachers have been in receipt of much advice and have been responsive to it, the problems have not gone away. Indeed, the position of language teaching in schools is as problematic as ever, certainly no less so (though perhaps not inordinately more so) than that of other subjects.

Meanwhile, the provision made for adult language learning has been relatively restricted and precarious. To some extent this is true of adult education in general. We expect our people to get their education over and done with quickly and to settle down to jobs, family and a quiet life! Once initial qualifications have been gained, we seem to value practical experience more than further study. This attitude is changing. Scientific and technical advance is now so rapid that, however much we may regret it, craft skills gained over long years of experience can become obsolete almost overnight. Instead of a thorough training for a particular craft or profession, initial education may be more appropriately directed towards giving the young person an understanding of himself and the developing world about him, and inner resources which will allow him to live a fuller life and adapt flexibly to changing conditions and roles as may be necessary. Such a person, living in such a world, will never reach the stage where his education is complete; the *abgeschlossene Bildung* of the German academic middle class becomes chimerical. This viewpoint has been recognised in recent British official policy documents and reports, though only to a limited extent. Thus the 1972 White Paper, while speaking of 'a broadly organised effort to enable all members of society, with their widely differing aspirations and capacities, once they have left school behind to learn where, when and what they want in the way that best suits them' (DES, 1972, p. 30) devoted no more than the most marginal attention (104, 105, 147) to adult education, pending the appearance of the Russell Report (DES, 1973). Regrettably, that report, with its narrow concentration on administrative minutiae and surprising lack of curiosity as to the content of adult education and the needs and motivations of adult learners, proposed no more than minor improvements and a very modest long-term expansion with no significant structural changes.

'Permanent education' has, however, been very much to the forefront of international educational thinking (OECD, 1973; UNESCO, 1973; CCC, 1972, 1973, 1974). A major project of the Council for Cultural Cooperation (CCC) of the Council of Europe, under the control of the Committee for Out-of-School Education and Cultural Development (CEES) has been devoted to a consideration of the structure and organisation of permanent and recurrent education – how are adults, who think they have put 'school' behind them, with all that it stands for, to be brought freely to consider the organised acquisition of new ideas, knowledge, techniques and skills as an on-going part of their ordinary lives, a continuing process of developing awareness and competence? How, on the other side, is society to provide and organise the resources to enable the awakened adult (awakened perhaps only as the result of a crisis, say redundancy) to acquire at short notice the new knowledge and skill he needs? Furthermore, how can systems be put together which will place at the disposal of the learner facilities geared to his specific needs and long-term interests, enabling him to study over extended periods with different degrees of intensity according to the exigencies and pressures of professional and private life, following a path which has a long-term strategy but a tactical progression through appropriate short-term objectives representing an 'aspiration... high enough for progress but low enough for success' (Torrey, 1971).

In September 1971 the CES convened a group of experts under the present author's direction, which has been engaged since then on an exploration of the nature and properties of a potential learner-centred, needs and motivation-based language learning system for adults in Europe organised along unit-credit lines. In its work, the expert group has followed the systems approach of educational technology (Richmond, 1970), an integrative approach which has the virtue of bringing together into a single conceptual framework the many different problems which face teachers of languages to adults (or indeed any category of learners). In this way its work and publications (cf. CCC refs in Section 5) act as a focus for the growing interest in language teaching. In fact, of course, the entire literature of the subject, however specialised and diversified, can be seen to contribute to a coherent picture if approached in this way.

3. The specification of objectives

In the wake of Bloom *et al.* (1956, 1964), the objectives of language learning have been more closely examined, especially from the behavioural point of view. That effective communication is the overall aim has been held by the majority of theorists since Viëtor (1888) and Sweet (1899) though the latter expected the intelligent adult learner to pass eventually to philological studies. However, the effect of the classical literary approach has remained strong in universities and in schools, so that proponents of 'direct' method have remained 'modernist' for almost a century. The advent of structural linguistics may have had some small influence in focusing attention back onto grammatical forms and in association with behaviourist theories of overlearning and the solipsistic environment of the language laboratory led away from communicative activity to a pursuit of efficient skilled speech production. English language teaching, strongly influenced by Palmer (1964), remained activity-oriented, though stiffened by phonetics and structural grammar.

More recently, the acceptance of a learner-centred, needs and motivation-based approach (CCC, 1973 a; Hanzell, 71) has led away from subject-oriented, quasi-absolute specifications to a concern with what is feasible for (Perren, 71) and appropriate to the learner. Moss (73) points out the dangers, even in a military context, of rigid behavioural objectives. Allen and Widdowson (74) point out the shift from grammatical to communicative aims, which Piepho (74) refines to the acquisition of communicative functions in situational teaching, embodying appropriate grammatical forms. Valette and Disick (1972), following Bloom, distinguish four parts to a performance objective: purpose, student behaviour, conditions and criterion, and establish separate taxonomies for subject-matter and affective, or attitudinal, objectives. These are then recombined into a five-stage development. The stages are (1) mechanical skills, (2) knowledge, (3) transfer, (4) communication, (5) criticism. The 'internal behaviour' of the student progresses from perception through recognition, reception, comprehension and analysis to evaluation, and his 'external behaviour' correspondingly moves from reproduction via recall, application and self-expression to 'synthesis' – the execution of original research or individual study. Whether any adult of reasonable experience and intelligence can pass amenably through these stages in sequence seems as highly dubious as performance level specifications which do not allow the beginner to understand (let alone make) jokes. Are we really to believe in a man (or woman) who can recognise all the characters in all written texts but not understand a word? But the conceptual scaffolding is useful. Of the major adult language-teaching organisations, the *Volkshochschulverband* in Germany and neighbouring countries has been particularly active in specifying clear objectives (Tietgens *et al.*, 1974, bibliography, pp. 281–4). Starting from defined syllabuses in terms of minimal vocabularies and grammatical inventories, the commissions of the VV have moved explicitly towards more differentiated communicative aims. The *Survey of curricula and performance* (James & Rouve, 1973) shows that the 40 modern-language syllabuses in further education they analyse lack declared objectives and rather employ expressions like 'ordinary everyday style', 'reasonable fluency', which 'are too subjective and ambiguous to be used as reliable indices between bodies'.

One of the most developed models is that of Bung (CCC, 1973 b), developed as part of the Council of Europe unit-credit project. This generalised model for the specification of operational language-learning objectives takes into account the situations the learner would face, the social functions he would want language to perform, the topics he would have to deal with, the notions he would have to express, the skills he would have to exercise, the grammar and vocabulary and phonetic system he would need to command, and the skilled actions by which all this is effected in speech. The general model has been developed, and fully exemplified for English, by J. van Ek (CCC, 1975). Van Ek gives a multi-dimensional specification of the minimal 'general' communicative ability which 'will allow learners to maintain themselves in most everyday situations, including situations for which they have not been specifically trained'. The specific class of learners envisaged are temporary visitors (or hosts) whose contacts will, on the whole, be of superficial, non-professional kind. Other variants may be derived by replacing certain items or classes of items, by others of similar weight. In this way, because it is so explicit, the 'threshold level' specification can act as a 'reference level' in a system of equivalences.

4. *Languages for special purposes*

A high proportion of adult learners correspond to van Ek's target audience. They are interested in developing their ability to make human contact with the foreigners whose language they are learning, but have no clear idea of the exact circumstances under which they will do so. They form the basis of most informal adult education classes in evening institutions, and most media-based systems are aimed at them. Much language teaching to adults has, however, specific vocational aims. A great deal of teaching and planning effort is devoted to such 'languages for special purposes' especially where intensive or part-time courses are offered in an institutional framework. The courses may be offered to non-specialist students in the fields concerned, or mounted as a service to industry. Some are directly organised by private industry or public services.

The most obvious characteristic of language used in a highly specialised context is its vocabulary (cf. Fries, 1945, p. 2). Numerous technical dictionaries and specialised vocabularies are published, monolingual, bilingual and multi-lingual. CREDIF has supplemented its basic scientific vocabulary (1972) with a number of specialised lexica. Pittman (74) warns against too heavy a concentration on vocabulary in specialised courses. For scientific and technical purposes the main concentration has been on how to achieve adequate information retrieval with minimal language learning. Dučkova and Beneš (68) describe tests to establish this minimal level. Reid (1970) proposes a method for scanning articles for bare information. Alford (68) proposes a minimal learning effort to cover basic morphology and high frequency lexicon so that computerised dictionary look-up will be feasible. Strevens (72) emphasises the need for conceptual planning as opposed to vocabulary teaching, especially in developing countries. Butler (72) shows how the internal articulation of a subject may indicate a natural order of grammatical progression within the language course. Gentilhomme (73) points out that linguistic and subject priorities may not correspond and advocates the teaching of a heuristic to the scientist. Swales (74) and Latal (74) explore the difficulties arising from the language teacher's lack of knowledge of or interest in scientific content. Herblin (75) describes a course aiming to develop an ability to construct scientific reasoning in the FL, while Baetens-Beardsmore (74) and MacKay (74) aim at spoken fluency to enable students to converse with other scientists. Coutts (75), dealing with intensive courses for airline personnel, discusses the use of simulation and role playing. The hotel and catering industry presents characteristic limited contact situations (Bung, CCC 1973; Combes, 1974; Coles & Land, 1973). Walker (1973) combines Russian language teaching with a technical introduction to Slavonic bibliography.

4. *Adult immigrants*

Immigrants and migrant workers form a special class of adult language learners. They are often disadvantaged, with severe social and educational problems in addition to their linguistic difficulties (Congleton, 68; Catani, 1975; SCRR, 1974). Most educational effort has centred on the children of immigrants, though this is best seen in a community context (Fischer *et al.* 72). For adults, the workplace has generally been the focus of contact (Winterscheidt, 72; Arbeitsgruppe, 1975) though volunteer schemes have been more directed to social integration (CRC, 1973) and the Pathway group in Southall aimed to 'gain the cooperation of employers by providing language courses which would make their non-English speaking employees more efficient workers as well as fulfilling wider aims for the individual and community' (Jupp & Hodlin, 1975, p. 1). No one, as Richards (73) point out, can be expected to learn the language of a social group if he is denied the means to join that group. As opposed to the near-ghetto conditions of temporary migrant workers in continental countries (especially Germany) with very limited contacts, which make the use of the host language almost a peripheral concern, immigrant doctors form a group in which language is a central tool and often a matter of life and death. Furthermore, the immigrant doctor is in a traditionally authoritarian position (Parkinson, 1973). The language problems of doctors have accordingly been more carefully investigated and catered for than any other group (Candlin *et al.* 1974).

5. *Methodology*

A large part of the literature on adult language learning is naturally concerned with method. The psycholinguistic basis for the choice of method has been discussed, though for the most part the discussions have been neutral as between adult and child learning and derivative from such more general psycholinguistic controversies as the 'audio-lingual habit theory' and the 'cognitive code-learning theory'. Thus Newmark and Reibel (69) base an exposure method on the claim that both children and adults are capable of deducing grammatical rules from a mass of linguistic material. Seliger (75), however, describes an experiment indicating that a group of adults taught by the deductive method performed significantly better on a long-term retention test than a group taught by the inductive method. This finding appears to be in line with the findings of Elek and Oskarsson (1972, cf. also Levin, 1972). Mueller (72) also reports superior results from a cognitive code learning course. Carroll (72) considers that the 'habit' theory will hold if 'functional habits' are brought in to supplement 'linguistic habits', and doubts whether adult language-learning ability is markedly less than that of children. Scovel (70), on the other hand, puts forward a theory that hemispherical dominance is established by the age of 12 after which naïve accentless learning is impossible – for the child language learning is a trait, for the adult a skill. In reply, Hill (71) emphasises the importance of cultural factors in America which militate against acquisition of an accent-free foreign language. She is close to the views of Christophersen (1973), who as a distinguished bilingual regards the primacy of the 'mother tongue' as a myth of monolingual societies. Kohls (72) reports an experiment to show that a purely oral method achieves inferior results with adult groups to a combination of aural and written work. He sees this as a consequence of the adults' strong inner model of the outer world and stable behavioural system. Stille (75) and Postovsky (75) report similar findings. Better progress is made by adults if auditory comprehension and writing precede oral production, to which there is a high positive transfer.

A number of works (e.g. Hay, 1973; Dunlop, 1970) continue to give sound advice to the adult class teacher, with suggestions for less formal ways of teaching (Hill & Fielden, 1974; Mullen, 1972; Cammack, 73; Druce, 74; Lindsay, 74). The need for a situational approach (Emsig, 68) leading to free expression (Bolinger, 73; Rivers, 73) and the ability to form conversational strategies (Potter, 72) and to think in the language (Leont'ev, 69 and 72; Makhmadova, 69) are increasingly emphasised. However, the change of emphasis from teaching to learning is apparent. Linguists have always emphasised 'study' and 'learning' (Sweet, 1964; Palmer, 1964; Fries, 1945; Moulton, 1966; Hall, 1966). Stern (75) identified the strategies of a good learner as: (1) positive learning strategies, (2) an active approach to the learning task, (3) a positive attitude to the language and its speakers, (4) sufficient linguistic knowledge about how to tackle a language, (5) ability to draw inferences and discover rules, (6) constant searching for meaning, (7) willingness to practice, (8) willingness to try to communicate in real situations, (9) self-monitoring and (10) developing the language as a separate system and learning to think in it. If only we were all like that! Motivation is further discussed by Vesely (74) and by McDonald and Sager (75) as well as Ingram (73), who sees it as necessary to carry the learner over the hard grind of boring practice. Raz (74) suggests, sensibly, that the students themselves be asked. Learner-centredness is demonstrated by the intense interest in individualised learning following the Stanford Conference (Altman & Politzer, 1972). Though the context is usually institutional, there is no reason why the principle of treating pupils like sensible adults should not be applied to sensible adults. In addition to self-instructional working, work in pairs (Zolotniskaya *et al.*, 73) and groups (Watts, 73) provides for social interaction and the exploitation of group dynamics and co-operative heuristic methods. The role of the teacher comes to be more that of counsellor (Titone, 73) and manager (Altman, 73). This development is emphasised by the use of technology. Less interest is now shown in the use of individual devices (see index section 10) than in the organisation of multi-media systems (Bishop, 72; Kuhn, 73). The use of mass media, and in particular broadcasting services, radio and TV, have dramatically increased the accessibility of languages to audiences previously untouched by adult education (cf. Bibliography section 10 and index section 11). The scale of course provision is very substantial (IZJB, 1969) and courses have steadily developed from motivating entertainment vehicles to sophisticated learning instruments embedded in multi-faceted systems (Hautamäkki, 1973; Innes, 1973). Television also affords unparalleled opportunities for combining cultural documentation with language teaching (BBC, 1973). Further means of reaching adult needs are afforded by distance teaching (Sdun, 69; Kaniščeva, 72; Goodman, 73) and intensive courses (index section 12).

Materials and courses directed towards adult learners are so many (CCC, 1969; Goethe-Institute, 1975) that to mention any is invidious. Alexander's *Mainline* may perhaps be mentioned as one attempt by an articulate (Alexander 1976, 68, 69) and clear-sighted course designer to reconcile functional and grammatical organisation, and to weld a series of courses into a single system. The 'backwash' effect of examination changes towards a more communicative approach is seen in Templer and Nettle (1974).

6. *Testing*

Techniques of language testing for the assessment of students' aptitude for language learning, for placement in courses, for monitoring their progress, including guided self-assessment as well as for assessing overall proficiency, have all come in for close examination (cf. Bibliography section 11, index section 16), together with the various techniques employed. Though much of the work has been directed at adults, little discussion has occurred of the specific differences between languages tests for adults and for children. Though the role of examinations in adult education remains contentious, some educationalists being opposed in principle to their intrusion and preferring techniques of guided self-assessment, the role of such major certificating bodies as the Cambridge Local Examinations Syndicate (LES, 1973) and the Volkshochschulverband in structuring learning is considerable and most would agree beneficial. Much remains to be done, however, to establish equivalences, clear criteria and objective specifications (James, 1973) and to introduce a learner-centred flexibility within an international system. The aim of the CCC unit-credit project is to create the basic prerequisites for such a system (CCC, 1973 a).

7. Teacher training

For the most part, teachers in adult education are part-time, recruited *ad hoc* for classes which appear to be a viable size. Their qualifications and experience are extremely various. Perhaps the full professionalisation of teachers is the most important contribution to the development of adult language learning that can be made. Training should certainly include learning management and creative counselling, and guidance to students in using multi-media systems. At present the specific training of teachers for adult language learners is almost totally neglected (apart from the EFL field (Wingard, 75), where the RSA Certificate in the Teaching of English as a Foreign Language performs a valuable service) – except that a high proportion of the books discussed above are read by practising teachers. *April 1975*

A Classified Bibliography on Adult Language Learning

1. BIBLIOGRAPHIES, ETC.

British Council (1973). *Theses and dissertations related to the teaching of English to speakers of other languages deposited with English universities 1961–72*. ETIC. Also Supplement to 1975.

Cantor, L. M. & Roberts, I. F. (1972). *Further Education in England and Wales*, Rev. edn. London: Routledge & Kegan Paul.

CILT/ETIC (1972). *A language-teaching bibliography*, 2nd edn. Cambridge University Press.

CILT (1976). *Language and language teaching: current research in Britain 1972–75*. London: Longman.

Department of Education and Science and Central Office of Information (1972). *Languages courses*. HMSO.

Essex University Appointments Board (1972). *Using languages*. Colchester: The Board.

Informationszentrum für Fremdsprachenforschung (1974). *Fremdsprachenunterricht in der Weiterbildung: Stand Juli 1973*. München: Hueber. (Spezialbibliographie, 1.)

Kelly, Thos. (ed.) (1974). *Select bibliography of adult education in Great Britain, including works published to the end of the year 1972,* 3rd edn. National Institute of Adult Education, Leicester.

Language Studies Ltd. (1972). *Every training manager's ABC of languages.* London: Language Studies Ltd.

National Institute of Adult Education (1974). *Research in adult education in the British Isles: abstracts and summaries, principally of master and doctoral theses presented since 1945,* by Alan H. Charnley. Leicester: NIAE.

Paulston, Rolland G. (ed.) (1972). *Non-formal education: an annotated international bibliography.* New York: Praeger.

Standing Conference on University teaching in the education of adults (1975). *Register of research in progress in adult education 1974 & 1975.* Manchester: Department of Adult Education, University of Manchester.

2. EDUCATIONAL POLICY AND PLANNING FOR ADULT EDUCATION

Byrne, Eileen M. *Planning and educational inequality.* Windsor: NFER, 1974.

Cleugh, M. F. (1970). *Educating older people.* 2nd edn. London: Tavistock Publications.

Clyne, P. (1972). *The disadvantaged adult: educational and social needs of minority groups.* London: Longman.

Commission on Post-secondary Education in Ontario (1972). *The learning society: report of the Commission on Post-secondary Education in Ontario.* Ministry of Government Services, Toronto.

Council of Europe: Council for Cultural Cooperation (CCC) (1973). *Permanent education: the basis and essentials.* Strasbourg.

—— (1974). *Some models of adult learning and adult change,* by A. M. Hubermann. Strasbourg.

—— (1972). *Today and tomorrow in European adult education,* by J. A. Simpson. Strasbourg.

Department of Education and Science (1972). *Education: framework for expansion.* HMSO.

—— (1973). *Adult education: a plan for development.* HMSO.

Organisation for Economic Cooperation and Development (OECD); Centre for Educational Research and Innovation. (1973). *Recurrent Education: a strategy for lifelong learning.* Paris: OECD.

UNESCO (1973). *Towards a conceptual model of lifelong education,* by George W. Parkyn. Paris: UNESCO.

3. PERIODICALS

English for Business: a language magazine for people at work. Box 5202, S-10244, Stockholm.

Modern Language Teaching: periodical of adult language teaching. Budapest.

Zielsprache Englisch, also *Zielsprache Deutsch, Zielsprache Französisch, Zielsprache Spanish.* All München: Hueber.

4. LANGUAGE USE, PLANNING, NEEDS AND DEMANDS

Alquist, P. (1968). *What needs do Swedes experience for proficiency in English?* UME-VB, bilaga 43, Stockholm.

Austin, J. (1975). *How to do things with words,* 2nd edn. Oxford University Press.

Bung, K. (1973). *The foreign language needs of waiters and hotel staff.* CCC/EES(73)16 rev. Strasbourg: Council of Europe.

Candlin, C., Leather, J. & Bruton, C. (1974). *Work in progress; reports I, II and III (English language skills for overseas doctors and medical staff).* University of Lancaster, mimeo.

Ehlich, K. & Rehbein, J. (1972). Sprache in einer Institution: das Speiserestaurant. In D. Wunderlich (ed.), *Linguistische Pragmatik.* Wiesbaden: Athenaion.

Emmans, K. *et al.* (1974). *The use of foreign languages in the private sector of industry and commerce.* York: Language Teaching Centre, University of York.

Evans, G. & Pastor, E. (1972). *Communication 12½: report of a field survey of language skills and real job needs.* Personnel Training Section, Swedish International Development Authority, Stockholm.

Falch, J. (1973). *Contribution à l'étude du statut des langues en Europe.* Quebec: Presses de l'Université Laval.

Fishman, J. A. (ed.). (1968). *Language problems of developing nations.* London, New York: Wiley.

—— (1974). *Advances in language planning.* The Hague, Paris: Mouton.

Larsson, J. (1969). The German language in parts of Swedish industry and commerce; a study in questionnaire techniques and an investigation of language needs. *Pedagogical and Psychological Problems*, no. 101, College of Education, Malmü.

London Chamber of Commerce (1972). *Report on the 'market survey' of the non-specialist use of foreign languages in industry and commerce.* London.

Richterich, R. (1971). *Analytical classification of the categories of adults needing to learn foreign languages.* (CCC/EES(71)55) Strasbourg: Council of Europe.

Ross, W. (1972). *Deutsch in der Konkurrenz der Weltsprachen.* München: Hueber.

Searle, J. (1970). *Speech acts.* Cambridge University Press.

Treffgarne, G. (1975). *The rôle of English and French as languages of communication between anglophone and francophone West African States: Africa Education Trust research project Jan. 1973–June 1974.* London: Africa Education Trust.

White, P. E. (1974). *The social impact of tourism on host communities: a study of language change in Switzerland.* Oxford: School of Geography, University of Oxford.

Wright, P. (1974). *The language of British industry.* London: Macmillan.

5. OBJECTIVES SPECIFICATION AND CURRICULUM DEVELOPMENT

Banathy, B. H. & Lange, D. L. (1972). *A design for foreign language curricula.* Lexington, Mass.: Heath.

Bloom, B. S. *et al.* (1956). *Taxonomy of educational objectives: the classification of educational goals. Handbook 1: Cognitive domain.* N.Y.: McKay.

Council of Europe, Council for Cultural Cooperation (1971). *Linguistic content, means of evaluation and their interaction in the teaching and learning of modern languages in adult education.* Strasbourg.

—— (1973 a). *Systems development in adult language learning.* Strasbourg.

—— (1975). *Systems development in adult language learning: the threshold level in a European unit-credit system for modern language learning by adults,* by J. A. van Ek, with an appendix by L. G. Alexander. Strasbourg.

Council of Europe, Committee for Out of School Education and Cultural Development (1973 b). *The specification of objectives in a language-learning system for adults,* by Dr K. Bung. (CCC/EES (73) 34). Strasbourg: Council of Europe.

—— (1974). *Modern languages in adult education: a unit-credit system.* Strasbourg.

Freihoff, R. & Takala, S. (1974). *A systematic description of language teaching objectives based on the specification of language use situations.* Jyväskylä.

James, C. V. & Rouve, S. (1973). *Survey of curricula and performance 1971–72. Chapter 2: further (adult) education.* London: Statistics supplements, 1975.

Kratwohl, D. R., Bloom, B. S. & Masia, B. (1964). *Taxonomy of educational objectives. Handbook II: affective domain.* N.Y.: McKay.

New York Board of Education Bureau of Curriculum Development (1972). *Teaching English as a new language to adults: scope and sequence: intermediate level.* N.Y.: The Board.

Oxford University Press (1975). *English language stages of attainment scale.* OUP.

Piepho, H. E. (1974). *Kommunikative Kompetenz als übergeordnetes Lernziel.* Dornburg-Frickhofen: Frankonius-Verlag.

Tietgens, H., Hirschmann, G. & Bianchi, M. (1974). *Ansätze zu einem Baukastensystem.* Braunschweig: Westermann.

Valette, R. M. & Disick, R. S. (1972). *Modern language performance objectives and individualisation: a handbook.* N.Y.: Harcourt & Brace.

6. LANGUAGES FOR SPECIAL PURPOSES

Association Internationale pour la Recherche et la Diffusion des Méthodes Audio-visuelles et Structuro-globales (AIMAV) (1973). *Modern language teaching to adults: languages for special purposes.* M. de Grève *et al.* (eds). Paris: Didier; Brussels: AIMAV.

Berth, E. (1971). *Fachsprache: eine Bibliographie.* Hildesheim.

Centre de Recherche et d'étude pour la Diffusion du Français (CREDIF) (1972). *Vocabulaire générale d'orientation scientifique (VGOS).* Paris: Didier.

Centre for Information on Language Teaching and Research (1974). *Teaching languages to adults for special purposes.* CILT. (CILTRAP, 11.)

—— (1975). *Survey of research and materials development in vocational uses of English, French and German.* CILT.

Coles, M. C. & Lord, B. D. (1973). *The Savoy English course for the catering industry.* London: Edward Arnold.

Combes, S. (1974). *Restaurant French: for hoteliers, restaurateurs and catering students.* 2nd edn. London: Barrie & Jenkins.

Finlay, I. F. (1973). *Language services in industry.* London: Lockwood.

Institut National pour la Formation des Adultes (1967). *Colloque sur l'enseignement des langues dans les Instituts Universitaires de Technologie, 5, 6, 7 Dec. 1967.* Nancy: INFA.

Institute of Modern Languages (1972–3). *Orientation in Business English: secretarial series.* 7 vols. Washington, D.C.: The Institute.

Kay, M. & Goodfellow, R. (1974). *Marketing petroleum products.* London: Collier-Macmillan.

Reid, R. E. (1970). *Chemistry through the language barrier: how to scan chemical articles in foreign languages; with special reference to Russian and Japanese.* London, Baltimore: Johns Hopkins Press.

Scottish Council for Commercial, Administrative and Professional Education (1973). *Report of the working party on language courses.* Edinburgh: SCCAPE.

Walker, G. P. M. (1973). *Russian for librarians.* London: Bingley.

7. LANGUAGES FOR ADULT IMMIGRANTS

Arbeitsgruppe 'Deutscher Sprachenschein für ausländische Arbeiter' (1975). *Deutschunterricht für ausländische Arbeiter.* München.

Bureau pour l'Enseignement de la Langue et de la Civilisation Française à l'Etranger (BELC) (1972). *Les travailleurs étrangers: éléments de civilisation liés à la pratique de la langue: dossiers niveau 2.* Paris: BELC.

Catani, M. (1975). *L'alphabetisation des travailleurs étrangers: une relation dominant/dominé; postface de R. Jaulin.* Paris: Tema-Editions.

Community Relations Commission. *Language Teaching and Community Relations.*

—— (1973). *Voluntary language tutoring schemes: a list of organisers.* London: CRC.

Fuller, Helene R. (1971). *Wifetalk: dialogs prepared for foreign student wives.* Ohio.

Jupp, T. C. & Hodlin, S. (1975). *Industrial English: an example of theory and practice in functional language teaching.* London: Heinemann Educational.

Parkinson, Joy E. (1973). *Investigation into the language problems of overseas doctors and nurses.* London: The Author, Southwark College.

Select Committee on Race Relations and Immigration (1974). *Educational disadvantage and the educational needs of immigrants.* HMSO.

8. METHODOLOGY

Altman, H. B. & Politzer, R. L. (eds). (1972). *Individualising foreign language instruction.* Rowley, Mass.: Newbury House.

Bloomfield, L. About foreign language training. *Yale Review,* **4**, 625–41.

Bronstein, M. (1937). *L'enseignement des langues étrangères aux adultes.* Paris.

Bung, K. (1973). *Towards a theory of programmed language instruction.* The Hague, Paris: Mouton.

Cembalo, M. & Holec, H. (1973). Les langues aux adultes; pour une pédagogie de l'autonomie. *Mélanges Pédagogiques.*

Center for Applied Linguistics (1967). *A report of the developmental testing of a self-instructional French program.* Washington, D.C.: CAL.

Christophersen, P. (1973). *Second language learning: myth and reality.* London: Penguin.

Council of Europe (1975). *Education and Culture no. 28: Modern language learning by adults.* Strasbourg: The Council.

de Grève, M. *et al.* (1973). *Modern language teaching to adults.* Paris: Didier; Brussels: AIMAV.

Disick, R. S. (1975). *Individualising language instruction: strategies and methods.* New York: Harcourt & Brace.

Dunlop, I. (1970). *Practical techniques in the teaching of oral English.* Stockholm: Almqvist & Wiksell.

Elek, T. & Oskarsson, M. (1972). *Teaching foreign language grammar to adults: a comparative study.* Stockholm: Almqvist & Wiksell.

Fries, C. C. (1945). *Teaching and learning English as a foreign language.* Ann Arbor: University of Michigan Press.

Gougher, R. L. (ed.) (1971). *Individualisation of instruction in foreign languages: a practical guide.* Philadelphia: Center for Curriculum Development.

Hall, R. A. (1966). *New ways to learn a foreign language.* New York: Bantam.

Hay, M. (1973). *Languages for adults.* London: Longman.

Hill, L. A. & Fielden, R. D. S. (1974). *English language teaching games for adult students,* books 1 and 2. London: Evans.

Levin, L. (1972). *Comparative studies in foreign language teaching: the GUME project.* Stockholm: Almqvist & Wiksell.

Logan, E. (1973). *Individualised foreign language learning: an organic process: a guide to initiating, maintaining and expanding the process.* Rowley, Mass.: Newbury House.

Moulton, W. G. (1966). *A linguistic guide to language learning.* New York: MLA.

Mueller, T. H. & Niedzielski, H. (1966). *Basic French: a programmed course.* New York: Irvington.

Mullen, D. (1972). *LEREC: Learning English as a second language through recreation.* Prince Albert: Saskatchewan New Start Inc.

Najam, E. E. (ed.) (1966). *Language learning: the individual and the process.* Bloomington: Indiana University; The Hague: Mouton.

Nida, E. A. (1957). *Learning a foreign language: a handbook prepared especially for missionaries.* Rev. edn. New York: Friendship Press.

Palmer, H. E. (1964). *The principles of language study* (1921). Reprinted London: OUP.

Richmond, W. K. (1970). *The concept of educational technology.* London: Weidenfeld.

Sprissler, M. & Weinrich, H. (eds.) (1972). *Fremdsprachenunterricht in Intensivkursen.* Stuttgart, Berlin: Kohlhammer.

Sweet, H. (1964). *The practical study of languages: a guide for teachers and learners* (1899). Reprinted London: OUP

Thorndike, R. L. (1973). *Reading comprehension in fifteen countries: an empirical study.* New York; London: Wiley; Stockholm: Almqvist & Wiksell.

Torrey, J. W. (1971). Second language learning. In C. E. Reed (ed.), *The learning of language.* New York: Appleton-Century-Crofts.

Viëtor, W. (1888). *Der Sprachunterricht muss umkehren!* Heilbronn.

Zamoysten, Habria (1974). *Do-it-yourself English: a comprehensive course.* Warszawa: Panstwowe Wydawnictwo Naukowe.

9. MATERIALS AND COURSES

Alexander, L. G. (1974-5-. *Mainline.* London: Longman.

—— (1976). Where do we go from here? A reconsideration of some basic assumptions affecting course design. *ELT,* **30**, 2, 89–103.

Council of Europe (CCC, CEES) (1969). *Modern language teaching to adults: course books and equipment specifically designed for use in adult education activities.* Strasbourg: The Council.

Goethe-Institut: Arbeitsstelle für wissenschaftliche Didaktik, Informations- und Dokumentationsstelle (1975). *Arbeitsmittel für den Deutschunterricht an Ausländer 10. Auflage.* München: Goethe-Institut.

10. MEDIA-BASED LANGUAGE TEACHING

Barnes, N. (1970). Research into television language broadcasts. *Educational Television International,* 193–196.

BBC (1972). *The Belcrest File.* BBC and OUP.

—— (1973). *Reportage: France: a look at France today.* BBC.

—— (1973). *Reportage: Germany: a look at Germany today.* BBC.

Corder, S. P. (1960). *English language teaching and television.* London: Longman.

Cremona, J. (1971). In G. E. Perren and J. L. M. Trim (eds), *Applications of linguistics. Papers from the 2nd Int. Cong. of Applied Linguistics.* Cambridge University Press.

Further Education Advisory Council for the United Kingdom (1972). *BBC Further Education: an introduction.* BBC.

Hauttamäki, Sirkka K. (1973). Radio and television language courses – final tests in vol. 3 of *Proceedings of 3rd International Congress of Association Internationale de Linguistique Appliquée* (AILA). Heidelberg: Groos.

Hickel, R. (1965). *Modern language teaching by television.* CCC, Strasbourg.

Innes, Sheila (1973). The BBC's further education language provision: an overview. Vol. 3 of *Proc. of 3rd AILA Congress.* Heidelberg: Groos.

Internationales Zentralinstitut für das Jugend- und Bildungsfernsehen (1969). *Television*

language courses: a compilation of 255 courses and series in 20 different countries in
Fernsehen und Bildung 4, 1-2 plus supplement 1971. München: Hueber.
UNESCO International Bureau of Education (1973). The TEVAC case: an experiment
in adult education using the multi-media system. UNESCO Paris.

11. TESTING

Cambridge Local Examinations Syndicate (1973). *Cambridge examinations in English:
changes of syllabus in 1975.* Cambridge.
Lado, R. (1964). *Language testing.* London: Longman.
Levine, J. (1976). An outline proposal for testing communicative competence. *ELT*,
30, 2, 135-44.
Rust, W. B. (1973). *Objective testing in education and training.* London: Pitman.
Valette, R. M. (1967). *Modern language testing: a handbook.* New York: Harcourt & Brace.
—— (1969). *Directions in foreign language testing.* New York: MLA.

12. THE TRAINING OF TEACHERS OF LANGUAGES TO ADULTS

Kramm, H.-J. (1973). *Analyse und Training fremdsprachlichen Lernverhaltens: Ansätze für
die berufsbezogene und praxisnahe Ausbildung von Fremdsprachlehrern.* Basel: Beltz.
Lugton, R. C. (ed.) (1970). *Preparing the EFL teacher: a projection for the 70s.* Philadelphia, Pa.: Center for Curriculum Development.
Perren, G. E. (ed.) (1968). *Teachers of English as a second language: their training and
preparation.* Cambridge University Press.

Classified index to abstracts related to adult language learning published in Language Teaching Abstracts 1968–75 or Language Teaching & Linguistics: Abstracts 1975

1. *General*   Hegedüs 69–250, Abbott 71–238, Lee 72–170, Levy 74–59
2. *Policy*   Murray 68–59, Rée 73–103 and 75–114, Harries 70–72, Prator 70–277,
   Welmers 71–181, Kerr 73–99, Ross 73–107, Lind 73–96, Sharma 73–97, Halsall
   73–259, MacMillan 74–68, Bormann 74–91.
3. *Language use and needs*   Wallwork 68–62, Girard 71–71, Gutknecht 71–154, King
   71–158, Emmans 72–112, Shukla 71–356, Lewis 72–80, Garrard 75–61, Banjo 72–163,
   Gage 72–204, Wong 72–205, Denison 71–345, Châlon 73–25, Stölting 73–187,
   Liem 69–173.
   Politeness   Levenston 69–172
   Trilingualism   Haggis 74–180, Mkilifi 74–22
   Spheres of oral communication   Skalkin 74–196
   Women's place   Lakoff 74–4
3 a. *Immigrants*
   General   Congleton 68–51, Condon 75–131, Richards 73–186
   Instruction at place of work   Winterscheidt 72–363
4. *Objectives*   Lademann 69–310, Günter 70–129, Allen 70–150, Artemov 71–194,
   Piepho 74–44, Allen and Widdowson 74–277, Gorosch 71–30, Perren 71–198,
   Hanzell 71–309, Roberts 73–33, Moss 73–184
5. *Languages for special purposes*
   Vocational learning   Pitman 74–280

Technical and scientific Dučkova and Beneš 68–114, Alford 68–328, Agnen *et al.* 60–204, Stern and Rudovski 69–331, Baumbach 70–54, Mitrofanova 70–87, Brown 70–215, Schmitz 70–363, Gould and Stern 72–94, Strevens 72–120 and 74–33, Butler 72–353 and 75–73, Meyer *et al.* 73–219, Gentilhomme 73–291, Becker 73–286 and 74–25, Baetens-Beardsmore 74–207, Mackay 74–210, Swales 74–211, Latal 74–213, Herblin 75–71, Pickard 75–293
Medical Lidvall 68–82, Artemov 69–38
Industrial Coutts 75–60, Binyon 73–63
Agricultural Rumszewicz 68–324
Businessmen Nixon 69–156
Administrators Bertrand and Imperatrice 69–158
Military Rocklyn 68–205

6. *Psycholinguistic aspects of adult language learning* Jakobovits 69–130, Zimnyaya 70–320, Scovel 70–350, Reply by Hill 71–310, Slama-Cazacu 72–26, Taylor *et al.* 72–28, Cromer 74–251, Carroll 75–31, Oller 75–235
Psychological position of foreigners living abroad Matragos 74–179
Hearing difficulties of foreigners James and Mullen 74–131

L1 learning and L2 learning Donague 69–216
Sentence length and imitation Hener 72–43
Natural sequence Bailey, Maddon and Krachen 75–252

7. *Motivation* Ingram 73–260, Raz 74–48, Vesely 74–112
8. '*Interlanguage*' *of learners* Nemser 72–21, Corder 72–25, Schinker 73–118, Svoboda 75–289
False beginners Schertz 69–182
Role of culture (incl. literature) Debyser 68–67, Baird 70–66, Fowler 72–239 and 335, Smith 73–54

9. *Methodology*
General Aupèche 68–64, Newmark 69–39, Wolfe 69–223, Prator 71–163, Palmer 72–292, Schumann 73–205
Syllabus design Hayes 74–188, Wilkins 74–189
Systems organisation Bishop 72–233, Kuhn 73–31, Richardson 74–72, Jameson 74–266
Conscious learning v. activity Apelt 72–116, Carroll 72–117, Hayes *et al.* 68–292, Apelt 70–31, Mueller 72–20.
Grammar, inductive v. deductive Newmark and Reibel 69–124, Seliger 75–188
TGG and language learning Contreras 69–215
Word-counts Engels 69–96
Classroom technique Emsig 68–134
Translation Mounin 69–98, Burling 69–122
Roles of oral and written language Kohls 72–53, Stille 75–65, Postovsky 75–130
Auditory comprehension training Bowen 75–66, Hughes 75–67
Use of theatre Cammack 73–137, Druce 74–63, Lindsay 74–64
Pronunciation training Coates and Regdon 75–191, Lebel 75–193, Schnitzer 75–194
Speed of utterance Schäfer 69–55, Higgins 69–254
Free expression Bolinger 73–208, Rivers 73–285
Conversation Potter 72–350, Thacker 73–276
Thinking in an FL Leont'ev 69, 148, 72, 300, Makhmudova 69–184
Simplified language Politzer 71–321, Reinert 71–322, Richards 72–209, Roux 72–348
Individualised learning Smith 72–133, Massey 72–228, Steiner 72–229, Jarvis 72–230, Altman 73–113, Everett 73–214, Fisher 74–46, Clarke 74–130, Valette 74–276

J. L. M. Trim

Pair work in language laboratory   Zolotniskaya *et al.* 73–280
Group learning   Watts 73–128
Community-based learning   Fischer *et al.* 72–354
Counselling   Titone 73–261
Self-instruction   Silva and Ferster 68–43, Taillon 69–155, Loveland 71–64, Connolly 73–282, Bauer 74–71
Learning strategies   Stern 75–255
Simulation and case-studies   Paton 75–148
Hypnopoedia   Burch 69–138
Need for Research   Carroll 69–128

10. *Use of technology*
Language labs.   Friedmann 68–129, Ratté 69–248, Jalling 74–206, Olechowski 71–234, Fahre 72–64
Writing lab.   Baskoff 70–67
Videotape   Cammach and Richter 68–223
Telephone   Gorosch 68–37
Local radio   70–241
Shortwave radio   Lalby 72–153
SAID   Lane 68–210
Souvag-lingua   Schneider 69–92, Horga 75–137
Laryngograph   Abberton 74–128

11. *Media*   Higgins 69–153, Behrens 70–367, Schneider 71–232, Apel 71–340, Kelley 73–33, Sherrington 75–56

12. *Intensive courses*   Donskov 74–42, Swain 75–149, Sprissler 75–189, Kohl 70–247, van Abbé 71–323, Denig 74–41
Distance teaching   Sdun 69–223, Kanisčeva 72–246, Goodman 73–114

13. *Materials, authentic*   Blanc 72–300

14. *Dictionaries*   Sazanova 73–223, Ledésert 74–13, Beattie 74–192, Burchfield 74–229, Novikov 74–231

15. *Course construction*   Alexander 68–124, 69–44, Schäpers 72–361

16. *Testing*
General   Catford 69–132, Hill 69–133, Nehls 70–42, Nusenks 70–227, Roy 70–229
Aptitude   Lasch 68–211, Chastain 70–143, Kollarik 73–265, Novak 74–106
Placement   Breitung *et al.* 75–178
Proficiency   Davies 68–52, Pendlebury 71–73, Darnell 71–150, Hardin 71–207, Raasch 72–272, Brosch 72–351, Vidal 74–214
Progress   Gommes-Judge 68–115, Brings 71–205, Upshaw 72–126, Dünwell 73–263, Levine 72–79
Oral   Robinson 71–210, Stoldt 73–143, Bachmann 74–35
Dictation   Oller 72–31
Noise-masking   Johansson 74–102
Cloze test   Oller and Conrad 73–38, Oller 74–185

17. *Teacher training*   Meyer and Strecher 75–126, Wingard 75–127

LANGUAGE DEVELOPMENT

Paul Fletcher and Michael Garman

Department of Linguistic Science, University of Reading

1.

Intensive work on child language development within a linguistic framework, over the past decade or so, has provided detailed information, under the traditional headings of phonology, grammar and, more recently, semantics, concerning the elements and structures which appear in the language of children at different ages. The most obvious contribution of linguistics to these studies has been the provision of a framework within which to characterise child utterances. In addition to this essentially methodological contribution, linguistics has also supplied a theoretical dimension in the form of an innateness hypothesis (see Chomsky, 1965, especially chapter 1; Chomsky, 1975; for a detailed critique see Derwing, 1973). The most widely used interpretation of this hypothesis has been to equate the child's competence, or linguistic ability, with structural descriptions supplied by (largely) generative grammars written for sets of the child's utterances. It is by now a truism that an interpretation of the child's linguistic ability solely in terms of the internal structure of sentences is too narrow (Campbell & Wales, 1970). Current research on the child's learning of communication skills widens this perspective (Shatz & Gelman, 1973; Keenan, 1975; Sachs & Devin, 1976). It is also true that there has been perhaps an overemphasis on the child's acquisition of syntax and phonology, rather than on how the child learns, via the functions of language, the ways to express meaning in form (Halliday, 1975). Nevertheless, it does seem to be the case that the child learns forms of ever-increasing complexity. This learning needs to be described and explained, and grammars are apparently useful devices for these purposes. In what follows we propose to review the advantages and disadvantages of using linguistic descriptions for children's language, at least as far as syntax and phonology are concerned. For semantics, enjoying a recent revival under the impetus of, for example, Clark's semantic feature hypothesis (Clark, 1973), we propose to restrict ourselves to a synthesis of the as yet rather sketchy modern accounts of the development of vocabulary.

2. *Phonology*

The child's development of a sound system has recently been the focus of lively theoretical debate and fruitful descriptive work (for a summary see Ingram, 1976). The pioneering contribution to the field was Jakobson (1968), a translation of a work originally published in 1941. This was an attempt to relate the child's phonological development to phonological theory by comparing the acquisition of contrasts with implicational laws which 'govern the synchrony of all languages of the world' (p. 51). For example, according to the evidence then available to Jakobson, fricatives do not develop in child language before stops; similarly, there are no languages without stops, whereas languages do exist in which fricatives are not known. Jakobson made quite specific predictions about the order in which contrasts would be acquired by children, after the establishment of the initial consonant vs. vowel opposition in a CV syllable. This opposition is, he says, represented by /p/, 'the diffuse stop with maximal reduction in its energy output', and /a/, the open vowel which 'represents the highest energy output of which the human vocal apparatus is capable' (Jakobson & Halle, 1956, p. 37). For consonants, nasal–oral contrasts are then expected, followed by labial–dental oppositions. For the vowels, open–close contrasts will precede front–back, and so on. Later empirical studies indicate that there is some value in Jakobson's predictions, and his suggestion that the child advances to the adult sound system by a progressive feature-based differentiation of contrasts has gained wide acceptance. More recent work, however, raises questions which alter the Jakobsonian picture, in terms both of the range of data considered relevant to phonological acquisition, and of the nature of the explanations adduced.

2.1. *Phonological development and generative phonology*

The direct descendants of Jakobson are those linguists who have dealt with phonological development within a quasi-generative framework, concentrating on (*a*) the relationship between the child's phonetic form and a presumed underlying representation of it (UR), which is often considered to be the adult surface form; and (*b*) changes in the child's phonetic realisations over time (see, for exemplification, Smith, 1973; Stampe, 1969). Morphological relationships are of course not generally dealt with, since they are not relevant for the child's phonology until considerably later; for an experimental approach to internal morphophonemic rules in older children, see Moskowitz (1973). For views of how changes in phonetic realisation are achieved, see Stampe (1969) and Smith (1973, chapter 3). Under (*a*), studies deal with what would traditionally be called allophonic relationships, and with phonotactics. Ingram (1974) relates the child's UR to its pronounced form by means of substitution rules and phonotactic rules. A substitution rule is segment-specific; if a child pronounces *yes* as [les], the /j/-[l] relationship is dealt with by a substitution rule. If *dog* turns up as [gɔg] (see Smith, 1973, p. 222; Ingram, 1974, p. 60), a phomotactic rule of 'back assimilation' or 'velar harmony' relates the UR to the child's form.

The selection of URs is crucial, of course, for this kind of approach. The simplest assumption is that the child uses the adult surface form for this purpose: Smith (1973, pp. 134 ff.) argues that this accounts for the child's ability to discriminate minimal pairs which he cannot distinguish in his production. This is the (anecdotally) well-attested 'wabbit' phenomenon (see Kornfeld & Goehl, 1974, for a discussion of what this might entail), in which a dialogue like the following goes on between the adult and child:

Adult: what's that? (pointing to a picture of a rabbit)
Child: that's a [wæbɪt]
Adult: a [wæbɪt]?
Child: no, [wæbɪt], not [wæbɪt]

Smith's discrimination data is gathered from only one child, and it is probably significant for his conclusions that his systematic analysis of the child's phonology did not begin until the child had reached two years. It will be clear from the discussion of perception which follows that there is abundant evidence that the child's URs at the earlier stages of phonological development cannot be the adult surface forms, at least not under any interpretation that holds that the child has a full system of contrasts for these forms. For a brief discussion of phonological development from 1;4 in terms of more abstract URs, which are distinct from the adult URs, see Fudge (1969, pp. 262 ff.).

2.2. *The role of perception*

The relevance of perceptual factors is a matter of dispute. Smith (p. 134) maintains that the child 'does not begin to speak until he has learned to perceive at least the majority of the contrasts present in the adult language' (see also Braine, 1974, p. 284). An opposing view, based on a prosodic analysis of production data, appears in Waterson (1970). In addition, several recently published experimental studies indicate that the child's perceptual system is not capable of the range of adult discriminations before the productive system begins developing. Garnica (1973; following Schvachkin, 1973, which is a translation of his original 1948 work) supplies experimental evidence from children aged between 1;5 and 1;10 for a developmental progression in perceptual ability. Schvachkin had found that the order in which Russian children developed their ability to perceive phonemic contrasts was strikingly similar to the order for productive development hypothesised by Jakobson. Garnica's results for English show some similarity to those for Russian. For instance, nasal–liquid and

123

nasal–glide oppositions are acquired at roughly the same time for each language. But there are a number of dissimilarities, which leave Garnica sceptical about Schvachkin's hypothesis of a universal order of acquisition for perception and production. Despite the differences between the two studies, we are still left with evidence for gradual perceptual development up until the end of the second year. Since we know that the child is producing recognisable lexical items well before this age (see for example Nelson, 1974), it seems reasonable to assume that perception must play a part in the development of the phonological system, and that perceptual factors must be built in to any adequate explanation of this development.

There is further experimental evidence which lends support to this view, from Edwards (1974). Her results indicate that children may not perceive some contrasts until as late as 3;0. An interesting feature of this study is that she has perception and production data from the same children, enabling her to establish the relationship between a particular perceptual opposition and its productive counterpart. She demonstrates that, while it is often the case that the perceptual contrast precedes a productive contrast for a particular phonemic pair, the order of acquisition in perception and production is not always the same. For instance, /l/-/r/ may be acquired earlier than /w/-/j/ in perception, but the other way round in production. The relationship between the two aspects of the child's ability is not simple and direct.

In spite of the methodological difficulties in successfully establishing whether or not a child can discriminate a given contrast (see Barton, 1975), there seems to be little doubt that adequate explanations of phonological development, especially during the second year of life, will need to take into account perceptual factors (for a general review of speech perception in children, see Gilbert, 1975).

2.3. *Regularity or variability?*

One of the predictions of a Jakobsonian type of hypothesis is that a feature contrast, once made, will generalise to all the segments to which it is relevant. There does seem to be evidence available for generalisation; thus Smith (1973) is able to argue for what he calls 'across the board' changes in his son's phonetic representations. For example, once the child had learned to produce sequences of a consonant plus /l/ (which he used to represent /Cl/ and /Cr/ clusters), he applied this representation to a number of words within a short time. Smith is sure that his son did not re-analyse some of these words AFTER starting to use the [Cl] form, which would suggest a piecemeal word-by-word change, with the child extending the new pronunciation to items as he hears them produced by the adult; and suggests that this evidence also supports the view that the child's UR is essentially the adult form (see also Stampe, 1969, p. 446).

There is, however, other data available which suggests variability rather than generalisation as the rule, at least for some periods of development. Olmsted (1971) shows for a sample of 100 children aged from 1; 3 to 4; 6 a high degree of variability in the phonetic realisation of adult phonemes for spontaneous speech. The children in this sample did not learn phones across the board, nor substitute one and only one phone for the adult target: 'In fact, though the kinds of errors are predictable within limits, there were . . . periods within the process of acquisition when the child got the phone right part of the time, and committed errors part of the time, relative to the same target' (p. 134). Further light is shed on this question, at least for the earlier stages of language acquisition, by Ferguson and Farwell (1975): they looked at longitudinal data of three children, from about 1; 0, until their total productive lexicon individually reached about 50 words. They found considerable variation in some phonetic forms, but stability in others. As they point out, the existence of variable phonetic forms causes difficulties in determining phonological contrastiveness. There may be no minimal pairs to establish a particular contrast with respect to a set of words having the same initial consonant in the adult language, simply some words beginning with one phone, some with another, and others varying between the two. They conclude from this that 'it is often impossible to make well-motivated claims about phonological contrasts in the usual sense at these early stages, as some might wish to do' (p. 431).

3. *Syntax*

It would be impossible to attempt a summary, in the space available, of the work done in this field over the past decade. Fortunately, the work of Roger Brown and his associates, which has had such an influential role in the area, is dealt with at some length for the first two of Brown's stages of development in Brown (1973). Useful collections of articles on syntactic development are to be found in Brown (1970), Huxley and Ingram (1971), Ferguson and Slobin (1973) and Bar-Adon and Leopold (1971). A general summary of the course of syntactic development can be found in chapter 4 of Crystal, Fletcher and Garman (1976). Overall, there is a wealth of empirical work, and a considerable amount of theorising. We shall restrict our discussion to some selective examples which illustrate the problems involved in writing grammars to account for syntactic development.

3.1. *The beginnings of syntax?*

After a period in which they produce single-item utterances (Bloom, 1974), children begin to produce utterances which consist of two 'words' within a single tone-group. The question is whether these combinations represent a rudimentary syntax, and the majority of scholars in this field have given a positive response (e.g. Braine, 1963; McNeill, 1966; Bloom, 1970; Brown, 1973). More recently, however, dissenting voices have been heard (Matthews, 1975; Howe, 1976). The issue concerns the reliability of the claims made by grammars about the child's syntactic 'knowledge', particularly if these grammars are formulated in terms of rules. The nature of the grammars written for data at the two-element stage has in fact changed radically over a rather short period, and to some extent has mirrored changing fashions in theoretical linguistics. Braine wrote an essentially distributional Pivot grammar for his data. A corpus was analysed into P_1+O, $O+O$ and $O+P_2$ utterance types, where O refers to a large 'open' class of (individually) relatively infrequent items, and P_1 and P_2 designate small, positionally restricted classes of much more frequently occurring items. This kind of description turned out to be not even observationally adequate (see Bowerman, 1973, p. 43), and was superseded by 'richer' characterisations. Bloom (1970), for example, suggested using the parental/adult interpretation, the 'expanded' utterance, as a base structure from which the child's 'reduced' utterance is to be seen as transformationally derived. This procedure can disambiguate, for example, two instances of the utterance *mummy sock*: one where mummy is putting on the sock, and another where the sock belongs to mummy. If information about context is used in this way, and such utterances are treated as constructional homonyms, they can be given distinct structural descriptions. For Bloom's approach (and for other 'rich' characterisations: see Bowerman, 1973, pp. 197 ff., using case grammar; and Brown, 1973, pp. 172 ff., using a restricted set of semantic functions), context is of course not the only relevant evidence: it is crucial that the child shows sensitivity to word-order by (to use the same example) not producing instances of *sock mummy* as well as *mummy sock*.

There are several difficulties with the 'rich' interpretations of child syntax prevalent in the literature. The first is that there is no necessary link between the parental interpretation of what the child is saying and the child's syntactic (or syntactic/semantic) ability (see Howe, 1976). This attempt to circumvent the difficulty of discovering the child's linguistic intuitions is therefore potentially unreliable. Nor can much weight be placed on the apparent consistencies of word-order. In the first place this may be a sampling accident. Bloom's children were recorded for eight hours over a three- or four-day period every six weeks. There is at least some possibility that crucial data was lost. (For a potentially more reliable data-gathering technique, see Wells, 1974.) This is, however, not the most serious criticism that can be made: there is some indication from experimental studies that word-order consistencies in production do not show up in comprehension testing. A study by de Villiers and de Villiers (1974) found that 'children in early Stage I (MLU 1·00–1·50) were unable to make use of word-order to comprehend reversible active sentences' (p. 15) – for the definition of his stages and the importance of MLU (mean length of utterance), see Brown (1973, pp. 53 ff.).

While considerations of sampling, and the results of comprehension studies suggest overestimation of the child's linguistic ability by researchers, at least during early Stage I, the possibility also exists that an eagerness to fit the data to a preconceived pattern can underestimate the child's ability. The problem of estimating what is 'grammatical' for the child is not an easy one; Wall (1972) points out that, by excluding some child utterances from her analysis, Bloom (1970) has discarded some potentially interesting or troublesome data – 'one thinks of Fleming throwing away his Petri dishes because they were mouldy' (p. 22). What Bloom did was to exclude, as non-productive, any utterance types that occurred less than five times in the data. Wall's point is by no means trivial: the dangers of trying to fit the data into an established grammatical framework, and then using the constructs of the grammar to 'explain' the child's language ability, are endemic in this field. It is possible that at some points during Brown's Stage I the child's ability is being overestimated; it is perhaps true that at others it is underestimated. What is virtually certain is that it cannot be adequately explained by any approach which uses the constructs of an adult grammar based on data from the child's output only (see Derwing & Baker, 1975, for a detailed exposition of a similar point of view in relation to morphological development).

3.2. *Later syntax*

Though much of the work on syntax development has concentrated on Stage I, there is information available about later stages. As the child's language becomes more complex, there is an understandable tendency to focus on very specific areas of the grammar for research purposes: for example, questions (Klima & Bellugi, 1966); tag questions (Brown & Hanlon, 1970); relative clauses (Sheldon, 1974). There is a report available on the development of complex sentences generally (Limber, 1973), and also some information in Menyuk (1969). Similar questions to those encountered in the previous section can be posed about the reliability of grammars written for data from older children.

One approach to the potentially distorting effect of the grammar as a reflection of the child's ability appears in R. Clark (1974). In the context of a concern with the role of psychological processes in syntactic development, she gives several examples of devices used by her child, Adam, to minimize the effort involved in sentence production and reception. For example, her child would incorporate a part of the previous adult utterance into his own production, following his mother's *we're all very mucky* with *I all very mucky too*. Clearly, for the production of this utterance Adam does not have to organise the data from scratch. From a number of similar examples, Clark comes to the conclusion that 'it may not be appropriate to give such sequences the fullest possible syntactic analysis' (p. 5).

The application of syntactic analyses to child data has had apparently useful results, however. The successive grammars written by Klima and Bellugi (1966) for the acquisition of questions suggests that children eventually learn transformations. (For an explicit statement of the assumption that children operate in terms of transformations, see Chomsky, 1975, pp. 30–5). This intimate link between grammatical rules and language development is reiterated, for questions in English, by Hurford (1975). He accounts for a child's mistakes in learning questions (e.g. *what's that is?*) by suggesting that the child had 'internalised an imperfect version of the adult rule' (p. 301). There is, however, increasing scepticism about transformational accounts of language learning: Prideaux (1976) takes issue with Hurford by offering an alternative explanation of the data in terms of 'functionally based surface generalisations' (p. 6). The child does not learn deep structures and transformational rules for mapping these onto surface structures, but extracts generalisations from surface structures about 'the relative linear ordering of constituents in various types of sentences'. (See Bever, 1970, and Garman, 1974, for essentially similar, though differently expressed views. For another reply to Hurford, see Kucjaz, 1976.)

A rather different view of the relationship between transformations and cognitive processes is expressed in Ingram (1975). He does not question the importance or relevance of transformations for language learning – rather the reverse. His concern is that by using transformations to account for complex sentences in children's language when they first appear, it is rather easy to overestimate their linguistic ability at that stage. His arguments rest on the assumption of a close relation between the stages of cognitive development as postulated by Piaget, and language development. He claims that a close examination of complex sentences reveals that they do not 'have the same grammatical origin as their adult counterparts' (p. 104). Children seem to use, overwhelmingly, simple juxtaposition to relate two sentences to one another up until the age of 6;0 or so. For example, children,· aged 3;0 to 6;0 tend to tie two propositions together with a conjunction, rather than embedding one into the other – *once there was a little boy and he went for a walk in the woods* is much more likely than *once there was a little boy who went for a walk in the woods*. Ingram argues that the transformational relationships of two propositions requires a reversible operation, and that the child achieves this cognitive ability at around the age of 7;0. This assertion of the dependence of linguistic ability on particular cognitive developments is not uncontroversial, of course. To take another area of syntax (which admittedly involves semantic factors), that of the development of modal auxiliaries in English: it appears that modal logical notions of possibility, probability, and necessity are not developed until the age of 7;0 at least (Le Bonniec, 1970). Yet we can find instances of modals used epistemically before this age (see Rosen & Rosen, 1973, p. 46, for an example of a child using the *must* of necessity; and Palmer, 1974, pp. 102 ff. for the meaning of 'epistemic' in relation to modals). We might therefore be somewhat sceptical about Ingram's close linking of a specific theory of cognitive development with the development of transformations, quite apart from any doubts about transformations themselves as internalised operations. Nevertheless his paper is another valuable reminder of the impossibility of considering language development as a purely linguistic issue.

4. *Semantic and cognitive development*

We are concerned here with the relationship that holds between *linguistic schemas* and *object/action schemas* generally, and shall focus particularly on *word schemas*, in the earliest stages of development. Unfortunately, much work remains to be done in the field. One wants to know not only how many items are acquired during a particular stage, but what sort of items they are. The great difficulty here, of course, is that in the absence of a well-developed syntax, it is just impossible to speak of nouns, verbs, adjectives, prepositions, etc., in the sense in which these are defined for the adult system. We can, certainly, refer to properties of the relevant objects/activities which seem to be referred to by particular early words; but while it may be possible to trace the development of certain referring terms into later noun/verb categories, we can be sure that not all early words will suit themselves to our descriptive convenience. For example, Bloom (1973) points out that the first words the child produces frequently may not typically be object names; and Carter (1975) shows in some detail the at first sight surprising development of the words *more* and *my/mine*, in the speech of one child, from a free-varying set of vocalisations around 1;0 accompanying a reaching gesture (the whole comprising what she calls a sensorimotor 'object request' behaviour pattern), into a phonologically and semantically stable and distinct pair of words around 2;0.

4.1 *Receptive and productive vocabulary*

Huttenlocher (1974) has a number of relevant points to make concerning the study of early words, which we may consider here. (*a*) There is a quantitative discrepancy between receptive and productive vocabulary, and we cannot talk about vocabulary growth sensibly by just looking at what the child produces. (*b*) Most importantly, she found no evidence for overextension of word meanings in comprehension, even where the same children did show it productively. Thus, a child might clamber over daddy, playing a game of naming parts of the body, but labelling them all as, say, *nose*; yet the same child may well not over-extend receptively, showing instead one of three other behaviour patterns – a failure to respond at all (in the case where the part for which a name is requested has no word in the child's vocabulary); or inconsistent responding (calling it now a *mouth*, now a *nose*, etc., if it is only partly known); or correct responding. (*c*) She also reports her subjects as *seeking* objects in response to words before 1;0. This is clearly of great interest, in view of Piaget's position (Piaget, 1954, 1962) in respect of children's lack of 'object permanence' up to 1;6. Thus, of Kristen, at 0;10.24, Huttenlocher notes that 'When I first see Kristen, she responds systematically to "Mommy" and to "Canterbury" (her cat). Wherever in the room either of them are located, if she is asked for one of them, she will look around, until her gaze becomes arrested when the appropriate object is found' (p. 350). Two points have to be stressed here: first, a cautionary note about the apparent novelty of such a finding, which actually seems to be close to the observation of Laurent's behaviour during stage 4 (0;8–1;0) of the sensorimotor period, when visibility of the target object is no longer essential to reaching behaviour (Piaget, 1952); and secondly the reasonableness of Huttenlocher's interpretation of the child's behaviour at this stage in saying that it must involve (*pace* Piaget) actual mental representation of the subject on the part of the child. She supports her interpretation as follows: 'The case for the child's actually representing object properties to himself is stronger when the child responds to a word by going directly to the object even when it is out of view. This type of response appeared first for objects which occupied fixed positions in the child's home. For example, we asked Wendy [between 0;10.13 and 1;2.17 in the study] "Where are the fish?" and she crawled some 15 feet around a large barrier to find them' (p. 362).

4.2 *The semantic feature hypothesis*

Let us now consider a little further the implications of overextension of word meanings, and Huttenlocher's finding that this seems to occur productively but not receptively. Over-extensions have been frequently reported in the literature. Piaget (1962) describes early words as 'still essentially sensory-motor in that they are capable of generalisation and of application to an increasing number of objects', and yet 'intermediary between the schemas of sensory-motor intelligence and conceptual schemas' (1962, p. 220). From her own point of view, E. Clark (1973) proposed a semantic feature hypothesis (SFH) of word-meaning development, in terms of which overextension was a sign of an incompletely feature-specified word. As Haviland and Clark (1974) explain, in the context of applying the SFH to the acquisition of English kinship terms, 'This hypothesis, derived partly from the type of semantic theory discussed by Bierwisch (1967), proposed that children's earliest word-meanings do not match those of the adults around them because the lexical entries for the words are incomplete' (p. 23). Thus, if a child acquires [do] as the word for a dog, it might well (the theory goes) simply be a term which marks the salient aspect(s) of the animal for the child – say, the presence of four legs and a tail; then, having just these features of meaning and no others, it will not be surprising to us if we find the child using this word also of cows, mice, sheep, etc. But, on acquiring, say, [mu] for a cow, one might discover that the difference for this child between the meaning of [do] and that of [mu] consisted in the presence or absence of the feature 'horned'. And in this case we should expect to find [do] now relegated to dogs, cats, mice, sheep (ewes and lambs), and [mu] to be applied to cows, goats, rams, deer (the horned variety), etc. Now, Huttenlocher points out that the SFH is put forward in respect of overextensions relating specifically to word-meanings – 'it is not claimed that the child's perceptual categorisation of objects initially involve few features; e.g. that he cannot distinguish between dogs and horses' (1974, p. 357). But, the argument then proceeds, if the SFH relates specifically to word-meanings, why does it not account for the observations concerning receptive vocabulary?

4.3. *Stages in the acquisition of words*

Now we must tie some strands together. It seems that we have to recognise the following logical-cum-developmental stages in the early acquisition of word-meanings:

(*a*) An early sensorimotor stage, where the child may or may not have a few stable object/action schemas, but certainly has reasonably consistent mental representations of notions such as those which are encoded by *more, my/mine, no,* etc. (cf. Bloom, 1973), and also has a range of vocalisations which may eventually become differentiated and stable before the notions become precise (Carter, 1975). We probably have to allow for alternative patterns of development at this stage: see Nelson (1973), Dore (1974) and Rosenblatt (1975) on the distinction between referential, descriptive terms and attitudinal, interpersonal terms in early vocabulary.

(*b*) A later sensorimotor stage, where the child rapidly develops certain stable object/action schemas, of which some become encoded as distinctive vocalisations. Of course, early object/action schemas may not be isomorphic with later ones (Huttenlocher, 1974); and the encoding is probably initially carried out on the basis of certain salient features in the object/action schemas. That is, the 'meaning' of the earliest words for object/action schemas will be a DESCRIPTION OF THE OBJECT/ACTION as the child has perceived it. At this stage, therefore, we have no intermediate representation between the sound schema and the object/action schema. It is at this stage that underextension of meaning may occur (see Reich, 1976, for an example of such underextension); and also at this stage many object words will be proper names, e.g. 'Mommy, Daddy, the pet, and various animal words for particular stuffed animals' (Huttenlocher, 1974, p. 356).

Notice that we are here allowing for Huttenlocher's observation that 'it certainly appears that children may possess a considerable capacity for mental representation of object properties in the period before they name many objects' (p. 366). While it is possible that the mental representations of notions encoded by *no, more*, etc. are 'simpler' in some way, we also have to consider the alternatives, which include (i) the possibility that the child becomes 'TOTALLY PREOCCUPIED WITH OBJECTS/ACTIONS' and is initially unaware of their link to words; (ii) the possibility that until a 'MATURATION OF COMMUNICATIVE FUNC-TION' takes place, the child does not realise that words associated with objects/actions can be used to communicate with other people; and (iii) the possibility that it is EASIER TO RETRIEVE words linked to mental representations such as are encoded by *no, more*, etc. than those linked to object/action schemas, because these latter tend to be packed fairly tightly into highly organised domains (Huttenlocher, 1974, p. 366).

(*c*) Thirdly, a stage where an intermediate level of representation is built up between the sound schema (which is thus far synonymous with word schema) and its object/action schema. This is the semantic representation of the word, so that the word schema now comprises two sub-schemas, the semantic schema and the sound schema. This detachment of the meaning of the word from the properties of the object/action is crucial for appropriate use of the vast majority of apparently purely referential terms; the meaning of *mummy* and *daddy*, for example, will be detached from the child's particular exemplars of these kinship relations; and terms such as *cup* and *glass* will no longer be distinguished according to such purely physical attributes as '± handle' or '± transparent substance', but will acquire semantic representations to allow for the flexibility of reference that is so noticeable a characteristic of adult use (see Andersen, 1975, where three stages in the acquisition of terms for the cup/glass field are recognised: first, one term for the whole field; then, a rigid distinction between the two terms on the basis of the physical properties of the referents; finally, adult-like flexibility).

One of the most important points to notice about the growth of semantic representations is that, while it probably only becomes possible in the pre-operational period, the progression from a sensorimotor type of definition to a semantically mediated type is doubtless observable in the acquisition of word-meanings well on into the language acquisition process, and even into adulthood; one might even want to call words such as proper names inherently sensorimotor, in the sense of the term used here.

Of course, a feature notation can be argued for with respect to both of these types of representation; and it is perhaps necessary to draw an explicit parallel here between meaning structure and sound structure, in the following way. In sound structure we have to recognise perceived phonetic features (either auditory or articulatory), which are qualitatively different from phonological features (which are dependent upon language-specific sound contrasts);

similarly, in meaning structure we have to distinguish between what we may call 'cognitive' features (characteristic of the early stages, features of the perceived object/action), and 'semantic' features (characteristic of the period when stable forms for stable mental representations coexist in the vocabulary and start to define themselves partly in relation to each other, in growing word-networks).

Thus, we are setting aside a picture of word-meanings growing feature by feature, replacing it with one where words start off fully specified with cognitive features which gradually get replaced by more and more semantic ones. According to this account, the fully-specified meaning of a word, in one set of features or the other, is available from the earliest stage for receptive use: hence, we find no over-extension receptively, where the major process involved is *recognition*. On the other hand, in productive use, where the major process is *retrieval*, we should expect overextension to occur, as a function of the smaller space in memory occupied by word schemas as compared to object/action schemas, and the difficulty of selecting an item out of a more tightly packed domain (Huttenlocher, 1974, pp. 366–7). It seems no great distance from this position to the one outlined in Bowerman (1976), where also Bloom (1970, 1973), Bowerman (1974), Schlesinger (1974) and Dore (1975) are cited in support. But we should stress that there is currently much discussion about the nature of the distinction which is encoded in the terms 'cognitive' and 'semantic' – in itself a fair example of linguistic form being in advance of present understanding.

5.

Much has necessarily been omitted from this account. In particular there are some areas of current inquiry which hold much promise and which we have only touched on: the relationship between linguistic and cognitive abilities (see Cromer, 1974, for a review); individual variation in children's development (Ramer, 1976); the relationship of the mother's speech ('motherese') to that of the developing child (Snow, 1973; Ferguson & Snow, 1977). There seems little doubt that these and other current enterprises will shed light on what is still the central problem, the child's constant development of more complex forms.   *July 1976*

References

Andersen, E. (1975). Cups and glasses: learning that boundaries are vague. *JChLang*, **2**, 79–103.

Bar-Adon, A. & Leopold, W. (1971). *Child language: a book of readings*. Englewood Cliffs: Prentice-Hall.

Barton, D. (1975). Statistical significance in phonemic perception experiments. *JChLang*, **2**, 297–8.

Bever, T. (1970). The cognitive basis for linguistic structures. In Hayes (1970), 279–354.

Bierwisch, M. (1967). Some semantic universals of German adjectivals. *Foundations of Language*, **3**, 1–36.

Bloom, L. (1970). *Language development: form and function in emerging grammars.* Cambridge, Mass.: MIT Press.

Bloom, L. (1973). *One word at a time.* The Hague: Mouton.

Bloom, L., Hood, L., & Lightbrown, P. (1974). Imitation in language development: if, when, and why. *Cognitive Psychology*, **6**, 380–420.

Bowerman, M. (1973). *Early syntactic development.* London: Cambridge University Press.

Bowerman, M. (1974). Learning the structure of causative verbs. *Papers and Reports on child language development*, **8**, 142–78. Stanford University Committee on Linguistics.

Bowerman, M. (1976). Semantic factors in the acquisition of rules for word use and sentence construction. In D. Morehead & A. Morehead (eds.), *Directions in normal and deficient child language.* Baltimore: University Park Press.

Braine, M. (1963). The ontogeny of English phrase structure: the first phase. *Language*, **39**, 1–14.

Braine, M. (1974). On what might constitute learnable phonology. *Language*, **50**, 270–99.

Brown, R. (1973). *A first language.* London: George Allen & Unwin.

Brown, R. & Hanlon, C. (1970). Derivational complexity and order of acquisition in child speech. In Hayes, 11–54.

Campbell, R. & Wales, R. (1970). The study of language acquisition. In J. Lyons (ed.), *New horizons in linguistics.* Harmondsworth: Penguin.

Carter, A. (1975). The transformation of sensorimotor morphemes into words: a case study of the development of 'more' and 'mine'. *JChLang*, **2**, 233–50.

Chomsky, N. (1965). *Aspects of the theory of syntax.* Cambridge, Mass.: MIT Press.

Chomsky, N. (1975). *Reflections on language.* New York: Pantheon Books.

Clark, E. (1973). What's in a word? On the child's acquisition of semantics in his first language. In Moore (1975), 65–110.

Clark, R. (1974). Performing without competence. *JChLang*, **1**, 1–10.

Cromer, R. (1974). The development of language and cognition: the cognition hypothesis. In B. Foss (ed.), *New perspectives in child development.* Harmondsworth: Penguin.

Crystal, D., Garman, M. & Fletcher, P. (1976). *The grammatical analysis of language disability: a procedure for assessment and remediation.* London: Edward Arnold.

Derwing, B. (1973). *Transformational grammar as a theory of language acquisition.* London: Cambridge University Press.

Derwing, B. & Baker, W. (1975). Meaning and other factors in the learning of morphological rules. Paper presented at McGill University, Dept. of Psychology.

DeVilliers, J. & DeVilliers, P. (1974). Competence and performance in child language: are children really competent to judge? *JChLang*, **1**, 11–22.

Dore, J. (1974). A pragmatic description of early language development. *JPsycholingRes*, **3**, 343–50.

Dore, J. (1975). Holophrases, speech acts and language universals. *JChLang*, **2**, 21–40.

Edwards, M. (1974). Perception and production in child phonology: the testing of four hypotheses. *JChLang*, **1**, 205–20.

Ervin-Tripp, S. (1964). Imitation and structural change in children's language. In E. Lenneberg (ed.), *New directions in the study of language.* Cambridge, Mass.: MIT Press.

Ferguson, C. & Farwell, C. (1975). Words and sounds in early language acquisition. *Language*, **51**, 419–39.

Ferguson, C. & Slobin, D. (1973). *Studies of child language development.* Holt, Rinehart & Winston.

Ferguson, C. & Snow, C. (eds.) (1977). *Talking to children*. London: Cambridge University Press.
Fudge, E. (1969). Syllables. *Journal of Linguistics*, **5**, 253–86.
Garman, M. (1974). On the acquisition of two complex constructions in Tamil. *JChLang*, **1**, 65–76.
Garnica, O. (1973). The development of phonemic speech perception. In Moore, 215–22.
Gilbert, J. H. V. (1975). Speech perception in children. In A. Cohen & S. Nooteboom (eds.), *Structure and process in speech perception*. Berlin: Springer-Verlag.
Halliday, M. (1975). *Learning how to mean – explorations in the function of language*. London: Edward Arnold.
Hayes, J. (ed.) (1970). *Cognition and the development of language*. New York: John Wiley & Sons.
Haviland, S. & Clark, E. (1974). 'This man's father is my father's son'. A study of the acquisition of English kin terms. *JChLang*, **1**, 23–47.
Howe, C. (1976). The meaning of two-word utterances in the speech of young children. *JChLang*, **3**, 29–48.
Hurford, J. (1975). A child and the English question-formation rule. *JChLang*, **2**, 299–301.
Huttenlocher, J. (1974). The origins of language comprehension. In R. Solso (ed.), *Theories in cognitive psychology: The Loyola Symposium*. Potomac, Md.: Lawrence Erlbaum Associates.
Huxley, R. & Ingram, E. (eds.) (1971). *Language acquisition: models and methods*. New York & London: Academic Press.
Ingram, D. (1974). Phonological rules in young children. *JChLang*, **1**, 49–64.
Ingram, D. (1975). If and when transformations are acquired by children. In Daniel P. Dato (ed.), *Georgetown University Round Table on Languages and Linguistics, 1975*. Washington: Georgetown University Press.
Ingram, D. (1976). *Phonological disability in children*. London: Edward Arnold.
Jakobson, R. (1968). *Child language, aphasia, and phonological universals*. The Hague: Mouton.
Jakobson, R. & Halle, M. (1956). *Fundamentals of language*. The Hague: Mouton.
Keenan, E. (1974). Conversational competence in children. *JChLang*, **1**, 163–84.
Klima, E. & Bellugi, U. (1966). Syntactic regularities in the speech of children. In J. Lyons & R. Wales (eds.). *Psycholinguistic Papers*. Edinburgh: Edinburgh University Press.
Kornfeld, J. & Goehl, H. (1974). A new twist to an old observation: kids know more than they say. In A. Bruck, R. Fox & M. LaGaly (eds.), *Papers from the parasession on natural phonology*. Chicago Linguistic Society.
Kuczaj, S. (1976). Arguments against Hurford's AUX-copying rule. *JChLang*, **3**.
LeBonniec, G. (1970). *Étude génétique des aspects modaux du raisonnement*. Paris: Laboratoire de Psychologie. École Pratique des Hautes Études (VIe Section).
Limber, J. (1973). The genesis of complex sentences. In Moore, 169–86.
McNeill, D. (1966). Developmental psycholinguistics. In F. Smith & G. Miller (eds.), *The genesis of language*. Cambridge, Mass.: MIT Press.
Matthews, P. (1975). Review of Brown, *A first language. Journal of Linguistics*, **11**, 322–42.
Menyuk, P. (1969). *Sentences children use*. Cambridge, Mass.: MIT Press.
Moore, T. E. (ed.). (1973). *Cognitive development and the acquisition of language*. London, New York: Academic Press.
Moskowitz, B. A. (1973). On the status of vowel shift in English. In Moore, 223–60.
Nelson, K. (1973). *Structure and strategy in learning to talk*. Monogr. Soc. Res. Ch. Dev. 38.
Olmsted, D. (1971). *Out of the mouth of babes*. The Hague: Mouton.

Olmsted, D. (1974). Review of Smith, *The acquisition of phonology*. *JChLang*, **1**, 133–7.

Palmer, F. R. (1974). *The English verb*. London: Longman.

Piaget, J. (1952). *The origins of intelligence in children*. New York: International Universities Press.

Piaget, J. (1954). *The construction of reality in the child*. New York: Basic Books.

Piaget, J. (1962). *Play, dreams and imitation in childhood*. New York: Norton.

Prideaux, G. (1976). A functional analysis of English question acquisition – a response to Hurford. *JChLang*, **3**.

Ramer, A. (1976). Syntactic styles in emerging language. *JChLang*, **3**, 49–62.

Reich, P. (1976). The early acquisition of word meaning. *JChLang*, **3**, 117–23.

Rosen, C. & Rosen, H. (1973). *The language of primary school children*. Harmondsworth: Penguin Books.

Rosenblatt, D. (1975). Learning how to mean: the development of representation in play and language. Paper presented to the conference on the biology of play, Farnham.

Sachs, J. & Devin, J. (1976). Young children's use of age-appropriate speech styles in social interaction and role-playing. *JChLang*, **3**, 81–98.

Schlesinger, L. (1974). Relational concepts underlying language. In R. Schiefelbusch & L. Lloyd (eds.), *Language perspectives: acquisition, retardation and intervention*. Baltimore: University Park Press.

Shatz, M. & Gelman, R. (1973). *The development of communication skills: modification in the speech of young children as a function of listener*. Monograph of the Society for Research in Child Development, no. 38.

Sheldon, A. (1974). The role of parallel function in the acquisition of relative clauses in English. *Journal of Verbal Learning & Verbal Behavior*, **13**, 272–81.

Shvachkin, N. (1974). The development of phonemic speech perception in early childhood. In Ferguson & Slobin (1973), 91–127.

Sinclair, H. (1971). Sensorimotor action patterns as a condition for the acquisition of syntax. In Huxley & Ingram, 121–29.

Slobin, D. (ed.) (1971). *The ontogenesis of language*. Academic Press.

Smith, N. V. (1973). *The acquisition of phonology: a case study*. London: Cambridge University Press.

Snow, C. (1972). Mothers' speech to children learning to talk. *Child Development*, **43**, 549–65.

Stampe, D. (1969). The acquisition of phonetic representations. *Papers from the fifth regional meeting of the Chicago Linguistic Society*, 443–53.

Wall, R. (1972). Review of Bloom, *Language development*. *Language Sciences*, **19**, 21–7.

Waterson, N. (1970). Child phonology: a prosodic view. *Journal of Linguistics*, **7**, 179–212.

Waterson, N. (1971). Some views on speech perception. *Journal of the International Phonetic Association*, **1**, 81–96.

Wells, G. (1974). Language development in pre-school children. *JChLang*, **1**, 158–62.

THEORIES GRAMMATICALES ET PEDAGOGIE DES LANGUES

Eddy Roulet

Institut de linguistique de l'Université de Neuchâtel (Suisse)

Abstract

The problem of the applications of grammatical theories to language teaching occupied a prominent place in applied linguistics in the Sixties. This article reviews the most important publications of the period on the subject. It shows how structural and transformational-generative grammars, often applied too directly and crudely, were accorded too dominant a place in language teaching methodology; they were later integrated into pedagogic grammars, which take into account the acquisition and use of the language as an instrument of communication.

'A central question in the application of linguistics to the teaching of foreign languages involves the conversion of a scientific grammar into a pedagogical grammar' (Saporta, 1968, 81).

Le problème posé par Sol Saporta a indéniablement marqué une période du développement de la linguistique appliquée à l'enseignement des langues, qu'on peut situer schématiquement entre 1960 et 1975; il suffit, pour s'en assurer, de voir le grand nombre d'ouvrages publiés sur ce thème aux Etats-Unis (Thomas, 1965; Aurbach *et al.*, 1968; Lester, 1970; Diller, 1971), en Allemagne (Carstensen, 1966; Erlinger, 1969; Hundschnurscher *et al.*, 1970; Mindt, 1971; Roth, 1971) et en France (Csécsy, 1968; Combettes *et al.*, 1970; Roulet, 1972; François, 1974) et les centaines de contributions à des revues ou à des ouvrages collectifs. Avant 1960, les préoccupations des linguistes appliqués ignoraient généralement les théories linguistiques et se situaient davantage au niveau des techniques de présentation du matériel pédagogique (méthodes audio-linguales, exercices structuraux pour le laboratoire de langues), ce d'autant que la conception de l'apprentissage dominante condamnait toute référence explicite à la grammaire. Aujourd'hui, sous l'effet du passage d'une pédagogie de l'enseignement à une pédagogie de l'apprentissage centrée non plus sur le maître, le cours, la technologie audio-visuelle ou le système de la langue seconde, mais sur l'élève, avec ses besoins langagiers, ses motivations et ses stratégies de l'apprentissage spécifiques (voir Roulet, 1976), la grammaire, sans perdre de sa pertinence, retrouve une place plus modeste en linguistique appliquée, non plus *deus ex machina*, mais auxiliaire important de l'acquisition de la compétence de communication.

Quels rôles, dans l'intervalle, les théories et les descriptions grammaticales ont joué dans la pédagogie des langues, c'est ce que nous tenterons de présenter schématiquement, en passant en revue les publications les plus significatives de cette période (nous laissons de côté, faute de place et parce qu'elles ont été ou seront traitées dans les articles concernant ces domaines, les applications des théories grammaticales en analyse contrastive, analyse des erreurs, etc.).

Les années cinquante et soixante sont marquées, en linguistique, par l'apparition et le développement de nombreuses théories grammaticales: distributionnelle (Harris), tagmémique (Pike), fonctionnelles (Martinet, Tesnière) et générative transformationnelle (Chomsky), pour ne citer que celles qui ont le plus influencé l'enseignement des langues. Conçues comme des grammaires scientifiques, en dehors de toute préoccupation didactique, elles vont connaître rapidement un vif succès en linguistique appliquée à la pédagogie des langues, sous les effets conjugués de plusieurs facteurs: apparition de besoins langagiers nouveaux privilégiant la maîtrise de la langue parlée, prise de conscience par les enseignants des lacunes des grammaires scolaires traditionnelles, désir des linguistes de quitter leur tour d'ivoire pour jouer un rôle dans la société!

La première phase de ce mouvement est caractérisée par une condamnation radicale, mais qui ne tardera pas à se révéler excessive, des grammaires traditionnelles, et une adhésion sans réserve aux nouvelles grammaires structurales. A la grammaire traditionnelle, on reproche un certain nombre de 'mystifications' (*fallacies*) inventoriées en particulier par Levin (1960): (*a*) la mystification sémantique: par exemple la définition des parties du discours par la signification (être, objet, état, action) qu'on leur prête; (*b*) la mystification logique ou l'illusion d'une coïncidence entre les catégories grammaticales et celles de la raison; (*c*) la mystification du latin, modèle des grammaires des langues modernes; (*d*) la mystification historique, caractérisée par la prise en compte de faits diachroniques étrangers au système actuel de la langue; (*e*) la mystification de l'écrit, ou le refus de prendre en considération la langue parlée; (*f*) la mystification normative ou la prescription d'une norme obsolète et le mépris de l'usage actuel.

Les grammaires structurales devraient permettre d'échapper à ces mystifications des grammaires traditionnelles et fournir aux pédagogues de meilleures descriptions car elles étudient la langue parlée en usage et prennent en considération le seul aspect objectif, observable et vérifiable du langage: la forme. Francis (1954) ne craint pas d'affirmer que les linguistes ont enfin trouvé la grammaire précise et complète qui va supplanter définitivement la grammaire traditionnelle dans le description et l'enseignement des langues.

Examinons, pour évaluer cette assertion, un ouvrage qui constitue une excellente illustration de cette approche et qui est très révélateur aussi bien de son apport que de ses lacunes. Sous le titre *De la linguistique à la pédagogie: le verbe français*, Csécsy (1968) présente une description distributionnelle systématique de la morphologie du verbe en français parlé et en dégage des implications pédagogiques. Compte tenu des différences considérables, mais le plus souvent ignorées, entre le système de la langue écrite et celui de la langue orale en français, l'ouvrage est de la plus grande utilité pour l'enseignant. En revanche, on ne peut manquer d'être frappé par l'absence totale de traitement de deux aspects du verbe qui sont essentiels dans l'acquisition d'un emploi correct: l'inventaire des constructions syntaxiques (compléments nominaux ou propositionnels) dans lesquelles les verbes peuvent entrer et la description des valeurs sémantiques (temporelles, aspectuelles, etc.) que les formes étudiées peuvent prendre dans le discours. A quoi bon connaître des formes verbales si on ne sait pas comment les combiner avec des syntagmes nominaux et des propositions complétives ni les utiliser à un certain temps et à un certain mode grammaticaux pour transmettre un contenu sémantique donné?

Il est vrai que toutes les descriptions structurales ne s'en tiennent pas, comme celle de Csécsy, à la morphologie, et présentent aussi des structures syntaxiques sous la forme de 'chaînes de cases' (pour reprendre l'expression de Delattre, 1966) ou de tables de substitution (voir Valdman, 1961). Mais du fait de leur attachement à la forme, à la structure de surface de l'énoncé, il leur arrive souvent de confondre des constructions différentes et de conduire ainsi les apprenants à des généralisations abusives et erronées (voir les exemples du cours de Lado et Fries: *English sentence patterns*, analysés par Jacobson, 1966). Malheureusement, l'engouement pour les grammaires structurales est tel qu'on refuse de saisir leurs limites et Wyler (1967) est un des seuls à attirer l'attention des pédagogues sur le danger d'accorder une place centrale dans l'élaboration d'un cours de langue à une grammaire qui ne prend en considération que la forme et néglige la signification, élément moteur de toute acquisition.

La deuxième phase du développement des théories grammaticales à l'enseignement est marquée par une condamnation aussi catégorique, et sans doute aussi excessive que précédemment pour la grammaire traditionnelle, des grammaires structurales et un vif intérêt pour la grammaire générative transformationnelle. A peine adoptées par les linguistes appliqués et une partie des enseignants, recyclés précipitamment, les grammaires structurales essuient de telles critiques de Chomsky et de ses disciples qu'elles cèdent le pas à la grammaire générative transformationnelle, considérée à la fois comme plus explicite et plus complète, puisqu'elle fournit des règles permettant en principe d'engendrer toutes les phrases grammaticales d'une langue et de rendre compte d'ambiguïtés syntaxiques qui échappaient à une analyse distributionnelle.

En dépit d'une mise en garde de Chomsky lui-même, en 1964, aux pédagogues rassemblés à la Northeast Conference, contre les dangers d'un emploi prématuré de la grammaire générative transformationnelle dans l'enseignement (Chomsky, 1966), les tentatives d'application vont se multiplier rapidement dans trois directions: (*a*) initiation des enseignants à la théorie générative transformationnelle de 1957 et au traitement qu'elle propose de certains éléments de grammaire anglaise, accompagnée de discussion de quelques implications méthodologiques pour l'enseignement de la langue maternelle (Thomas, 1965) ou seconde (Roth, 1971); (*b*) manuels d'anglais, langue maternelle, reprenant littéralement, dans une présentation didactique, les règles de *Syntactic structures* (cours programmé de Roberts, 1964) ou manuels d'anglais langue seconde utilisant des règles génératives transformationnelles (Rutherford, 1968); (*c*) 'Applications non techniques de la grammaire générative transformationnelle' (Mueller *et al.*, 1968) sous la forme d'exercices de transformation d'une phrase simple en une autre phrase simple, ou de phrases simples en une phrase complexe, sans référence au cadre théorique de Chomsky, ni aux règles formelles.

Ces tentatives d'application soulèvent d'emblée un certain nombre de problèmes (étudiés en particulier par Helbig, 1969; Lester, 1970; Roulet, 1972; Arndt, 1972; et Allen, 1974); nous n'en retiendrons ici que quatre:

(1) les auteurs justifient généralement le choix de la grammaire générative transformationnelle dans leurs applications à l'enseignement avec l'argument que c'est le meilleur modèle de grammaire disponible; or, si la grammaire de Chomsky paraît supérieure aux autres du point de vue de la démarche scientifique, il ne faut pas oublier qu'elle reste très inférieure à la grammaire traditionnelle dans l'étendue des faits décrits (voir la comparaison de Mindt, 1971); cela est dû en particulier au fait que beaucoup des descriptions proposées visent davantage à mettre à l'épreuve la théorie qu'à développer nos connaissances sur une langue. Ces limites des descriptions génératives transformationnelles constituent un inconvénient sérieux pour le pédagogue. En outre, la grammaire sur laquelle s'appuient les auteurs, à savoir le modèle de 1957, est déjà remplacée, au moment même où paraissent les premiers manuels, par une deuxième version (1965), que Chomsky lui-même juge plus adéquate et qui abandonne précisément les éléments empruntés par les pédagogues, en particulier les concepts de phrases-noyaux et de transformations généralisées. L'argument de la description la meilleure se révèle à double tranchant et va entraîner certains à une poursuite sans fin aux derniers développements. Le seul moyen d'éviter ces écueils des applications, c'est, comme nous le verrons avec Lakoff (1969), de ne pas attendre de la grammaire générative transformationnelle des descriptions toutes faites, constamment remises en question dans leur forme et dans leur contenu, mais des instruments heuristiques propres à favoriser la découverte du fonctionnement de la langue.

(2) le problème de l'adéquation de la théorie se pose d'ailleurs d'une manière plus aiguë, qui ne sera ressentie et exprimée clairement que dans les années soixante-dix, si l'on excepte un article prémonitoire du sociolinguiste Gumperz

en 1965. Si la grammaire générative est plus adéquate que les grammaires traditionnelle et structurale, elle reste une grammaire de la phrase et du système de la langue et ne peut fournir par conséquent qu'un apport limité à une pédagogie qui ne vise pas seulement la maîtrise du système grammatical mais celle de l'emploi de la langue comme instrument de communication. ʻIt seems necessary, at least for the purpose of applied linguistics, to reopen the question of the relationship between linguistic and social facts. More specifically, the question arises: given a grammatical analysis of the languages involved, what additional information can the sociolinguist provide in order to enable the language teacher to give his students the skills they need to communicate effectively in a new society?ʼ (1965, 84). Cette réflexion de Gumperz annonce déjà le mouvement, qui se confirme aujourd'hui, de relativisation de l'apport des descriptions grammaticales dans la pédagogie des langues et d'intégration de ces descriptions dans le cadre plus vaste de l'emploi de la langue comme instrument de communication (voir Candlin, 1973).

(3) le développement d'une théorie linguistique plus adéquate que les grammaires traditionnelles et structurales est soumis, selon Chomsky, à deux exigences: utilisation d'une métalangue formalisée, d'origine logico-mathématique, qui seule permet d'expliciter et, le cas échéant, de falsifier les règles de la grammaire; postulation d'un niveau plus abstrait de structure, qui seul permet de rendre compte de généralisations fondamentales de la grammaire d'une langue. On peut se demander légitimement si ses deux exigences, conditions indiscutables du progrès scientifique en linguistique, sont directement compatibles avec les exigences de l'enseignement; il n'est pas du tout évident que l'enfant puisse travailler au niveau d'abstraction du linguiste ni que l'étude de règles formelles ou de schémas arborescents corresponde à ses stratégies d'apprentissage; il en va de même de la progression, qui est sans doute déterminée par bien d'autres facteurs que l'ordre des règles syntagmatiques et transformationnelles (cf. Lamendella, 1969); en dépit des résultats d'expériences comme celle d'Isačenko (1966), conduites, il faut le préciser, avec des étudiants de niveau universitaire, on peut douter de la possibilité de généraliser ces applications directes des descriptions génératives transformationnelles.

(4) si, conscient des difficultés soulevées par l'application directe des règles d'une description générative transformationnelle à l'enseignement, le pédagogue se contente d'applications informelles du type ʻtransformer une phrase active en une phrase passiveʼ, on ne voit pas très bien ce que ce type de transformation ʻnaïveʼ, qui existait bien avant Chomsky, apporte de nouveau et en quoi il peut se recommander de la grammaire générative transformationnelle. Huot (1974) met en évidence tout ce qui sépare les transformations de Harris et de Chomsky des exercices de transformations des manuels qui prétendent appliquer ces théories linguistiques et conclut son analyse d'un exercice sur les constructions relatives en français langue maternelle par cette remarque, qui a une valeur plus

générale: '. . . cet exercice est un mauvais exercice transformationnel (. . .); il habitue juste les élèves à se servir d'équivalences sémantiques approximatives; il ne leur apprend rien sur le fonctionnement du français contemporain car, entre les phrases qu'on leur propose et celles qu'on attend qu'ils fournissent, il n'y a vraisemblablement pas de relation *syntaxique*. Il ne peut en aucune façon leur donner une réelle maîtrise de la langue' (28).

Toutes ces critiques avaient d'ailleurs été formulées très clairement dans les années 1969–1970 par deux des têtes de file de la linguistique générative, Robin Lakoff et Bruce Fraser, tous deux engagés, parallèlement à leurs recherches théoriques, dans des recherches appliquées à l'enseignement à la Language Research Foundation de Cambridge, Mass. Lakoff (1969) et Fraser (1970) sont convaincus de l'apport de la grammaire générative transformationnelle à l'enseignement, mais pas sous la forme simpliste qui a prévalu jusque là. Lakoff est particulièrement sévère à l'égard de manuels comme ceux de Roberts (1964) et Thomas (1965): 'These authors are not really using transformational grammar; they are using only its hollow shell of formalism; they are not employing rationalism at all, but resorting to new forms of the same old mumbo-jumbo; they have substituted one kind of rote learning for another, and the new kind is harder than the old. Their treatments do not allow scope for presenting the sorts of facts I have been talking about any more than did the structuralists' treatment allow them to do so, and for much the same reasons. Rather than teaching students to reason, they seem to me to be teaching students to use new formulas. Instead of filling in patterns of sentences – surface structures – students have to learn patterns of abstractions – the rules themselves. And these rules are, without exceptions, fakes' (1969, 129). Robin Lakoff démontre clairement que la formulation transformationnelle du passif ne rend pas mieux compte de cette construction que les descriptions traditionnelles et que la formalisation de la règle n'a qu'un avantage, à savoir de montrer que celle-ci conduit à la génération de nombreuses phrases agrammaticales, donc qu'elle est fausse. L'intérêt de la grammaire générative transformationnelle pour le pédagogue ne réside selon elle ni dans la métalangue, qui peut changer, ni dans les règles, encore très insuffisantes, mais dans les instruments heuristiques qu'elle fournit pour observer la structure de l'énoncé et dans les observations même informelles qu'elle permet de dégager. Fraser (1970) estime aussi que les résultats des recherches linguistiques n'ont pas à être communiqués directement à l'étudiant, mais que la grammaire générative transformationnelle peut aider le maître à comprendre le fonctionnement de la langue, à condition qu'on tienne compte des perspectives nouvelles ouvertes dans le domaine de l'emploi de la langue par Austin et par Searle, en particulier sur les présuppositions et les actes de langage.

On trouve néanmoins, récemment, des applications plus judicieuses de la grammaire générative transformationnelle. Nous mentionnerons tout d'abord la thèse de Sophie Moirand (1973), qui est le seul ouvrage, à notre connaissance, à faire le parcours complet de la description générative transformationnelle à l'élaboration et à l'utilisation de matériel pédagogique sans présenter une conception directe et simpliste des rapports entre théorie et pratique. Moirand traite des nominalisations en français, un sujet de prédilection des générativistes car il se prête à un traitement systématique au plan grammatical de phénomènes traités marginalement comme relevant du vocabulaire dans les descriptions traditionnelle ou structurale. Elle commence par établir les règles de génération et de transformations qui permettent de dériver les nominalisations d'action et d'agent d'une proposition sous-jacente enchâssée dans la principale, non pour les enseigner telles quelles aux étudiants, mais pour mieux saisir en tant que pédagogue les processus syntaxiques en jeu. L'apprentissage des nominalisations par les étudiants en français langue seconde commence par le repérage de syntagmes nominalisés dans des textes de journaux et par l'observation, qui échappe à une description générative, du rôle anaphorique des nominalisations dans le discours; il se poursuit par la saisie d'ambiguïtés syntaxiques, la découverte de la proposition sous-jacente et des règles de nominalisation pour aboutir à la production et à l'utilisation de nominalisations dans le discours. Ce qui est exemplaire, dans cette approche, c'est l'emploi modéré et judicieux de la grammaire générative transformationnelle dans le seul domaine où elle est pertinente: l'exploration de processus syntaxiques, et le refus de s'en tenir à son seul apport, pour la description (voir la perspective discursive adoptée) comme pour l'enseignement des nominalisations.

Autre exemple intéressant, mais qui illustre une perspective différente, d'utilisation de la grammaire générative transformationnelle, l'ouvrage de Le Goffic et Combe McBride (1975) sur *Les constructions fondamentales du français*, qui s'inspire des travaux de Gross, plus proche de la grammaire transformationnelle de Harris que de celle de Chomsky. Partant de l'observation de l'insuffisance des informations fournies par les grammaires traditionnelles et distributionnelles sur les constructions des verbes français (voir Csécsy, 1968), ils dressent un inventaire systématique de toutes les constructions possibles des verbes du français fondamental avec des syntagmes nominaux ou des propositions complétives. Ils proposent ainsi un classement syntaxique des verbes français, sans négliger d'établir, chaque fois que c'est possible, des corrélations avec des propriétés sémantiques (verbes de perception, d'opinion, de volonté, etc.), classement qui constitue pour l'enseignant un instrument précieux pour l'analyse d'énoncés et l'élaboration de matériel pédagogique. Dans cet exemple d'application, on laisse de côté tout l'appareil formel de la grammaire transformationnelle pour ne retenir que des informations sur la langue française.

Dans une perspective analogue, mais plus orientée vers l'étude des propriétés sémantiques, on relèvera les différentes tentatives d'application de la grammaire de cas de Fillmore, un développement plus récent de la théorie générative

143

(Brown, 1971; Platt, 1972; Zimmermann, 1972; Kreidler, 1974). Zimmermann résume bien, dans les conclusions pédagogiques de son article, l'apport de la grammaire de cas: 'Das Rollenkonzept scheint sich aus folgenden Gründen für den Sprachunterricht nutzbar machen zu lassen: (1) Die Rollen sind intuitiv faßbare übereinzelsprachliche Kategorien. (2) Verben werden nicht mehr als isolierte lexikalische Einheiten gelehrt und gelernt, sondern mit Hilfe einfacher Beziehungen wie Kausativität und Konversität in systematischem Zusammenhang gesehen. (3) Die Verbindung von Prädikat und Rollenstruktur führt zur Erkenntnis einer Typologie einfacher Satztypen. (4) Die bei vielen synonymen Verben vorhandenen Unterschiede zwischen dem Deutschen und Englischen (Präpositionalphrasen gegenüber Subjektivierung) ergeben eine natürliche Strukturierung für ein – und zweisprachiges Übungsmaterial' (1972, 178). Peu importe ici que, du point de vue de la science linguistique, la grammaire de cas soit encore loin de répondre aux exigences d'explicitation et de falsification, si elle constitue un instrument heuristique utile pour le pédagogue.

Les recherches récentes tendent d'ailleurs à montrer que bien des régularités dans les processus syntaxiques ne se laissent saisir et expliquer qu'au plan sémantique, ce qui n'est pas sans importance pour la pédagogie. Dirven (1975) montre que la sémantique générative permet d'appréhender, de manière plus éclairante que la grammaire générative transformationnelle, les caractéristiques de certaines classes de semi-auxiliaires anglais et de guider ainsi l'apprenant dans la découverte des généralisations nécessaires au maniement correct de ces verbes.

Relevons aussi à ce propos que la sémantique générative, intégrant l'apport d'Austin et de Searle, contribue à développer l'étude d'éléments de l'énoncé qui jouent un rôle capital dans la communication, mais qui avaient été complètement occultés par les grammaires structurale et générative transformationnelle, à savoir les verbes et adverbes modaux et performatifs, qui expriment le point de vue du locuteur et définissent un certain type de rapport avec l'interlocuteur. Lee (1973) et Charolle (1976) montrent tout l'intérêt de cette approche pour la pédagogie de la langue maternelle ou d'une langue seconde. Mais on est encore loin des grammaires du texte et du discours réclamées par Widdowson (1973).

La théorie générative transformationnelle n'a pas seulement influencé la pédagogie au plan de la description des langues, elle a joué aussi un rôle déterminant, au plan méthodologique, dans le passage d'une pédagogie de l'enseignement à une pédagogie de l'apprentissage. Le petit ouvrage de Diller (1971) montre comment les positions prises par Chomsky dans le débat traditionnel entre conceptions empiriste et rationaliste de l'acquisition du langage doivent conduire en pédagogie des langues secondes à l'abandon de la méthodologie structuro-behavioriste (*audio-lingual habit*) qui a dominé dans les années cinquante et soixante en faveur d'une méthodologie cognitiviste (*cognitive code learning*), plus ouverte aux capacités de découverte et de réflexion de l'apprenant. Au plan de la grammaire, qui nous intéresse plus directement ici, l'opposition va se cristalliser entre une conception dite inductive ou implicite de l'enseignement, où explication et réflexion sont condamnées au profit des exercices structuraux, et une conception déductive ou explicite, qui accorde une large place aux explications, souvent avec référence à la langue maternelle. Il convient de noter à ce propos la série d'expériences comparatives conduites en Suède depuis une dizaine d'années sur l'enseignement de la grammaire de l'anglais et qui a donné lieu à la publication de nombreux ouvrages et articles (nous ne mentionnerons ici que Ellegård, 1973; Von Elek & Oskarsson, 1973*a*, *b*; et Björneberg, 1974). Les expériences successives conduites avec des groupes d'apprenants différents (des lycéens de douze ans aux adultes) et des matériaux pédagogiques illustrant des approches méthodologiques différentes semblent montrer la supériorité, du point de vue des résultats et de l'attitude des apprenants, des cours accordant une large part aux explications.

Toujours dans la perspective psycholinguistique ouverte par Chomsky, mais avec des intentions, des méthodes et des conclusions bien différentes, on mentionnera les expériences conduites par Dulay et Burt (1973) sur l'acquisition de l'anglais langue seconde par des enfants. Observant que les enfants apprenant l'anglais langue seconde font les mêmes erreurs de syntaxe que les enfants acquérant l'anglais langue maternelle et que des enfants de langues maternelles différentes adoptent le même ordre d'apprentissage de certains faits grammaticaux en anglais, les auteurs en concluent que le processus de l'apprentissage est contrôlé par les stratégies de l'enfant et qu'il suffit d'exposer celui-ci à des situations de communication naturelles pour assurer l'apprentissage. Elles répondent ainsi catégoriquement par la négative à la question qui sert de titre à leur article: 'Should we teach children syntax?'

Que penser des résultats et des conclusions de telles expériences? Il paraît difficile de les généraliser, compte tenu du nombre très limité de faits grammaticaux étudiés dans l'un et l'autre cas, de la situation expérimentale assez éloignée de l'enseignement habituel (enseignant réduit au rôle de présentateur, dans les expériences suédoises, pour neutraliser les variables personnelles) ou du statut particulier des cobayes (enfants chicanos et portoricain établis aux Etats-Unis dans l'expérience de Dulay et Burt). Aussi Pit Corder (1975) suggère-t-il de développer les observations sur la manière dont les enfants apprennent la grammaire en classe et il propose comme instrument d'investigation un modèle de l'apprentissage en trois étapes: formation d'hypothèse, vérification, pratique. Dans cette perspective, écrit Corder, 'the formal learning of grammar is one of *guided discovery*: the learner hypothesises, the teacher tries to guide his hypothesising to a greater or lesser degree, effectively or ineffectively' (1975, 170). Le problème revient dès lors à déterminer les types, le mode d'organisation et la quantité de guidage à apporter à l'apprenant. Dans un tel modèle de l'acquisition de la grammaire, l'apprenant est au centre du processus, sans pour autant être abandonné à lui-même, comme dans la conception de Dulay et Burt.

Adamczewski reprend et développe les suggestions de Pit Corder dans un article au titre révélateur 'Le montage d'une grammaire seconde': 'Le vrai problème', écrit-il, 'se trouve enfin posé, comment aider l'élève à monter sa grammaire?' (1975, 32). Il répond à cette question en posant deux conditions fondamentales: (1) l'enfant doit être amené à découvrir par l'enseignement de la langue maternelle les principes qui commandent le système et l'emploi de cette langue en particulier et des langues en général; il doit acquérir corollairement les instruments heuristiques qui l'aideront à acquérir des langues secondes; (2) cette découverte ne doit pas se limiter à la structure de surface, à la linéarité de l'énoncé, comme dans la plupart des manuels en usage dans l'enseignement des langues maternelles et secondes; il convient en particulier de doter l'apprenant des instruments lui permettant de saisir les phénomènes de l'énonciation, qui seuls éclairent des faits grammaticaux traités de manière très inadéquate dans les manuels (emploi des verbes modaux, de certains adverbes, des temps, etc.).

L'apprenant n'ayant en principe pas accès, par sa situation et sa formation, aux travaux des linguistes, il convient d'élaborer à son intention, pour guider son apprentissage, des 'grammaires pédagogiques', pour reprendre le terme utilisé par Saporta (1968). Noblitt (1972) en donne la définition suivante: 'A pedagogical grammar (PG) is a formulation of the grammar of a foreign language with the objective of the acquisition of that language; it embodies these considerations which are relevant as the learner is put in contact with that which is to be learned' (316). Cette définition met clairement l'accent sur le rôle central de l'apprenant dans une grammaire pédagogique, comme d'ailleurs celle de Corder (1974): 'it refers to "a way of thinking about" or "representing" these categories of the target language grammar which have been validated by linguistic research so that they can become accessible to the learner' (168). Peut-être conviendrait-il de préciser dans l'une et l'autre que la grammaire en question n'est pas seulement une grammaire du système, mais une grammaire de l'emploi de la langue. Krzeszowski (1976), un des premiers à avoir élaboré une grammaire pédagogique dans le sens de la définition de Corder, affirme clairement: 'any pedagogical grammar must contain some generalisations concerning the use of the presented grammatical forms, i.e. the description of the *pragmatic functions* of these forms' (voir aussi Candlin, 1973). On peut se demander dès lors si une grammaire pédagogique, comme le laisse entendre la définition de Corder, n'a à présenter que des informations validées par les recherches linguistiques. Krzeszowski (1976) reconnaît que sa grammaire pédagogique, conçue comme ouvrage de référence à l'intention des étudiants polonais apprenant l'anglais, n'est dérivée que partiellement des résultats des recherches théoriques de l'équipe du Polish–English Contrastive Project et qu'il n'a pas hésité à utiliser toutes les informations d'autres sources qui pouvaient aider l'apprenant. L'ouvrage montre bien comment des descriptions encore très tentatives et fragmentaires des linguistes (nous pensons en particulier au domaine des actes de langage et des postulats de conversation) peuvent être utilisées informellement avec profit dans la pédagogie.

S'il fallait dégager, à l'intention du linguiste appliqué et du pédagogue, une leçon des tentatives d'application des théories grammaticales à l'enseignement de ces quinze années, nous l'emprunterions au dernier article de Robin Lakoff (1975), qui constitue une remarquable mise au point: 'If he (the applied linguist) is clever, and a good teacher, and a sensitive linguist, he will work around the theory, pay it lip-service, use some concepts from it but not others, and thus be successful in his efforts despite the theory that is supposed to be his salvation. But it's silly to be a slave to any theory, especially one that isn't appropriate, and it's silly to twist facts to match some idealisation of the way language ought to be, but isn't; and it's silly to burden oneself with theoretical mechanisms that one must pick his way around, mechanisms that fight his intuition rather than support it. This has gone on too long, and really ought to stop' (321).   *October 1976*

Bibliographie

Nous donnons ici seulement les références des ouvrages et des articles qui nous paraissent les plus importants. On trouvera une bibliographie plus complète pour la période jusqu'à 1971 dans Roulet (1972) et pour ces dernières années, avec d'excellents commentaires, dans Hausmann (1975, 11–104).

Adamczewski, Henri (1969). La grammaire générative transformationnelle et l'enseignement des langues vivantes. *Bulletin pédagogique IUT*, 1–37.

Adamczewski, Henri (1975). Le montage d'une grammaire seconde. *Langages*, **39**, 31–50.

Allen, J. P. B. (1973). Applied grammatical models in a remedial English syllabus. In S. P. Corder & E. Roulet (eds), *Theoretical linguistic models in applied linguistics.* Bruxelles: AIMAV et Paris: Didier, 91–106.

Allen, J. P. B. (1974). Pedagogic grammar. In J. P. B. Allen & S. P. Corder (eds), *Techniques in applied linguistics.* Londres: O.U.P., 59–92.

Allen, J. P. B. & Widdowson, H. G. (1975). Grammar and language teaching. In J. P. B. Allen & S. P. Corder (eds), *Papers in applied linguistics.* Londres: O.U.P., 45–97.

Arndt, Horst (1972). Tendenzen der transformationellen Schulgrammatik in Deutschland. *Linguistik und Didaktik*, **17**, 247–65.

Aurbach, J., Cook, Ph. J., Kaplan, R. T. & Tufte, V. J. (1968). *Transformational grammar: a guide for teachers.* Rockville (Maryland): English Language Series.

Björneberg, Björn (1974). *A follow-up study in teaching foreign language grammar.* Gothenburg: School of Education, 87 p.

Borissevic, Pavel (1975). Einige Probleme der Grammatik für den Fremdsprachenunterricht. *Deutsch als Fremdsprache*, **12**, 150–7, 234–40.

Brekle, H. E. (1970). Allgemeine Grammatik und Schulunterricht. *Linguistik und Didaktik*, **1**, 48–55.

Brown, T. Grant (1971). Pedagogical implications of a case grammar of French. *IRAL*, **9**, 229–44.

Candlin, Chris (1973). The status of pedagogical grammars. In S. P. Corder & E. Roulet (eds), *Theoretical linguistic models in applied linguistics*. Bruxelles: AIMAV et Paris: Didier, 55–64.

Carstensen, Broder (1966). *Die 'Neue' Grammatik und ihre praktische Anwendung im Englischen, Forschungsbericht, Bemerkungen, Bibliographie*. Francfort: Moritz Diesterweg.

Charolles, Michel (1976). Exercices sur les verbes de communication. *Pratiques*, **9**, 83–107.

Chevalier, J.-Cl. (1970). Grammaire, linguistique et enseignement des langues. *Langues modernes*, **64**, 33–48.

Chomsky, Noam (1966). Linguistic theory. In *Northeast Conference Reports: Language teaching: broader contexts*. Menasha, Wisconsin, 43–9.

Combettes, B., Demarolle, P., Copeaux, J. & Fresson, J. (1970). *L'analyse de la phrase, contribution à une application pédagogique des théories linguistiques modernes*. Nancy, C.R.D.P.

Contreras, Helen (1967). Transformational grammar and language teaching. *Revista de linguistica aplicada*, **5**, 1, 6–17.

Corder, S. P. (1974). Pedagogical grammar or the pedagogy of grammar? In S. P. Corder & E. Roulet (eds), *Linguistic insights in applied linguistics*. Bruxelles: AIMAV et Paris: Didier, 167–73.

Csécsy, Madeleine (1968). *De la linguistique à la pédagogie: le verbe français*. Paris: Hachette/Larousse.

Delattre, P. (1966). La notion de structure et son utilité. *Le français dans le monde*, **41**, 7–11.

Delesalle, Simone (1974). L'étude de la phrase. *Langue française*, **22**, 45–67.

Delesalle, Simone & Aeschimann, Jeannie (1975). *La grammaire à l'école élémentaire*. Paris: Larousse, 134 p.

Diller, J. C. (1971). *Generative grammar, structural linguistics and language teaching*. Rowley: Newbury House.

Dirven, R. (1975). The relevance of generative semantics for language teaching. In S. P. Corder & E. Roulet (eds), *Linguistic insights in applied linguistics*. Bruxelles: AIMAV et Paris: Didier, 27–44.

Dulay, Heidi C. & Burt, Marina K. (1973). Should we teach children syntax? *Language Learning*, **23**, 245–58.

Ellegård, Alvar (1973). L'enseignement explicite et implicite de la grammaire des langues étrangères. *Bulletin CILA*, **18**, 47–57.

Von Elek, Tibor & Oskarsson, Mats (1973 a). *Teaching foreign language grammar to adults – a comparative study*. Stockholm: Almquist & Wiksell, 242 p.

Von Elek, Tibor & Oskarsson, Mats (1973 b). *A replication study in teaching foreign language grammar to adults*. Gothenburg, School of Education, 67 p.

Erlinger, Hans-Dieter (1969). *Sprachwissenschaft und Schulgrammatik, Strukturen und Ergebnisse von 1900 bis zur Gegenwart*. Düsseldorf: Pädagogischer Verlag Schwann.

Francis, W. Nelson (1954). Revolution in grammar. *Quarterly Journal of Speech*, **40**, 299–312; repris ds H. B. Allen (1964), *Readings in applied English linguistics*. New York: Appleton–Century–Crofts, 2e ed.

François, Frédéric (1974). *L'enseignement et la diversité des grammaires*. Paris: Hachette, 219 p.

Fraser, Bruce (1970). Linguistics and the EFL teacher. In R. C. Lugton (ed.), *Preparing the EFL teacher: a projection for the 70's*. Philadelphie: The Center for Curriculum Development, 1–27.

Gross, Maurice (1971). Grammaire transformationnelle et enseignement du français. *Langue française*, **11**, 4–14.

Grunig, Blanche-Noëlle (1972). Pour la définition d'une grammaire d'enseignement (langue étrangère). In Jeanne Martinet (ed.), *De la théorie linguistique à l'enseignement de la langue*. Paris: P.U.F., 219–44.

Gumperz, J. J. (1975). Linguistic repertoires, grammars and second language instruction. *Monograph Series on Languages and Linguistics*, **18**, 81–90.

Hausmann, Franz Joseph (1975). *Linguistik und Fremdsprachenunterricht 1964–1975, Ausführliche kommentierte Bibliographie für Schule und Hochschule (mit besonderer Berücksichtigung des Französischen)*. Tübingen: TBL Verlag Gunter Narr.

Helbig, Gerhard (1969). Zur Applikation moderner linguistischer Theorien im Fremdsprachenunterricht und zu den Beziehungen zwischen Sprach- und Lerntheorien. *Deutsch als Fremdsprache*, **1**, 15–27; repris sous le titre Zur Anwendbarkeit... *Sprache im technischen Zeitalter*, **32**, 287–305.

Helbig, Gerhard (1975). Bemerkungen zum Problem von Grammatik und Fremdsprachenunterricht. *Deutsch als Fremdsprache*, **12**, 325–32.

Hundsnurscher, F. *et al.* (1970). *TSG Transformationelle Schulgrammatik*, Göppingen: Verlag Kümmerle.

Huot, Hélène (1974). Théorie et pratique de la notion de transformation. *Langue française*, **22**, 16–44.

Isačenko, M. (1966). Les structures syntaxiques fondamentales et leur enseignement. In *Actes du premier colloque international de linguistique appliquée*. Nancy, 252–66.

Jacobson, Rudolfo (1966). The role of deep structures in language learning. *Language Learning*, **16**, 153–60.

Kandiah, T. (1970). The transformational challenge and the teacher of English. *Language Learning*, **20**, 151–82.

Kreidler, Charles W. (1974). Case grammar and language teaching. In J. Quistgaard, H. Schwartz & H. Spang-Hanssen (eds), *Proceedings of the third AILA Congress*, III. Heidelberg: Julius Groos, 436–50.

Krzeszowski, T. P. (1976). English reference grammar for Polish learners. In S. P. Corder & E. Roulet (eds), *Theoretical approaches in applied linguistics*. Bruxelles: AIMAV et Paris: Didier.

Lakoff, Robin (1969). Transformational grammar and language teaching. *Language Learning*, **19**, 117–40.

Lakoff, Robin (1975). Linguistic theory and the real world. *Language Learning*, **25**, 309–38.

Lamendella, John T. (1969). On the irrelevance of transformational grammar to language pedagogy. *Language Learning*, **19**, 255–70.

Lee, D. A. (1973). Modal 'auxiliaries' in generative grammar – some pedagogic implications. *ITL*, **20**, 19–30.

Le Goffic, Pierre & Combe McBride, Nicole (1975). *Les constructions fondamentales du français*. Paris: Hachette/Larousse, 175 p.

Lester, Mark (ed.) (1970). *Readings in applied transformational grammar*. New York: Holt, Rinehart & Winston.

Levin, Samuel R. (1960). Comparing traditional and structural grammar. *College English*, **21**, 260–65; repris in H. B. Allen (1964), *Readings in Applied English Linguistics*. New York: Appleton–Century–Crofts, 2e éd., 46–53.

Meyer, Hans-Lothar (1970). Zur Anwendung der Transformationsgrammatik im Englischunterricht. *Linguistik und Didaktik*, **2**, 137–54.

Mindt, Dieter (1971). *Strukturelle Grammatik, generative Transformationsgrammatik und englische Schulgrammatik*. Francfort: Moritz Diesterweg, 221 p.

Moirand, Colette Sophie (1973). *Les nominalisations verbo-affixales*. Thèse de 3e cycle. Université de Besançon.

Newmark, Leonard (1970). Grammatical theory and the teaching of English as a second language, ds Lester, Mark, *Readings in applied transformational grammar*. New York: Holt, Rinehart & Winston, 210–18.

Noblitt, James S. (1972). Pedagogical grammar: towards a theory of foreign language materials preparation. *IRAL*, **10**, 313–31.

Pape, Sabine & Zifonun, Gisela (1971). Grammatik und Lateinunterricht. *Linguistik und Didaktik*, **8**, 262–78.

Peterson, H. (1971). Überlegungen zur Anwendung der generativen Transformations-grammatik im Englischunterricht an deutschen Schulen. *Der Fremdsprachliche Unterricht*, **18**, 25–48.

Platt, Heidi (1972). Case theory and its application to language teaching. *ITL*, **15**, 31–45.

Reinertsen Lewis, Karen (1972). Transformational generative grammar: a new consideration to teaching foreign languages. *Modern Language Journal*, **56**, 3–10.

Ritchie, William C. (1967). Some implications of generative grammar for the construction of courses in English as a foreign language. *Language Learning*, **17**, 45–69, 111–31.

Roberts, Paul (1964). *English Syntax, Alternate Edition, A programmed introduction to transformational grammar*. New York: Harcourt, Brace and World.

Roth, Elmar (1971). *Transformationsgrammatik in der englischen Unterrichtspraxis*. Francfort: Diesterweg, 160 p.

Roulet, Eddy (1970). Les modèles de grammaire et leurs applications à l'enseignement des langues vivantes: trad. angl.: Grammar models and their applications in the teaching of modern languages. Strasbourg: Conseil de l'Europe. Miméo; trad. franç. reprise in *Revue des langues vivantes*, **37** (1971), 582–604, et *Le Français dans le monde*, **85** (1971), 6–15; trad. angl. reprise in *Contact*, **18/19** (1972), 21–35.

Roulet, Eddy (1972). *Théories grammaticales, descriptions et enseignement des langues*. Bruxelles: Labor, Paris: Nathan. Trad. néerl: *Grammatica, taalbeschrijving en onderwijs*, Bruxelles: Labor (1972). Trad. angl.: *Linguistic theory, linguistic description and language teaching*. Londres: Longman (1975).

Roulet, Eddy (1974). Vers une grammaire de l'emploi et de l'apprentissage de la langue. In J. Quistgaard, H. Schwarz & H. Spang-Hanssen (eds), *Proceedings of the third AILA Congress*, III. Heidelberg: Julius Groos, 24–37.

Roulet, Eddy (1976). L'apport des sciences du langage à la diversification des méthodes d'enseignement des langues secondes en fonction des caractéristiques des publics visés. *Etudes de linguistique appliquée*, **21**, 43–80.

Saporta, S. (1966). Applied linguistics and generative grammar. In Valdman, A., *Trends in modern language teaching*. New York: McGraw Hill, 81–92.

Scott, Charles T. (1969). Transformational theory and English as a second language/dialect. *Monograph Series on Languages and Linguistics*, **22**, 75–86.

Spolsky, Bernard (1969). Linguistics and language pedagogy – applications or implications? *Monograph Series on Languages and Linguistics*, **22**, 143–55.

Thomas, Owen (1965). *Transformational grammar and the teacher of English*. New York: Holt, Rinehart & Winston.

Valdman, Albert (1961). *Applied linguistics: French, a guide for teachers*. Boston: D. C. Heath & Co.

Widdowson, H. G. (1973). Directions in the teaching of discourse. In S. P. Corder & E. Roulet (eds), *Theoretical linguistic models in applied linguistics*. Bruxelles: AIMAV et Paris: Didier, 65–76.

Wilkins, D. A. (1974). Notional syllabus and the concept of a minimum adequate grammar. In S. P. Corder & E. Roulet (eds), *Linguistic insights in applied linguistics*. Bruxelles: AIMAV et Paris: Didier, 119–28.

Wyler, Siegfried (1967). Zur Integration der strukturellen Grammatik in den traditionellen Unterricht. *Der Fremdsprachliche Unterricht*, **3**, 12–21.

Wyler, Siegfried (1970). Generativ-transformationelle Grammatik und Schul-Grammatik. *Bulletin CILA*, **11**, 33–51.

Zimmermann, Rüdiger (1972). Die Kasusgrammatik in der angewandten und kontrastiven Linguistik. *IRAL*, **10**, 167–78.

Zydatiss, Wolfgang (1975). Lernprobleme im Englischen und ihre Behandlung in einer didaktischen Grammatik. *Linguistik und Didaktik*, **21**, 1–21.

FOREIGN LANGUAGES FOR YOUNGER CHILDREN: TRENDS AND ASSESSMENT

H. H. Stern and Alice Weinrib

Modern Language Centre, Ontario Institute for Studies in Education

1. Introduction

The teaching of languages to younger children has been a fascinating but confusing story of ups and downs over the last 25 years. It offers an excellent illustration of the intricate and sometimes problematical relationship between theory, research, educational practice and language policy. It has increasingly become a puzzle and a worry to educational policymakers and administrators in many parts of the world. However, the experience of the last two decades in this area should now lead to more informed decisions contributing to better language learning. For the purpose of this article, 'younger children' are approximately five to ten years old and are in 'primary' or 'elementary' school. (Although this paper does not address itself specifically to pre-school second language learning, many of the principles discussed are equally applicable to that area.)

2. Historical background

The broad trend in most educational systems up to about 1950 was to regard languages as a natural part of secondary education. Although there have been exceptions to this trend such as in colonial education and education in some countries of immigration (Andersson, 1969; Stern, 1967), learning foreign languages was generally a mark of privileged or advanced schooling. Primary schooling was in the vernacular. This fact was reaffirmed as a basic principle of education by UNESCO (1953).

Several factors in the history of language teaching contributed to the development of a foreign-language component in the education of younger children. They were, above all, the demand for a radical improvement in language learning, the wish to exploit the young child's supposedly greater language-learning abilities, and the desire to enrich the educational experience of primary-school children. Foreign Languages in the Elementary School (FLES) were first vigorously advocated in the U.S.A. where the dissatisfaction with language teaching in high schools was most acute (Andersson, 1953). Similar movements also took place in other countries. As a result of these educational developments, many attempts have been made over the past two and a half decades to take languages out of their relatively exclusive position as high-school subjects and the study of literature at university, and to include them in the education of younger children.

Two international meetings organised by the UNESCO Institute for Education in Hamburg in 1962 and 1966 (Stern, 1967; 1969) demonstrated a sustained and increasing interest in many aspects of second-language teaching and bilingual education for younger children in many areas of the world. They also emphasised the need for empirical and evaluative research, and more factual survey data. The results of such studies, it was hoped, would yield answers to some of the fundamental unanswered questions related to this issue and give the movement a firmer basis and direction. In particular, there was an expressed need for inquiries on the starting age, the amount and distribution of time, and the approach to teaching in relationship to achievement, attitudes and cost.

Two promising international studies on the teaching of French and English as foreign languages which were also initiated in Hamburg in the '60s, have unfortunately yielded little information about foreign-language teaching in the early grades. These studies were launched by the International Association for the Evaluation of Educational Achievement (IEA) as part of their Six Subject Survey. The aim of *The teaching of French as a foreign language in eight countries* (Carroll, 1975) was to measure and interpret proficiency at several major stages of schooling ranging from primary to pre-university. At the primary level, the intention had been to study 10-year-olds with the equivalent of two years of French instruction. However, such students were found only in the United States and even there only in very small numbers, because 'relatively few schools in the U.S. offer foreign language study to young children' (Carroll, 1975). Among these students, the previous amount of French instruction they had received was so varied that interpretations of the limited test data could be made only with caution. Similarly, in *The teaching of English as a foreign language in ten countries* (Lewis & Massad, 1975), the intention to test 10-year-olds was abandoned because the number of 10-year-olds who had been taught English for at least 18 months in the countries studied, was not large enough to ensure a satisfactory sample. In short, schools where a foreign language is introduced systematically before grade five are very much the exception in the large majority of countries.

In spite of this, in the course of the last 10 years, several new and significant national developments in this area of language education have taken place. Experimentation has continued and taken new directions and a few major studies have been completed. What began as simply a lowering of the starting age for second language with adjustments in teaching methods and curriculum materials, now includes various forms of 'bilingual education'. Within the compass of this article, it is possible only to refer to a few selected examples of research and development in U.S.A., Canada, Great Britain, France and a few other countries of Western Europe.

3. Recent trends

U.S.A.

The FLES movement in the United States now has a history of at least 25 years, documented by Andersson (1953, 1969), JeKenta & Fearing (1968) and Birkmaier (1973). There has been a marked decrease in the number of FLES programmes over the past few years (Fernandez, 1973). We learn, for example, that

> 'the field is faced with a myriad of problems while seeking its place in the education of our youth. It is faced with financial problems, lack of sufficiently trained language teachers, a sometimes unsympathetic unilingual audience, and a lack of well-developed sequential foreign language materials... Many foreign language programs have fallen by the wayside because of inadequate planning. Nevertheless, there exist today many good foreign language programs in the elementary school.' (Je Kenta & Fearing, 1968.)

A review of American studies on FLES confirms the conflicting picture suggested by the above quotation. Some studies show that FLES raises the level of performance in a language (Oneto, 1968; Vocolo, 1967); others, that FLES programmes are poorly planned and ineffective, and therefore not worth the expenditure of funds (Kunkle, 1972; Oller, 1974). FLES is no longer seen, as it was by many American educators some 10 or 15 years ago, as the most important way of improving second-language proficiency. Improvements and innovations are looked for at the high-school level and in universities by catering more clearly to the individual interests and capabilities of students and by paying more attention to humanistic and affective aspects in foreign-language education (e.g. Fryer, 1975).

FLES has been overshadowed by the concern for the education of language and ethnic minorities leading to the introduction of bilingual education programmes. The Bilingual Education Act of 1968 which made possible the funding of bilingual education projects has become a landmark in this development, as the National Defense Education Act of 1957 had been for language teaching generally in the previous decade.

Bilingual education in the U.S.A. has generally a twofold purpose: (1) to establish the right to use and retain the vernacular in education (for example, Spanish or Navaho), and (2) to provide a more humane and pedagogically more realistic approach to the learning of English as a second language by ethnic minorities. This transitional, compensatory function of many bilingual education programmes as an introduction to English has been severely criticised by

Gaarder (1971), Kjolseth (1972) and others, who have repeatedly emphasised that the whole point of bilingual education is language retention and the development of the United States as a multilingual nation. This criticism, together with the dissatisfaction of language minority communities, has led to a shift in emphasis and even new legislation; many bilingual education programmes which formerly aimed at rapid assimilation into the mainstream, now strive for language preservation and cultural enrichment.

Several valuable studies and reports on bilingual education in the U.S.A. provide a good picture of the situation (Alatis, 1970; Alatis & Twaddell, 1976; Andersson & Boyer, 1970; Cohen, 1975; Fishman, 1976 *a*, *b*; Gaarder, forthcoming; John & Horner, 1971; Paulston, 1975; Spolsky, 1972). Reports of particular bilingual programmes for Spanish speakers that have been evaluated generally indicate favourable results. Spanish-speaking students instructed bilingually develop language skills in Spanish and English, and perform as well in content areas as students schooled unilingually. Native English speakers in such programmes learn a second language (Spanish) and do not appear to lag in either language arts or other subjects.

In brief, the FLES movement has declined in the United States. But through bilingual education for minorities, second-language education is available for some younger children.

Canada

In Canada some of the same influences that have led to a review of language teaching in many parts of the world have also been at work. But they have had a special impetus there because of the two official languages, English and French. Canada is trying to come to grips with its most important problem of national unity, namely the interaction between the English and French national groups. The language aspect of this interaction is the subject of much concern and research. The impressive work of the Royal Commission on Bilingualism and Biculturalism which resulted in an influential six-volume report (1967) gave direction to government policy. Canada also has an active Commissioner of Official Languages, a position that is unique in the world, whose responsibilities are to ensure the recognition of the status of the official languages, and report annually to Parliament on matters pertaining to the activities of this Office (Commissioner of Official Languages, 1971–76). Dr Keith Spicer, the Commissioner, believes in 'putting the language priority on our children instead of on public servants' (Commissioner of Official Languages, 1975).

In connection with the expectation of bilingual government services, the *Report of the Independent Study of Language Training in the Public Service* (Bibeau, 1976) has yielded a very detailed appraisal of the effectiveness of second-language programmes implemented for federal civil servants in response to the Official Languages Act of 1969. The summary report and supporting studies (12 volumes) make proposals for improving specific aspects of the language-training programme in the federal Public Service which was regarded as too costly and not effective enough. The Report suggests that ultimately the future of language in Canada lies in better second-language education in schools – although not necessarily in primary schools – rather than in an expensive programme of basic language instruction in the Public Service.

There is, in fact, considerable emphasis currently being placed on second languages at the primary level, particularly in the provinces of Quebec and Ontario. The interest among Anglophone parents in the improvement of French instruction for their children has enormously increased. During the past 10 or 15 years many school systems have attempted to reform the French programmes by introducing 'oral French' into the primary schools (Canadian Education Association, 1969). In the province of Ontario in 1975, French was studied by 28 per cent of the pupils in kindergarten, 38 per cent in grades 1 to 6 and 87 per cent of the pupils in grades 7 and 8 (Ontario Ministry of Education, 1975).

In spite of all this activity, Canadian educators and the public are not satisfied with the results. They feel that 20 minutes of French a day over a period of two or more years in the elementary schools does not lead to any substantial achievement for those who start early. Canadian educators have argued in favour of extending downwards the starting age, providing more time for French per day, and intensifying the approach to second-language learning. These arguments, together with a realistic appreciation of the relative ineffectiveness of 20 minutes of French a day, have led over the past decade to extensive classroom experimentation in Montreal, Ottawa, Toronto and other places throughout Canada.

The experiments deal with different permutations of second-language learn-ing, but basically they explore differences in the *age* at which the second language is begun, variations in the *amount of time* given to it and in the *approach* to the teaching of French. For starting ages or grades, the range of experimentation is from kindergarten to grades 8 or 9, for time from 30, 40, 60, and 90 minutes per day to 50 per cent of the school day and even the whole school day in French. For approach, experiments range from the 'formal' teaching of French as a subject to different combinations of the formal approach with the 'functional' use of French as a medium of teaching. French may be used as the medium all day, part of the day, or in one or several subjects – usually referred to respectively as 'full immersion,' 'partial immersion,' or 'extended French.' (We refer here to the schooling of anglophone children. Children of francophone parents are offered education in French.)

Immersion programmes are becoming an important approach to language learning in Canadian schools (Bilingual Education Project, 1976). Their proto-type is the 'home-school language switch' programme of the St Lambert elementary school which has become widely known through the evaluative research of Dr W. E. Lambert and colleagues of McGill University in Montreal. The St Lambert classes have been in operation since 1965. The studies on the evaluation of this project have reported very favourable results (Bruck, Lambert & Tucker, 1974; Lambert & Tucker, 1972; Tucker, 1976) and aroused widespread interest. In the province of Ontario, especially in Ottawa, similar programmes have been introduced in kindergarten and the early grades. The Bilingual Education Project of the Modern Language Centre of the Ontario Institute for Studies in Education has assisted and evaluated these programmes (Swain & Barik, 1976). Other large-scale research and development experiments in 'full' and 'partial French immersion' and in 'extended French,' in the federal capital area of Ottawa have been applied with promising results to thousands of children at different age levels from the infant school upwards.

The Ottawa experiments provide an interesting example of a large-scale research and development project in which a ministry of education, local school authorities and several research teams co-operated in an attempt to improve second-language learning in an entire school system. The findings of these experiments (Edwards & Smyth, 1976; Halpern *et al.* 1976; McInnis & Donoghue, 1976; Swain & Barik, 1976; Trites & Price, 1976) have been summarised and reviewed in a report by Stern *et al.* (1976). They are also discussed in a special issue of the *Canadian Modern Language Review* (Harley, 1976) which includes comments on these studies by Burstall, Carroll and Rivers. A summary of the research to date and of future research directions in immersion education has appeared as the proceedings of a national research colloquium published in another special issue of the *Canadian Modern Language Review* (Swain & Bruck, 1976). The results of these experiments are reassuringly similar. A radical increase in the opportunities to use French in the classroom leads within a few years to a fairly serviceable knowledge of the language but not to full bilingualism. No long-term deterioration in mother-tongue skills and general education are noted. The recommendations related to these various new directions have been developed in an interesting and concise Ministerial Committee report on the teaching of French in Ontario (Ontario Ministry of Education, 1974).

In Canada, then, it has not been found satisfactory to place languages into the education of younger children at the rate of 15 to 20 minutes a day. On the other hand, an increase in the provision of French in the form of 'immersion' programmes, particularly 'early immersion', is proving much more promising.

Great Britain

British educators became interested in languages in primary education around 1960. This interest was expressed on a nationwide scale when the pilot scheme for the teaching of French in the primary schools was launched in 1963. The principal aim of this project was to study in a realistic way the practicality of introducing French at the age of eight (instead of the more usual start at 11) in a wide variety of schools. Two interim reports (Burstall, 1968, 1970) and the final report by the National Foundation for Educational Research (Burstall *et al.* 1974) have provided the evaluation of this 10-year experiment.

The expectation of the pilot scheme was (1) that the earlier start would make French as a second language available to a much larger section of the school population across the entire ability range than previously; (2) that it would ultimately lead to a substantial improvement in French at the secondary stage of education than was previously possible, when French was taught only during the secondary phase of schooling, and (3) that it would offer a better chance for more prolonged programmes at the secondary stage in other languages, such as Spanish, German and Russian.

Some 125 primary schools in England and Wales in 15 selected areas participated in the pilot scheme. They started teaching French as a second language at the age of eight and undertook to provide continuing French instruction on the assumption that it would continue throughout the pupils' secondary education. In the evaluation, three large samples of pupils were studied. Groups 1 (5,300 pupils) and 3 (6,000 pupils) were investigated for five years, from ages 8 to 13, three years in the primary school and two years in the secondary school; group 2 (5,300 pupils) was studied the longest, from 8 to 16, three years in the primary school and five years in the secondary school. These experimental groups were compared with two types of comparison groups: one comparison group was composed of children of the same age as the experimental children but who had started French at the usual age of 11-plus, that is three years later, and the other group was composed of students who were older than the experimental children but who had an equivalent period of years of exposure to French. The study included the measurement of achievement in French, the assessment of teachers' and students' attitudes to the learning of French in the primary schools, classroom observations, and questionnaires addressed to head masters, teachers, and pupils.

The feasibility of languages within the primary school was amply demonstrated by the pilot study. The consensus was that the introduction of French had no negative effect on the work of the primary school. However, its effect as a stimulus to other languages at the secondary stage was disappointing. Far from leading to an increase in other languages, the secondary schools which received primary school pupils with French tended to restrict the language component in their programme to French alone.

The most controversial outcome was the evaluation of the French achievement of the experimental groups. The NFER report emphatically denied that pupils taught French from the age of eight revealed any substantial gains in achievement when compared with pupils who had started three years later. The report concluded that 'the weight of the evidence has combined with the balance of opinion to tip the scale against a possible expansion of the teaching of French in primary schools' (Burstall *et al.* 1974).

In a brief, cogently argued critical review, Bennett (1975), while praising the NFER report as an example of laudable long-term educational research, questions whether 'the design and analysis produced evidence strong enough to provide a basis for decision-making' and seems to conclude that it does not. He queries certain aspects of the research design and opposes the interpretation of the main findings. Buckby (1976) also argues against treating the report as the definitive evaluation of French in British primary schools. The NFER report has further resulted in much debate about future directions (e.g. Doe, 1976 a). Several writers in the press have interpreted it as the death sentence of primary French. '"Le parlez-vous" is out' was one British headline. The supporters of primary French, however, did not accept this verdict and questioned whether British policy-makers 'are yet ready for the formulation and implementation of anything approaching a national policy on the teaching of French in primary schools' (Robinson, 1975). Against this, others have argued in support of the NFER report that one must be realistic and accept the fact that early learning has not proved to be a cost-effective answer to the language problem. Another more cautious opinion has been that the results do not, for the present, warrant the expansion of primary French as a universal practice. Instead there should be further experimentation with different time distributions of French. Also, there are those who have argued on educational grounds 'that French should continue to be taught in primary and middle schools', but that the weaknesses revealed by the NFER report should be eradicated. This is the view expressed by language educators who were invited to a conference organized by H.M. Inspectorate in March 1975, to consider the implications of the NFER report (D.E.S., 1975).[1]

Lastly the debate arising out of the NFER report has been viewed as a polarisation between the vested interests of members of the language-teaching profession in the continuation of primary French, and those of policy-makers who feel the necessity to restrict public spending.

In spite of all the criticisms and concerns that the NFER report has engendered it should be pointed out that – given the difficulties of carrying out evaluative research of this kind – it is undoubtedly an outstanding example of a longitudinal study yielding enormous amounts of valuable information and insights on the teaching and learning of languages by younger children and many of the problems presented in the process. The findings and implications of this report have been widely discussed across Europe (Council of Europe, 1974,

[1] For representative views of language advisers, see NALA, 1976.

1977) and in North America (e.g. Burstall, 1975*a*; Stern, 1976*b*; Stern, Burstall & Harley, 1975). The Nuffield Foundation has recently set up a Working Party to review comprehensively the national impact of the pilot scheme for the teaching of French in British primary schools, and to consider the situation against the background of current developments in Europe. A report is expected later this year (Doe, 1976*b*).

From the above, we recognise in Britain a confrontation between one view favouring the continuation of languages in primary education and another which firmly rejects primary French as a useful contribution to foreign-language learning in schools.

France

The first national enquiry to determine the extent of early language teaching in France took place in 1964–65. It revealed 1,000 primary foreign-language classes (two-thirds German, mostly in Alsace, and one-third English). Also in 1964, the Ministry gave official support to the introduction of English at age eight in five towns, with some provision for teacher training and course materials. But no arrangements were made to evaluate and compare the achievement. In 1973, a five-year study of 1,000 children learning English from the age of eight was launched. In the meantime, German in kindergarten was becoming popular under the influence of a very active *Inspectrice Générale*.

The Ministry then became concerned about the proliferation of early language teaching and halted the horizontal growth of these programmes allowing only existing ones to continue through the grades. It also recognised the need to review the position in the whole country, with a view to formulating a national language policy.

The resulting inquiry by Girard (1974) revealed that 17,500 pupils in nursery schools and 76,500 pupils in primary schools were involved in foreign-language learning. Of these pupils, 48,000 were learning English, 42,000 German and 4,000 Spanish and Italian respectively. Generally, schools involved in second-language teaching were distributed all over the country, except for Spanish and Italian which tended to occur near the corresponding frontier. On the whole, however, early language teaching was still very limited, involving only about 1·5 per cent of the school population.

In the same inquiry, language teachers in secondary schools were asked to assess various aspects of early second-language learning, based on their experiences with students learning a second language at the primary level. Contrary to expectations, a strong majority favoured early language learning and felt that pupils had benefited from their early experience. In his direct classroom observations, Girard was not as optimistic. He judged about one-third of the classes to be efficient, one-third tolerable and one third inadequate. Girard concluded his report with a list of basic conditions necessary for satisfactory early second-language learning. His view appears to be that early second-language teaching should not be expanded unless all possible efforts can be made to create the right conditions for its successful implementation.

On the basis of the Girard study, it can be said that second-language teaching in the early grades is not widespread in France, and is not likely to expand in the near future. Small-scale investigations have taken place from time to time, but languages at the primary level are regarded with caution.

Other European countries

Like France, many other countries are to some degree involved in the teaching of foreign languages at the primary level (e.g. Titone, 1972). Most of these countries have in common a concern for more effective second-language learning. To this end, many experiments on the early introduction of a second language have been planned or conducted. Unfortunately, with a few exceptions, documentation of these investigations is not readily accessible as was discovered in a recent study of current practices in foreign-language teaching in 50 countries from around the world (UNESCO/FIPLV, 1975). A well documented study was carried out by Gompf (1975) in the Federal Republic of Germany, based largely on a wide-ranging review of recent experiments in Germany and elsewhere, and on her own personal experience as a teacher, course developer and teacher trainer in the State of Hesse. Gompf's study indicates that the teaching of English as a second language to younger children encounters the same kinds of problems in Germany that have already been reported in other parts of the world. In Sweden, the EPÅL project (Holmstrand, 1975) is investigating the advantage of introducing English in grade one instead of the well established beginning in grade three, i.e. around age nine. This project is also involved in the development of English teaching materials, and a study of the impact of learning English on immigrant children.

The Council of Europe has sponsored or co-sponsored several meetings on early language teaching in Europe. In 1972, a group of European language educators at an AILA/FIPLV seminar in Uppsala, organised by the Council of Europe and the National Board of Education of Sweden, endorsed a working paper on trends and new directions in language teaching for younger children (Stern, 1972). This seminar gave firm support to the principle of language teaching to younger children; at the same time it identified a number of needed improvements, particularly in teaching methodology, curriculum design and teacher training. Brief accounts of early language teaching in several European countries is given in the proceedings of a symposium held at Wiesbaden in the German Federal Republic (Council of Europe, 1974). The delegates at this conference expressed dissatisfaction with the state of modern-language teaching in Europe. Although they recognised that there are 'no decisive theoretical or experimental conclusions regarding the best age,' they recommended that the learning period should be extended at the beginning with a starting age of eight or nine, provided proper educational conditions, and continuity could be guaranteed.

A renewed attempt to come to grips with the question of the early teaching of modern languages (ETML) in Western Europe was made at a 22-country European symposium held in Copenhagen in September 1976 (Council of Europe, 1977). The symposium was preceded by a questionnaire survey in 1975 of current practices in Europe (Hoy, 1975). According to Hoy, this survey 'would suggest that the European picture is one of a general trend towards lowering the starting age for modern languages.' The Copenhagen symposium once more endorsed ETML without, however, specifying a particular starting age. It recommended a number of new developments, e.g. to relate ETML to an ultimate standard of proficiency related to the Council of Europe's concept of a threshold level (van Ek, 1975), and to experiment with a programme proposed by Hawkins in which the primary school's role would be preparation for foreign-language learning. Such a programme would be elaborated jointly by the teachers of mother tongue, foreign language, music, movement and geography.

4. Assessment

The decline of FLES in America, the critique of the 20-minute oral French programme in Canada, the sobering findings of the NFER Report in Britain, the cautious recommendations of the Council of Europe Symposia (Council of Europe, 1974, 1977), and the conclusion of the study on French in eight countries that there is no special advantage 'in starting the study of a foreign language very early other than the fact that this may provide the student more time...' (Carroll, 1975), all point in the same direction: the provision of languages in the education of younger children has not come to be considered the *sine qua non* of effective language learning over the last 25 years. Its place in the curriculum of primary education continues to be a matter of debate and indecision.

To overcome this uncertainty, four main issues need to be clarified: (1) the optimal starting age; (2) time allowance; (3) language pedagogy; and (4) educational goals.

The optimal starting age

When languages for younger children were advocated in the '50s and '60s, this innovation was promoted with excessive expectations. Such over-optimism, it should be noted, was not encouraged by the UNESCO studies (Stern, 1966, 1967, 1969). The chief claim was that the early years of life before puberty were the best, even 'critical' years for second-language learning. To the much cited neurological or biological arguments of Penfield (1953, 1965), Penfield & Roberts (1959), and Lenneberg (1967), Schumann (1975) has added an affective theory which contributes a new and important dimension to previous arguments. It attributes to the early years a greater social and emotional permeability of the 'language ego' (Guiora *et al.* 1972) than is available at later stages of life. A more cognitive argument for early second-language learning in terms of Piagetian stages of intellectual growth has been advanced by Krashen (1975) and Rosansky (1975). According to this point of view, the critical period of language development, first and second, ends with the end of the period of 'concrete operations', i.e. when the stage of 'formal operations' begins. In other words, adolescent abstract thinking precludes 'natural' language learning. Several of the other arguments for early learning have been placed into the context of early child development by Andersson (1973), one of the principal and most consistent American advocates of early language learning (e.g. Andersson, 1953, 1969).

Against these and other claims in favour of early second-language learning, there has been a constant stream of theoretical writings and some research evidence denying the specific advantages of the early years and advancing the claim that adults, too, can be effective language learners: e.g. Asher & Price (1967), Ausubel (1964), Burstall (1975a), Politzer & Weiss (1969), Smythe, Stennet & Gardner (1975), Thorndike *et al.* (1928), and van Parreren (1976). Macnamara (1973) has argued that children learn more and faster because they have more opportunities for language learning than adults; if an adult of 40 was freed of the preoccupations of work and supplied with a companion who devoted much time and energy to helping him to learn the language, that adult would learn as well as a young child from its mother. The NFER report (Burstall *et al.* 1974) reviewed the arguments favouring adults, and used the evidence of the British Primary French Scheme to support the view that greater cognitive maturity and learning experience are assets favouring the older learner. Others have challenged specific claims for early learning. For example, the argument based on the time-table of cortical lateralisation has been criticised by Krashen (1973); even the widely accepted advantage of younger learners in acquiring foreign-language pronunciation has not gone unquestioned (Olson & Samuels, 1974).

To end these arguments and counter-arguments, it is probably best to assume that no overall optimal age, operative for all conditions and all aspects of language learning, can be conclusively determined (Jakobovits, 1970; Stern, 1976b). Once the first language has been established, all age levels face similar second-language learning tasks and difficulties, and are likely to go through similar stages of second-language acquisition. Nevertheless, children and adults may differ developmentally in certain respects in their approach to second-language learning, but age-specific characteristics are only beginning to be studied systematically (e.g. Asher, 1972; Fathman, 1975; Krashen, 1976; Krashen *et al.* 1976). They can only be discovered by further observation and experiments and not by polemical arguments. More studies of the characteristics of different age levels of second-language learning are needed. In the present climate of research, they are more likely than ever to be made (Brown, 1974, 1976).

In the present state of our knowledge, the practical implication of this discussion is that on psycholinguistic grounds alone, second-language education could be placed anywhere in the curriculum. But 'instruction at an early age is *in itself* no guarantee of success' (Stern *et al.* 1976).

Time allowance and time distribution

Carroll's long-standing insistence on explaining attainment in a foreign language as 'a matter of the amount of time spent in learning' (e.g. 1962, 1969, 1975) has been repeatedly confirmed in recent studies such as the NFER research (Burstall *et al.* 1974), the IEA French study (Carroll, 1975) and particularly in the Canadian studies (Stern *et al.* 1976; Stern, 1976c) where time variations, ranging from 20 minutes per day to the whole school day in a foreign language have been investigated and have amply confirmed Carroll's thesis. If the language educator accepts the lessons of these recent investigations, he will consider the level of language achievement to be reached at a given stage of education, e.g. the CSE, or the GCE 'O' or 'A' level in Britain, or the European 'Threshold level' (van Ek, 1975), and estimate how much time is needed by the majority of students to reach this level. In view of this argument, the NFER report may be right in concluding that there is no overwhelming reason for starting French as a second language below 11-plus, *if* a satisfactory level can be reached without extending the total time allowance.

Besides the total amount of time allowed for language learning, another time aspect to bear in mind is its distribution. The Canadian experience suggests that a principle advocated and practised since the '60s, i.e. to make available from the early years of schooling small amounts of daily time for language learning, is not as effective as a more concentrated effort (Stern, 1976c; Stern *et al.* 1976). Making more time available as is done in 'immersion' programmes, particularly in 'early immersion' (e.g. Lambert & Tucker, 1972; Stern *et al.* 1976; Swain & Barik, 1976), can lead within two or three years to a level of language performance surpassing traditional expectations of language instruction. Even in these programmes, phenomena such as an 'immersion class dialect' (Selinker, Swain & Dumas, 1975; Swain & Bruck, 1976) and backsliding have been observed. These and other problems of second-language maintenance and development are now receiving attention (Spilka, 1976).

An appropriate time allowance and distribution cannot be determined *a priori*. It is a matter of trial-and-error accompanied by systematic evaluation in relation to stated objectives. But very small amounts of time, e.g. 15 or 20 minutes a day over several years, appear to be less productive and more difficult to organise than a more concentrated effort.

Language pedagogy

Experience in the teaching of languages to young children is now available internationally over the whole range of pre-secondary education. The presence of languages other than the mother tongue is no longer regarded as an anomaly or as an out-of-the-way experiment. While second-language learning in primary education has not become accepted as part of normal literacy, as was proposed in the First Hamburg Report (Stern, 1967), it is accepted as a practical educational possibility.

If we compare the teaching of foreign languages to younger children with the teaching of other primary subjects such as reading or mathematics, it is worth pointing out that although these subjects have been in the field much longer, they have by no means solved all their problems. It is not surprising to find that in the brief span of second-language teaching to younger children, this new area in the primary curriculum has also encountered problems and difficulties. Defenders and critics of early language teaching have noted a number of these, and there is little argument about what they may be: inadequate teacher preparation, lack of co-ordination between primary and secondary language teaching, inadequate integration of the language courses into the existing curriculum, insufficiently differentiated stages of language curriculum development, doctrinaire and limited methods, and unsatisfactory materials (Council of Europe, 1974, 1977; Buckby, 1976; Burstall *et al.* 1974; Stern, 1966, 1972, 1976 *b*). None of these difficulties are such that they could not be remedied by appropriate measures. Moreover, the difficulties in providing second-language instruction for younger children are no greater than those encountered in teaching languages to adolescents or adults.

Practical guidance is available in several useful works on language pedagogy for younger children (e.g. Donoghue, 1968; Finocchiaro, 1964; Gompf, 1975; Titone, 1972). A wide variety of curriculum materials incorporating valuable techniques for teaching younger children, particularly in English, French and Spanish, have been, and continue to be developed (e.g. Beile & Rutherford, 1975; Hawkes, 1974; Jenks, 1975; Weinrib, 1976; Wright & Betteridge, 1976). Somewhat spurious theories about language and language learning which in the '60s had imposed rigidity on the methodology of language teaching at the primary stage are being revised. In particular, the strict separation of skills, and the tabooing of reading and writing in the early stages of language learning are being re-examined. The methodological starkness of many language-teaching programmes produced under the influence of the audiolingual or audiovisual methods with a near exclusive emphasis on dialogue learning, repetition, and structure drill is being modified. A more flexible and intellectually more challenging approach, allowing for individual learner characteristics and interests, is gaining momentum (Council of Europe, 1977; Stern, 1976 *a*). Particularly promising for the development of language pedagogy at this level have been teaching experiments in which language learning has been associated with functional use, as in North American bilingual education programmes (Stern, 1976 *c*). While such bilingual education may not have universal application, it provides an important methodological lesson for language teaching to younger children, namely that 'a student can more effectively acquire a language when its learning becomes incidental to the task of communicating with someone about an inherently interesting topic' (Tucker, 1976).

In line with this trend of thought, the Copenhagen Symposium (Council of Europe, 1977) has recommended teacher exchanges, and visits to classes by children and adults who are native speakers of the target language. Current experience suggests that younger children are particularly responsive to informal opportunities for language acquisition. This is not to imply that older learners could not benefit from informal contacts nor that formal classroom teaching does not make a contribution to the younger learners. All language learning probably needs both: opportunities for formal classroom instruction and informal acquisition through use of the second language (Krashen, 1976; Stern, 1973 *b*), but the optimal balance between the two types of input may be different for younger and older learners and may vary in different environments.

Educational goals

Ultimately, the decision on the stage of education at which to introduce a second language is an educational, cultural and political one. There may be no overpowering reason in the biology of child development in favour of teaching languages to younger children. But there are no overpowering reasons against it either. It is a question, then, for the community and the school to ask whether or not they want the education of young children to be 'ethnocentric' and 'linguocentric'. In parts at least, this decision must be based on a sociolinguistic analysis of the society that wishes to plan its language education policy on rational grounds. An understanding of the role of a second language in a community, and an appreciation of its educational and cultural value are perhaps more important than the search for a psychologically or biologically optimal age. Unfortunately, hardly any studies of this nature have so far been made in association with early language teaching experiments.

In considering the place of a foreign language in the education of young children, it should further be borne in mind that a unilingual upbringing and education is not more 'natural' than a multilingual one; the emphasis on the vernacular as the sole medium of education is, after all, an artifact of the nineteenth century nation-state. In most countries, ethnic pluralism and linguistic contact are the rule and not the exception (e.g. Perren, 1976; Porsché, 1975; Stern, 1973c). It can be argued therefore that language education as well as other parts of the primary curriculum, e.g. social studies, should reflect this reality. There are many ways in which children could be sensitised to the existence of other languages, ranging from a simple language awareness programme, such as was recently proposed at the Copenhagen Symposium (Council of Europe, 1977), to the total immersion in the second language exemplified by the experimental programmes in some Canadian schools.

5. Conclusion

Although a much more circumspect attitude toward languages for younger children has been expressed everywhere, there is considerable reluctance among those involved in these pioneer efforts to view language teaching for younger children as a failure and to abandon it. A more realistic appreciation of the contribution of second-language learning to the language education of young children has been observed and a recognition of the need to spell out more precisely 'the conditions for success' (Council of Europe, 1977).

The guiding principle based on the considerations identified in this paper is to recognise that a language can be taught from any age upwards. Once this has been accepted, the decision at what stage in the educational process to introduce a foreign language can be governed by three criteria: (*a*) the estimated time necessary to reach a desired level of language proficiency by a specified stage in the school career of the majority of learners; (*b*) the educational value attributed to learning foreign languages at a given stage of the curriculum; and (*c*) the human and material resources required to develop and maintain an educationally sound and successful foreign-language programme.

We wish to give special thanks to Mr Peter Hoy who gave us invaluable assistance in obtaining information from the Council of Europe and the Nuffield Foundation, and to Dr Merrill Swain who read this paper and contributed many informative and incisive comments.   *January 1977*

References

Alatis, J. E. (ed.) (1970). *Bilingualism and language contact: anthropological, linguistic, psychological and sociological aspects.* Report of the 21st Annual round table meeting on linguistics and language studies. Washington: Georgetown University Press.

Alatis, J. E. & Twaddell, K. (eds.) (1976). *English as a second language in bilingual education.* Washington, D.C.: TESOL.

Andersson, T. (1953). *The teaching of foreign languages in the elementary school.* Boston: D. C. Heath.

Andersson, T. (1969). *Foreign languages in the elementary school: a struggle against mediocrity.* Austin, Texas: University of Texas Press.

Andersson, T. (1973). Children's learning of a second language: another view. *Modern Language Journal,* **57**, 5/6, 254–9.

Andersson, T. & Boyer, M. (1970). *Bilingual schooling in the United States.* Austin: Southwest Educational Development Laboratory.

Asher, J. J. (1972). Children's first language as a model for second language learning. *Modern Language Journal,* **56**, 3, 133–9.

Asher, J. J. & Price, B. S. (1967). The learning strategy of the total physical reponse: some age differences. *Child Development,* **38**, 1219–27.

Ausubel, D. P. (1964). Adults versus children in second-language learning: psychological considerations. *Modern Language Journal,* **48**, 7, 420–4.

Beile, Werner & Rutherford, Ramsey W. (1975). A model for the production of foreign language teaching materials. *IRAL,* **13**, 3, 209–27.

Bennett, S. N. (1975). Weighing the evidence: a review of *Primary French in the balance. British Journal of Educational Psychology,* **45**, 337–40.

Bibeau, Gilles (1976). *Report of the independent study of the language training programmes of the public service of Canada, Vols. 1–12.* Ottawa: Public Service of Canada.

Bilingual Education Project (1976). French immersion programs in Canada. *Canadian Modern Language Review,* **32**, 5, 597–605.

Birkmaier, E. (1973). Research on teaching foreign languages. In R. Travers (ed.), *Second handbook of research on teaching.* Chicago: Rand McNally.

Brown, H. Douglas (1974). Editorial. *Language Learning,* **24**, 2, v–vi.

Brown, H. Douglas (1976). Papers in second language acquisition. Special issue of *Language Learning,* **4**.

Bruck, M., Lambert, W. E. & Tucker, G. R. (1974) Bilingual schooling through the elementary grades: the St Lambert project at grade seven. *Language Learning,* **24**, 2, 183–204.

Buckby, M. (1976). Is primary French really in the balance? *Audio-Visual Language Journal,* **14**, 1, 15–21. (Also published in *Modern Language Journal* (1976), **60**, 7, 340–6.)

Burstall, C. (1968). *French from eight: a national experiment.* Slough: National Foundation for Educational Research.

Burstall, C. (1970). *French in the primary school: attitudes and achievement.* Slough: National Foundation for Educational Research.

Burstall, C. *et al.* (1974). *Primary French in the balance.* Slough: National Foundation for Educational Research.

Burstall, C. (1975a). French in the primary school: the British experiment. *Canadian Modern Language Review,* **31**, 5, 388–402.

Burstall, C. (1975b). Factors affecting foreign-language learning: a consideration of some recent research findings. *Language Teaching and Linguistics: Abstracts,* **8**, 1, 5–25.

Canadian Education Association (1969). *French programs offered in elementary schools: a CEA survey of 50 Canadian school boards. Education Canada,* June 1969.

Carroll, J. B. (1962). The prediction of success in intensive language training. In R. Glaser (ed.), *Training research and evaluation*. Pittsburgh: University of Pittsburgh Press.

Carroll, J. B. (1969). Psychological and educational research into second language teaching to young children. In H. H. Stern (ed.), *Languages and the young school child*. London: Oxford University Press.

Carroll, J. B. (1975). *The teaching of French as a foreign language in eight countries*. New York: John Wiley.

Cohen, Andrew D. (1975). *A sociolinguistic approach to bilingual education*. Rowley, Mass.: Newbury House.

Commissioner of Official Languages (1971–76). *Annual reports, 1970–75*. Ottawa: Information Canada.

Council of Europe (1974). *Symposium on the early teaching of a modern language, Wiesbaden, 11–17 November 1973*. Strasbourg: The Council.

Council of Europe (1977). *Symposium on modern languages in primary education, Copenhagen, 20–25 September 1976*. Strasbourg: The Council.

Department of Education and Science (1975). Report of an invitation conference organized by H.M. Inspectorate to consider the implications of NFER's report *Primary French in the balance*. London: D.E.S.

Doe, Bob (1976a). What about the after eights? *Times Educational Supplement*, May 3, 1976.

Doe, Bob (1976b). Europe backs primary French. *Times Educational Supplement*, January 10, 1976.

Donoghue, Mildred R. (1968). *Foreign Languages and the elementary school child*. Dubuque, Iowa: W. C. Brown.

Edwards, H. P. & Smyth, F. (1976). *Evaluation of second language programs*. Toronto: Ontario Ministry of Education.

Fathman, Ann (1975). The relationship between age and second language productive ability. *Language Learning*, **25**, 2, 245–53.

Fernandez, Laura B. (1973). The Spanish FLES picture in New York State. *Hispania*, **56**, 1, 111–14.

Finocchiaro, Mary (1964). *Teaching children foreign languages*. New York: McGraw-Hill.

Fishman, Joshua (1976a). Bilingual education: the state of social science inquiry. Paper prepared for the Center of Applied Linguistics Project on 'Cross-disciplinary perspectives in bilingual education.'

Fishman, Joshua (1976b). *Bilingual education: an international sociological perspective*. Rowley, Mass.: Newbury House.

Fryer, T. Bruce (1975). Free to explore: curricular developments. In Gilbert A. Jarvis (ed.), *ACTFL review of foreign language education*, 7. Skokie, Illinois: National Textbook Co.

Gaarder, A. Bruce (1971). Language maintenance or language shift: the prospect for Spanish in the United States. Paper presented at the Child Language Conference, Chicago, November 22–24, 1971.

Gaarder, A. Bruce (forthcoming). *Bilingual schooling and the survival of Spanish in the United States*. Rowley, Mass.: Newbury House.

Girard, D. (1974). Early language teaching in France. Unpublished paper.

Gompf, Gundi (1975). *Englischunterricht auf der Primarstufe*. Weinheim und Basel: Beltz.

Guiora, A. Z. *et al.* (1972). Empathy and second language learning. *Language Learning*, **22**, 1, 111–30.

Halpern, G. *et al.* (1976). *Alternative school programs for French language learning*. Toronto: Ontario Ministry of Education.

Harley, B. (ed.) (1976). Alternative programs for teaching French as a second language in the schools of the Carleton and Ottawa school boards. Special issue of the *Canadian Modern Language Review*, **33**, 2.

Hawkes, Nicholas (1974). Some considerations of principle for TEFL in the European primary school, 1974. ELT Documents, **3**, 14–21.

Holmstrand, Lars (1975). *An introduction to the EPÅL project.* Uppsala: Pedagogiska institutionen.

Hoy, P. H. (1975). *The early teaching of modern languages: a summary of reports from fifteen countries.* Strasbourg: Council of Europe.

Jakobovits, Leon A. (1970). *Foreign language learning: a psycholinguistic analysis of the issues.* Rowley, Mass.: Newbury House.

JeKenta, A. W. & Fearing, P. (1968). Current trends in curriculum: elementary and secondary schools. In E. Birkmaier (ed.), *Britannica review of foreign language education*, 1. Skokie, Illinois: National Textbook Co.

Jenks, Frederick L. (1975). Foreign language materials: a status report and trends analysis. In Gilbert A. Jarvis (ed.), *ACTFL review of foreign language education*, 7. Skokie, Illinois: National Textbook Co.

John, V. P. & Horner, V. M. (1971). *Early childhood bilingual education.* New York: Modern Language Association.

Kjolseth, Rolf (1972). Bilingual education programs in the United States: for assimilation or pluralism? In Bernard Spolsky (ed.), *The language education of minority children.* Rowley, Mass.: Newbury House.

Krashen, S. (1973). Lateralization, language learning, and the critical period: some new evidence. *Language Learning*, **23**, 1, 63–74.

Krashen, S. (1975). The critical period for language acquisition and its possible bases. *Annals of the New York Academy of Sciences.*

Krashen, S. (1976). Formal and informal linguistic environments in language acquisition and language learning. *Tesol Quarterly*, **10**, 2, 157–68.

Krashen, S. *et al.* (1976). Adult performance on the SLOPE test: more evidence for a natural sequence in adult second language acquisition. *Language Learning*, **26**, 1, 145–51.

Kunkle, John F. (1972). Now that FLES is dead, what next? *Educational Leadership*, **29**, 5, 417–19.

Lambert, W. E. & Tucker, G. R. (1972). *The bilingual education of children.* Rowley, Mass.: Newbury House.

Lenneberg, E. (1967). *Biological foundations of language.* New York: Wiley and Sons.

Lewis, Glyn E. & Massad, E. (1975). *The teaching of English as a foreign language in ten countries.* New York: John Wiley.

Macnamara, John (1973). Nurseries, streets and classrooms: some comparisons and deductions. *Modern Language Journal*, **57**, 5/6, 250–4.

McInnis, C. E. & Donoghue, E. E. (1976). *Research and evaluation of second language programs.* Toronto: Ontario Ministry of Education, 1976.

National Association of Language Advisers (1976). *Primary French in perspective: members' opinions and attitudes.* NALA, June 1976.

Oller, John W. (1974). The long-term effect of FLES: an experiment. *Modern Language Journal*, **58**, 1/2, 15–19.

Olson, L. L. & Samuels, S. J. (1973). The relationship between age and accuracy of foreign language pronunciation. *Journal of Educational Research*, **66**, 263–8.

Oneto, Alfred J. (1968). *FLES evaluation: language skills and pupil attitudes in Fairfield, Connecticut public schools.* Hartford, Conn.: Connecticut State Department of Education, Bulletin No. 106.

Ontario Ministry of Education (1975). *Education statistics Ontario.* Toronto: Ontario Ministry of Education.

Ontario Ministry of Education (1974). *Report of the ministerial committee on the teaching of French.* (The Gillin report.) Toronto: Ontario Ministry of Education.

Paulston, Christina Bratt (1975). Teaching English to speakers of other languages in the United States, 1975. Paper presented at the UNESCO meeting of experts on the diversification of methods and techniques for teaching a second language, Paris, September 15–22, 1975.

Penfield, W. (1953). A consideration of the neurophysiological mechanisms of speech and some educational consequences. *Proceedings of the American academy of arts and sciences,* **82,** 201–14.

Penfield, W. (1965). Conditioning the uncommitted cortex for language learning. *Brain,* 88.

Penfield, W. & Roberts, L. (1959). *Speech and brain mechanisms.* Princeton, N.J.: Princeton University Press.

Perren, G. E. (1976). Neglected mother tongues: some unknown dimensions of language diversity. *Times Educational Supplement,* October 8, 1976.

Politzer, R. & Weiss, L. (1969). Developmental aspects of auditory discrimination, echo response and recall. *Modern Language Journal,* **53,** 1, 75–85.

Porsché, Don (1975). Urteile und Vorurteile über Zweisprachigkeit im Kindesalter. *Linguistik und Didaktik,* **23,** 6, 179–89.

Robinson, J. A. (1975). Primary French: what next? *Times Educational Supplement,* March 21, 1975.

Rosansky, E. (1975). The critical period for the acquisition of language: some cognitive developmental considerations. *Working Papers on Bilingualism,* **6,** 93–100.

Royal Commission on Bilingualism and Biculturalism (1967). *Report of the royal commission on bilingualism and biculturalism, Books I–VI.* Ottawa: Queen's Printer.

Schumann, John H. (1975). Affective factors and the problem of age in second language acquisition. *Language Learning,* **25,** 2, 209–35.

Selinker, L., Swain, M. & Dumas, G. (1975). The interlanguage hypothesis extended to children. *Language Learning,* **25,** 1, 139–52.

Smythe, P. C., Stennet, R. G. & Gardner, R. C. (1975). The best age for foreign-language training: issues, options and facts. *Canadian Modern Language Review,* **32,** 1, 10–23.

Spilka, Irene V. (1976). Assessment of second-language performance in immersion programs. *Canadian Modern Language Review,* **32,** 5, 543–61.

Spolsky, Bernard (ed.) (1972). *The language education of minority children.* Rowley, Mass.: Newbury House.

Stern, H. H. (1966). FLES: achievement and problems. In A. Valdman (ed.), *Trends in language teaching.* New York: McGraw-Hill.

Stern, H. H. (1967). *Foreign languages in primary education.* London: Oxford University Press.

Stern, H. H. (ed.) (1969). *Languages and the young school child.* London: Oxford University Press.

Stern, H. H. (1972). Languages for younger children: recent trends and new directions. Working paper for the AILA/FIPLV seminar on teaching modern languages to the young child, Uppsala, February 23–25, 1972.

Stern, H. H. (1973 a). Bilingual education: a review of recent North American experience. *Modern Languages,* **54,** 2, 57–62.

Stern, H. H. (1973 b). Bilingual schooling and second language teaching: a review of recent North American experience. In J. W. Oller & J. Richards, *Focus on the learner.* Rowley, Mass.: Newbury House.

Stern, H. H. (1973 c). *Report on bilingual education.* Quebec: L'Editeur Officiel du Québec.

Stern, H. H. (1976 a). Mammoths or modules? *Times Educational Supplement,* October 8, 1976.

Stern, H. H. (1976 b). Optimal age: myth or reality. *Canadian Modern Language Review,* **32**, 3, 283–94.

Stern, H. H. (1976 c). The Ottawa–Carleton French project: issues, conclusions and policy implications. *Canadian Modern Language Review,* **33**, 2, 216–32.

Stern, H. H. *et al.* (1976). *Three approaches to teaching French.* Toronto: Ontario Ministry of Education.

Stern, H. H., Burstall, C. & Harley, B. (1975). *French from age eight, or eleven?* Toronto: Ontario Ministry of Education.

Swain, M. & Barik, H. C. (1976). *Five years of primary French immersion.* Toronto: Ontario Institute for Studies in Education.

Swain, M. & Bruck, M. (eds.) (1976). Immersion education for the majority child. Special issue of *Canadian Modern Language Review,* **32**, 5.

Thorndike, E. L. *et al.* (1928). *Adult learning.* New York: Macmillan.

Titone, R. (1972). *Bilinguismo precoce e educazione bilingue.* Rome: Armando.

Trites, R. L. & Price, M. A. (1976). *Learning disabilities found in association with French immersion programming.* Toronto: Ontario Ministry of Education.

Tucker, Richard G. (1976). Cross-disciplinary perspectives in bilingual education: linguistics review paper. Paper prepared in the Psychology Department of McGill University for the Center for Applied Linguistics in Washington.

UNESCO (1953). *The use of vernacular languages in education.* Paris: UNESCO.

UNESCO/FIPLV (1975). *Foreign language teaching and learning to-day.* Paris: UNESCO.

Van Ek, J. A. (1975). *The threshold level.* Strasbourg: Council of Europe.

Van Parreren, C. F. (1976). The psychological aspects of teaching modern languages. *IRAL,* **14**, 135–41.

Vocolo, Joseph M. (1967). The effect of foreign language study in the elementary school upon achievement in the same foreign language in high school. *Modern Language Journal,* **51**, 8, 463–9.

Weinrib, Alice (1976). French as a second language: kindergarten to grade 3. *Orbit,* **34**, 24–6.

Wright, A. & Betteridge, D. (1976). Writing a foreign language course: one project team's experience. *ELT Documents,* **2**, 15–23.

THE TEACHING OF ADVANCED READING SKILLS IN FOREIGN LANGUAGES, WITH PARTICULAR REFERENCE TO ENGLISH AS A FOREIGN LANGUAGE

C. J..Brumfit

Department of English as a Foreign Language, University of London Institute of Education

1

Formal schooling is inescapably bound up with literacy, and ever since foreign languages have been taught at all reading has been an essential part of the process (Kelly, 1969, chapter 5). In the twentieth century there has even been a specifically designated 'reading method' of teaching (Mackey, 1965, p. 149) with emphasis on the acquisition of new vocabulary through fluent reading. However, using reading as a means of teaching a foreign language is a different concern from the training of reading skills (Lim Kiat Boey, 1976), and a conscious interest in the process of reading in the foreign language at an advanced level is a product of very recent developments in psycholinguistics and pedagogy: there are only five references to reading in the index of as recent a survey of foreign-language teaching as Mackey (1965).

This situation is partly accounted for by the emphasis on oral procedures in teaching during the highly productive 1960s, but it is also the result of the fact that a methodology for teaching reading in a foreign language is dependent on a number of areas of study which are not directly involved with the teaching situation at all: reading occupies an undefined position midway between linguistic and cognitive studies. It is also unclear whether advanced reading work in a foreign language poses particularly different problems from advanced reading work in the mother tongue. Altogether, in spite of the fact that there have been in recent years a vast number of studies and commentaries on problems of initial literacy, there has been very little systematic discussion of advanced reading needs and abilities, either in first- or second-language situations. Yet there have been striking differences of approach between teachers of mother tongues and of foreign languages. These differences, however, have not been clearly articulated, and are far more the product of a range of unconscious assumptions about the second-language learning situation than of a carefully worked out theoretical position. Thus there are two main problems in attempting to survey the literature in the teaching of advanced reading skills.

First, while in recent years there has indeed been a great deal more discussion of this area than in the past, little of this has been more than anecdotal. Not only is there a lack of discussion of a rationale for teaching advanced reading, but published work itself reflects the lack of an agreed rationale by rarely concerning itself seriously with questions of purpose or justification, either in articles or textbooks. The few writers whose comments go beyond relatively trivial practical detail (e.g. Norris, 1970; King, 1976; Bright & McGregor, 1970, among methodology books; Munby, 1968, among textbooks) stand out very conspicuously. Second, as with any survey of methodological discussion, there are no clearly defined boundaries. Reading is usually taught in close association with writing, listening and speaking; there is an obvious continuity between initial reading and the development of more advanced skills, and much overlap of interest between mother-tongue teachers and foreign-language teachers, particularly when dealing with advanced reading skills. As a result of these two problems, it is necessary for this survey to be highly selective. Textbooks and general articles are included because they represent particular approaches to the teaching situation, or because they are of particular relevance even though they are concerned with peripheral areas – such as, on the practical side, mother-tongue teaching, and, at a more abstract level, the nature of the comprehension process. To survey all these fields would take us far away from the reading process itself, but to ignore them completely would be to limit discussion to the trivial.

2. *Preliminaries*

Comprehension models deriving from recent psycholinguistic research offer the beginnings of an account of what is involved in understanding a written text (Freedle & Carroll, 1972; Clark, 1975; Smith, 1975). How this relates to the needs of a learner coming from a different cultural and linguistic situation is still largely unexplored territory (but see Al-Rufai, 1969, 1976; Torrey, 1970; Rivers, 1972, pp. 104–6; Goodman, 1970). At the same time there has been very little recent investigation into the mechanical difficulties of foreign readers using advanced texts, though it has been noted that they reread as they advance more frequently than native readers (Oller & Tullius, 1973).

Sociological and anthropological considerations have also been little explored with direct relevance to the reading process in a foreign cultural or linguistic setting. Relationships between literacy and culture in general have been discussed (Goody & Watt, 1963), and many investigations (surveyed in D'Arcy, 1973) have been made of reading interests in the mother-tongue situation. There have been some similar investigations (Taiwo, 1975; Dimitrijević & Gunton, 1975; Jordan, 1975) in the second-language situation.

In the mother-tongue situation a clearer picture is beginning to emerge of a reading curriculum from the early stages to advanced work (Melnik & Merritt, 1972 *a*, *b*). A notion of reading as a process of creative interaction with the text, with the reader predicting the message increasingly accurately (Smith, 1971, 1973), provides the beginning of a theoretical basis. At the same time there is increasing awareness of perceptual and other problems associated with reading (surveyed in Vernon, 1971), and of the nature of linguistic comprehension (surveyed in Carroll, 1972). The foreign-language situation has not produced anything comparable. The need to grade and stage the advanced reading process (Rivers, 1968) has been noted, but most early discussion was restricted to the attainment of basic literacy in English (though West (1955) and Billows (1961) provide partial exceptions). Reading and writing have been discussed as two aspects of the same problem (Davies & Widdowson, 1974), but the most general analysis is that reflected in a separation of intensive and extensive reading. There is very little agreement on the precise relationship between these two terms, but it is universally accepted that intensive reading is concerned with close reading of texts and extensive reading is concerned with breadth rather than depth. A more convenient framework might be to distinguish between reading for accuracy and reading for fluency.

In methodological terms, there have been two main responses to reading problems. One, a predominantly American tradition, has been to break down the reading process, even when the goal has been fluency, and teach on the basis of a detailed analysis of types of reading skill (Lado, 1964; Harris, 1966; Plaister, 1968). This tradition has tended to concentrate on the production of appropriate muscular habits and has borne fruit in many faster reading and reading development courses (Fry, 1963). The alternative tradition has concentrated on cognitive and affective aspects of the reading process, with an emphasis on classroom activity and discussion.

3. *Intensive reading*

For many years certain forms of intensive reading were widely practised in schools: short passages in foreign languages were studied and translated as part of the process of classical training. Many of the assumptions of the translation approach seem to have been carried over into the intensive reading situation in mid-twentieth-century schools. The characteristic intensive reading exercise consists of a short passage which is used as a basis for activity to promote accurate reading. Much of the questioning which in the past has been offered on passages has been designed to check understanding without actually demanding translation, and discussion still rarely clarifies whether classroom procedures are intended to facilitate or to check comprehension (Munby, 1968). It has frequently been assumed that reading ability will develop naturally if the activity is insisted on, and that the main role of the reading passage is to provide exposure to language (Lockett, 1972) or to support the work in the general language course (Roberts, 1975). The passage was often a piece of 'good' writing for appreciation, but even so it was frequently seen as a device for introducing new vocabulary or – less frequently – for reinforcing syntax (Light, 1970). Many textbooks used passages for intensive reading as starting points for various sorts of language work, and there has been much discussion of ways of exploiting the 'passage' for non-reading purposes (Mackin, 1964–6; Taylor, 1971; Dunning, 1975). General discussion of classroom procedures (Murphy, 1969; Abiodun, 1975) improved greatly when, in the late 1960s, the text began to be seen as a 'context' for the development, by means of probing questions by the teacher, of strategies for the understanding of other texts. Before that time there had only been a few writers who had argued that the development of comprehension ability requires specific questioning strategies by the teacher (Gurrey, 1955). More recently, the nature of comprehension exercises has been widely discussed, both in useful surveys for the mother-tongue situation which have relevance to foreign-language teachers (Walker, 1974; Potts, 1976), and in writings for the foreign-language classroom (Davies & Widdowson, 1974). For example, Hurman (1974) discusses students using the text as a basis for developing their own oral responses; Moody (1976) develops a reconstruction of a text by means of prediction exercises; Lawrence (1975) uses frame-filling exercises, and a number of writers (Plaister, 1973; Cripwell, 1976; Radice, 1976) discuss the use of cloze procedures as a teaching device. Indeed, short passages for translation are again being produced (Chamberlin & White, 1975). The feature these writers share is the emphasis on discussion around a particular problem set up by the type of question provided on the passage. The most fruitful source of discussion, because it is both flexible and controllable by the teacher, is the multiple-choice question format (Munby, 1968; Hill, 1969; Munby & Brumfit, 1975; Isaacs, 1968). It has been claimed, however, that the detail and intricacy of the questioning trains skilful question answerers rather than skilful readers (Shook, 1977). Certainly the value of the most niggling multiple-choice questions is greatest to those who need to develop reading skills for academic purposes.

Recent developments in discourse analysis have led to more refined analyses of texts, while developments in designing courses for specific purposes have led to more precise clarification of goals of reading programmes. It is now possible to specify more precisely the linguistic and rhetorical skills necessary for the decoding of texts (Ingram & Elias, 1974; Catterson, 1971; Widdowson, 1973), though the extent to which the interpretation of what is decoded can be considered a linguistic operation is a matter of some uncertainty. Some attempts have been made to discuss cross-cultural discourse and rhetorical patterns (Kaplan, 1966; Nababan, 1976), and studies are also in progress of cultural attitudes to learning to read: members of non-literate cultures have less understanding of the reading process when they encounter it (Downing *et al.*, 1975). Again, implications of such studies for foreign-language teaching are not explored, but teaching texts and discussion based on developments in discourse analysis are appearing (Sim, 1973; Mountford, 1975; Allen & Widdowson, 1973–5). It has also been argued that the comprehension of logical relationships requires specific training in reading (Horn, 1971), and that such rhetorical and logical strategies can be adapted to the individual needs of the learner (Eskey, 1973).

Suitable texts should be enjoyable to the student, should be typical of what he will expect to read in later life (Baird, 1973), and should relate to his preferences and problems (Nation, 1974; Buckby, 1975).

When attempts are made to relate the reading passages to the reader's purposes in reading, deficiencies in pedagogy become most striking. It is mainly those preparing materials for advanced academic work who relate the questions specifically to anticipated language problems of the students, either with scientific materials (Jones & Roe, 1975; Allen & Widdowson, 1974) or with more general materials (Narayanaswamy, 1973; Kohl, 1973), and demand explicit awareness of the reading process from the learners. Otherwise discussion of this need is rare except in relation to the design of distractors for multiple-choice questions.

Most exercises assume that reading for exact understanding is all that is required. However, skimming (or reading for gist), reading for required information, and other sorts of selective processes are also necessary, as well as the ability to read fast when appropriate, to vary speed, and so on. In the 1960s many reading improvement courses, including films, reading pacers, etc., were devised (surveyed in Macmillan, 1965), but few attempted to integrate their work with the rest of the reading programme (Chapman-Taylor & Ballard, 1967). The emphasis was frequently on speed rather than appropriacy, however (Rudd, 1969), and even recent books frequently relate comprehension directly to speed (Hirasawa & Markstein, 1974).

An examination of reading textbooks on the market makes it clear that very few texts show evidence of having been constructed on a systematic basis at all. Two areas which obviously require investigation are those of the classification of comprehension skills in the foreign-language situation (examined in detail in Munby, 1977; also, more typically, in Vallette & Disick, 1972; also Corbluth, 1975), and the pedagogically-related task of analysing the appropriacy of particular question formulations and methodological strategies for the remediation of particular types of error. There appear to be two levels of misunderstanding of a text: a psychological level, which motivates a linguistic confusion (as when we allow our own strong opinions to lead us to misread a text towards our own bias), and the linguistic level, which is interpretable in terms of an overt linguistic signal (as when we fail to recognise the significance of a tense marker).

The line between these two is not always easy to draw, but clarification should lead to more systematic questioning and more effective teaching. Some books of multiple-choice questions on passages are based – through the distractors which have to be discussed – on predictions of probable misunderstandings (Munby, 1968). But other practices, for example the adding of spelling or syntactic errors to distractors (Eynon, 1970), are less easy to justify.

4. Extensive reading

If the purpose of intensive reading is to develop accuracy, there are at least two other aspects of reading to be touched upon. One is appropriacy, which has already been mentioned in relation to reading efficiency. The other is the development of fluency (Beattie, 1975).

Since 1926, when Longmans published a simplified edition of *Robinson Crusoe*, reduced texts in various forms have been normal in the foreign-language situation. Principles of simplification have been discussed in a variety of places (West, 1950, 1953, 1964; Bright & McGregor, 1970). Broadly, simplification has been on the basis of lexical counts (CILT, select lists 5 and 6). Most publishers in the foreign-language market now produce books which are graded lexically and syntactically, and most have private documents which indicate editorial policy, with lists of appropriate words and structures for different levels. General problems of preparing materials for reading are discussed in a number of places (Davies & Widdowson, 1974), but there have been many criticisms of the nature of the simplification process. The intellectual level of most reading materials has been attacked (Frechette, 1975); original materials, and less rigid grading, have been demanded (Saunders, 1973), and publishers have been asked at least to systematise the information they give about the readers they publish (Beattie, 1970). The organisation and preparation of readers has proved difficult to evaluate, though an attempt has been made to evaluate the kinds of glossing given to vocabulary items (Holley & King, 1971). Recently, a few books of short entertaining extracts have been published, in response to the demand for varied registers (Levine, 1971; Maley & Duff, 1976).

The role of the extensive reader in the curriculum has been surprisingly little discussed. It is generally assumed that it should lead on to the study of literature (Grant, 1975), or at least that it should be read for its impact and the response should be similar to that of a literature set book (Billows, 1961, chapters 10–11; Baird, 1976). This certainly presumes that there will be a class reader, like a set book, and much methodological discussion, such as suggestions about acting class readers (Paine & Parsons, 1970), assumes this. Organisation of extensive silent reading is much less recommended, though there are suggestions of how to organise it (Davies, 1975), perhaps with report forms to check reading (Bright & McGregor, 1970; Morris, 1972), or in relation to library work

(Isaacs, 1968; Narayanaswamy, 1973). Some reading programmes are specifically geared to study skills, and link extensive reading, library work and intensive work (Grant & Umoh, 1976; Yorkey, 1970).

It is apparent that extensive reading is often expected to lead on to the reading, if not the study, of literature. The role of literature in language teaching is one of the most discussed areas of teaching, and only a representative selection of recent writings can be mentioned here. There are a large number of general surveys of literature teaching problems in the foreign-language classroom (*Modern Language Journal*, 1972; Press, 1963, for example). The value of literature in the foreign-language classroom is usually taken for granted (e.g. Hoskins, 1976), or it is assumed that the aims in the foreign-language situation are the same as for the mother-tongue situation (Baird, 1969 with particular reference to poetry). Literature teaching has been defended because it is good for cultural development (Chamberlain, 1975), because it adds variety to the classroom and gives pleasure (Gelman, 1973), and because it leads to very effective discussion (Clutterbuck, 1970). On the other hand, it has been pointed out that literature is only one variety of language among many (Girard, 1970, chapter 5), and that the cultural implications of teaching traditional literature courses are much more serious than with language courses (Searle, 1972). It is widely taken for granted that literature and language naturally go together (Harrison, 1973, chapter 4; Moody, 1971), though the contrary view has been expressed (Burke & Brumfit, 1974). The presence of literature courses in some second-language situations has been defended on the grounds that it leads to the development of skills of criticism and discrimination which are socially useful (Brumfit, 1970), but this view has been attacked as 'sociological' and aesthetic justifications proposed instead (Pettit, 1971). Literature teaching has also provided the opportunity for an extension of discourse and rhetorical work by the application of stylistics to literary texts for the benefit of second-language learners (Haynes, 1976; Allen, 1976). On the whole, though, like the rest of the reading programme, literature teaching is taken for granted and questions are not often asked very penetratingly. Only rarely is there an attempt to place the role of literature in the context of the total language-teaching process (Littlewood, 1975).

5

It will be apparent from this account that the discussion of teaching methods is conducted at a low theoretical level if it is conducted at all. This is unavoidable, for teaching is not research, and classes will not wait until clarity has been achieved. Nonetheless it is to be hoped that within the next decade the teaching of advanced reading skills will have been placed on a much more systematic basis than it has been in the past.

Note: I would like to thank my students at London University Institute of Education who drew my attention to a number of reading textbooks.

April 1977

Addendum, July 1977

A few additions can be made: the reference to Jordan, 1975 should be supplemented by Jordan, 1974; Hamblett, 1977, surveys reading skills in secondary schools in Botswana and considers various tests of readability for teaching materials in English used in secondary schools; and Dentant & Standaert, 1976, discuss the use of literary texts in the training of advanced reading skills, and try to relate effective as well as cognitive objectives to the teaching programme.

References

Abiodun, E. A. (1975). The conduct of comprehension lessons in our secondary schools. *Journal of the Nigerian English Studies Association*, **7**, 1 and 2, 81–5.

Allen, Virginia French (1976). Some insights from linguistics for the teaching of literature. *English Teaching Forum*, **14**, 4, 17–21.

Allen, J. P. B. & Corder, S. Pit (eds.) (1974). *The Edinburgh course in applied linguistics*, vol. 3. London: Oxford University Press.

Allen, J. P. B & Corder, S. Pit (eds.) (1975). *The Edinburgh course in applied linguistics*, vol. 2. London: Oxford University Press.

Allen, J. P. B. & Widdowson, H. G. (eds.) (1973–5). *English in focus*: Glendinning, Eric H. (1973), English in mechanical engineering; Allen, J. P. B. & Widdowson, H. G. (1974), English in physical science; Maclean, Joan (1975), English in basic medical science; Mountford, Alan (1975), English in workshop practice. London: Oxford University Press.

Allen, J. P. B. & Widdowson, H. G. (1974). Teaching the communicative use of English. *IRAL*, **12**, 1, 1–21.

Al-Rufai, M. A. H. (1969). A study of the reading abilities and habits, in English and Arabic, of Baghdad University students. Unpublished Ph.D. thesis, University of London Institute of Education.

Al-Rufai, M. A. H. (1976). Ability transfer and the teaching of reading. *ELTJ*, **30**, 3, 236–41.

Baird, Alexander (1969). The treatment of poetry. *ELTJ*, **23**, 2, 166–73.

Baird, Alexander (1973). Varieties of English: some factors influencing text selection. *ELTJ*, **27**, 3, 250–7.

Baird, Alexander (1976). The study and teaching of literature. *ELTJ*, **30**, 4, 281–6.

Beattie, Nicholas (1970). What constitutes a 'good reader'? *Modern Languages*, **51**, 3, 108–15.

Beattie, Nicholas (1975). The uses of reading. In Hornsey, 1975, 270–7.

Billows, F. L. (1961). *The techniques of language teaching*. London: Longman.

Bright, J. A. & McGregor, G. P. (1970). *Teaching English as a second language*. London: Longman.

Brumfit, C. J. (1970). Literature teaching in Tanzania. *Journal of the Language Association of Eastern Africa*, **1**, 2, 38–44.

Buckby, M. (1975). What is to be read? In Hornsey, 1975, 252–69.

Burke, S. J. & Brumfit, C. J. (1974). Is literature language, or is language literature? *English in Education*, **8**, 2, 33–43.

Carroll, J. B. (1972). Defining language comprehension: some speculations. In Freedle & Carroll, 1972, 1–30.

Catterson, Jane H. (1971). Rhetoric and reading comprehension, or reading skills in search of a content. *McGill J. of Education*, **6**, 2, 125–32 (reprinted in Melnik & Merritt, 1972 *a*).

Chamberlain, A. (1975). The great god literature. *Babel*, **11**, 1, 27–30.

Chamberlin, Dennis & White, Gillian (1975). *English for translation*. London: Cambridge University Press.

Chapman-Taylor, Y. & Ballard, B. A. (1967). *Read and enjoy: a rapid reading practice book*. London: Nelson.

CILT (1976). Select list 5, Word lists based on frequency studies.

CILT (1971). Select list 6, Frequency studies in language and vocabulary: theory and methods.

Clark, Ruth (1975). Adult theories, child strategies and their implications for the language teacher. In Allen & Corder, 1975, 325–34.

Clutterbuck, J. G. (1970). A sixth-form German reading course. *Babel*, **6**, 3, 20–1.

Corbluth, Julian (1975). A functional analysis of multiple-choice questions for reading comprehension. *ELTJ*, **29**, 2, 164–73.

Cripwell, Kenneth R. (1976). What is a cloze test? How do I use it? *Modern English Teacher*, **4**, 1, 4–6.

D'Arcy, Pat (1973). *Reading for meaning*. 2 vols. London: Hutchinson Educational for the Schools Council.

Davies, Alan & Widdowson, H. G. (1974). Reading and writing. In Allen & Corder, 1974, 155–201.

Davies, Ann M. (1975). Organising reading work. In Hornsey, 1975, 278–82.

Dentant, J. & Standaert, R. (1976). The priority of affective aims in the teaching of literature in the secondary school curriculum and its consequences. *ITL*, **31**, 27–41.

Dimitrijević, N. & Gunton, D. (1975). A survey of reading habits and interests of learners of English in Belgrade. *ELTJ*, **30**, 1, 36–45.

Downing, John (1975). The international seminar: reading in differing languages and cultures. In Moyle, 1975, 240–2.

Downing, John, Ollila, L. & Oliver, P. (1975). Cultural differences in children's concepts of reading and writing. *B. J. Ed. Ps*, **45**, 3, 312–16.

Dunning, Roy (1975). Exploiting a text: French. In Hornsey, 1975, 99–121.

Eskey, David E. (1973). A model programme for teaching advanced reading to students of English as a foreign language. *Language Learning*, **23**, 2, 169–84.

Eynon, John (1970). *Multiple choice questions in English*. London: Hamish Hamilton and St George's Press.

Frechette, Ernest A. (1975). A critical survey of elementary and intermediate level French readers 1968–73. *MLJ*, **59**, 3–6.

Freedle, Roy O. & Carroll, John B. (eds.) (1972). *Language comprehension and the acquisition of knowledge*. Washington: V. H. Winston & Sons.

Fry, Edward (1963). *Teaching faster reading*. London: Cambridge University Press.

Gelman, Manuel (1973). Poetry and songs in the teaching of languages. *Babel*, **9**, 1, 13–15.

Girard, Denis (1972). *Linguistics and foreign language teaching*. Translated and edited by R. A. Close. London: Longman 1972.

Goodman, Kenneth S. (1970). Psycholinguistic universals in the reading process. In Paul Pimsleur & Terence Quinn, *The psychology of second language learning*. London: Cambridge University Press, 1971, 135–42.

Goody, J. & Watt, I. (1963). The consequences of literacy. In *Comparative studies in society and history*, vol. 5, 304–26, 332–45. Reprinted in Giglioni (ed.) *Language and social context*. London: Penguin 1972.

Grant, N. J. H. (1975). From rocking horse to Pegasus: the class reader in the lower secondary school. *ELTJ*, **29**, 3, 190–7.

Grant, N. J. H. & Umoh, S. O. (1976). *Reading for a purpose, Book 1*. London: Longman.

Gurrey, P. (1955). *Teaching English as a foreign language*. London: Longman.

Hamblett, Catherine Moon (1977). *A survey of reading skills in English government and grant-aided secondary school students in Botswana in 1976*. Ministry of Education, Republic of Botswana.

Harris, David P. (1966). *Reading improvement exercises for students of English as a second language*. Englewood Cliffs, N.J.: Prentice Hall.

Harrison, Brian (1973). *English as a second and foreign language*. London: Edward Arnold.

Haynes, John (1976). Polysemy and association in poetry. *ELTJ*, **31**, 1, 56–63.

Hill, C. P. (1969). Some notes on reading, comprehension and the use of multiple-choice items. University of London Institute of Education, mimeo.

Hirasawa, Louise & Markstein, Linda (1974). *Developing reading skills*. Rowley, Mass.: Newbury House.

Holley, Freda M. & King, Janet K. (1971). Vocabulary glosses in foreign language reading materials. *Language Learning*, **21**, 2, 213–19.

Horn, Vivian (1971). Advanced reading: teaching logical relationships. *English Teaching Forum*, **9**, 5, 20–2.

Hornsey, Alan (ed.) (1975). *Handbook for modern language teachers*. London: Methuen Education.

Hoskins, A. J. (1976). The accessibility of classical literature. *Didaskalos*, **5**, 2, 250–61.

Hurman, J. D. (1974). Oral exploitation of a text: from learning differences to teaching materials. *AVLJ*, **12**, 1, 41–8.

Ingram, D. E. & Elias, G. C. (1974). Bilingual education and reading. *RELC Journal*, **5**, 1, 64–76.

Isaacs, R. (ed.) (1968). *Learning through language, Teacher's book*. Dar es Salaam: Tanzania Publishing House.

Jones, Keith & Roe, Peter (1975). Designing English for science and technology programmes. In *ETIC Occasional Paper no. 3*, English for Academic Study, 1–45. London: The British Council.

Jordan, R. R. (1974). A survey of reading interests and reading abilities in some secondary schools in Sierra Leone. *W.Af.J. of Ed.*, **18**, 2, 219–40.

Jordan, R. R. (1975). The reading interests of lower secondary school children in Africa and Asia. *IATEFL Newsletter*, **40**, 31–2.

Kaplan, Robert B. (1966). Cultural thought patterns in inter-cultural education. *Language Learning*, **16**, 1–20.

Kelly, L. G. (1969). *Twenty-five centuries of language teaching*. Rowley, Mass.: Newbury House.

King, A. H. (1976). Advanced reading, some general principles. *IATEFL Newsletter*, **41**, 52–4.

Kohl, Herbert (1973). *Reading, how to*. New York: Dutton; London: Penguin Books 1974.

Lado, Robert (1964). *Language teaching: a scientific approach*. New York: McGraw-Hill.

Lawrence, Mary S. (1975). *Reading, thinking, writing*. Ann Arbor: University of Michigan Press.

Levine, Albert (ed.) (1971). *Penguin English reader*. London: Penguin Books.

Light, Timothy (1970). The reading-comprehension passage and a comprehensive reading programme. *ELTJ*, **24**, 2, 120–4.

Lim Kiat Boey (1976). A look at the teaching of reading in ESL. *RELC Journal*, **7**, 1, 8–12.

Littlewood, William T. (1975). Literature in the school foreign language course. *Modern Languages*, **56**, 127–31.

Lockett, Landon (1972). The role of reading at the intermediate level. *MLJ*, **56**, 7, 429–33.

Mackey, W. F. (1965). *Language teaching analysis*. London: Longman.

Mackin, R. (1964–6). *A course of English study*, Readers 1–3. London: Oxford University Press.

Macmillan, M. (1965). Efficiency in reading. *ETIC Occasional Paper no. 6*. London: The British Council.

Maley, Alan & Duff, Alan (1976). *Words!* London: Cambridge University Press.

Melnik, Amelia & Merritt, John (eds.) (1972 a). *The reading curriculum*. London: University of London Press in association with the Open University Press.

Melnik, Amelia & Merritt, John (eds.) (1972 b). *Reading: today and tomorrow*. London: University of London Press in association with the Open University Press.

Modern Language Journal (1972): **56**, The teaching of foreign literatures.

Moody, H. L. B. (1971). *The teaching of literature*. London: Longman.

Moody, K. W. (1976). A type of exercise for developing prediction skills in reading. *RELC Journal*, **7**, 1, 13–20.

Morris, J. (1972). Intensive reading. *ELTJ*, **27**, 1, 38–47.

Mountford, A. J. (1975). Discourse analysis and the simplification of reading materials for English for special purposes. Unpublished M.Litt. thesis, Edinburgh University.

Moyle, D. (ed.) (1975). *Reading: what of the future*. London: Ward Lock Education.

Munby, John (1968). *Read and think*. London: Longman.

Munby, John (1977). Designing a processing model for specifying communicative competence in a foreign language: a study of the relationship between communication needs and the English required for specific purposes. Unpublished Ph.D. thesis, University of Essex, Colchester.

Munby, John & Brumfit, C. J. (1975). A problem-solving approach to intensive reading. *IATEFL Newsletter*, **40**, 26–30.

Murphy, M. J. (1969). Comprehension. In Brian Tiffen (ed.), *A language in common*, chapter 14. London: Longman.

Nababan, P. W. J. (1976). Objectives and the syllabus of a foreign language reading course: English language teaching in higher education in Indonesia. *RELC Journal*, **7**, 1, 1–7.

Narayanaswamy, K. R. (1973). Reading comprehension at the college level. *Central Institute of English and Foreign Languages Monograph 8*. Madras: Oxford University Press.

Nation, I. S. P. (1974). Making a reading course. *RELC Journal*, **5**, 1, 77–83.

Norris, William E. (1970). Teaching second language reading at the advanced level: goals, techniques and procedures. *TESOL Quarterly*, **4**, 1, 17–36.

Oller, John W., Jr. & Tullius, James R. (1973). Reading skills of non-native speakers of English. *IRAL*, **11**, 1, 69–80.

Paine, M. J. & Parsons, A. J. (1970). Acting the reader. *ELTJ*, **25**, 1, 27–32.

Pettit, R. D. (1971). Literature in East Africa: reform of the A Level syllabus. *Journal of the Language Association of Eastern Africa*, **2**, 1, 19–26.

Plaister, T. (1968). Reading instruction for college level foreign students. *TESOL Quarterly*, **2**, 3, 164–8.

Plaister, T. (1973). Teaching reading comprehension to the advanced ESL student using the cloze procedure. *RELC Journal*, **4**, 2, 31–8.

Potts, John (1976). *Beyond initial reading.* London: Allen & Unwin.

Press, John (ed.) (1963). *The teaching of English literature overseas.* London: Methuen.

Radice, Francis (1976). The cloze procedure as a teaching technique. *Modern English Teacher,* **4**, 1, 6–7.

Rivers, Wilga M. (1968). *Teaching foreign language skills.* Chicago: University of Chicago Press.

Rivers, Wilga M. (1972). *Speaking in many tongues.* Rowley, Mass.: Newbury House.

Roberts, J. T. (1975). The 'session libre'. *AVLJ,* **13**, 1, 3–11.

Rudd, J. C. (1969). A new approach to reading efficiency, *ELTJ,* **23**, 3, 231–7.

Saunders, John (1973). Simplification: theory and practice. Unpublished M.A. paper, University of Lancaster.

Searle, Chris (1972). *The forsaken lover.* London: Routledge & Kegan Paul.

Shook, Ron (1977). Discourse structure in reading. *TESL Reporter* **10**, 2, 1–3 and 15.

Sim, D. D. (1973). Grammatical cohesion in English and advanced reading comprehension for overseas students. Unpublished M.Ed. thesis, University of Manchester.

Smith, Frank (1971). *Understanding reading.* New York: Holt, Rinehart & Winston.

Smith, Frank (ed.) (1973). *Psycholinguistics and reading.* New York: Holt, Rinehart & Winston.

Smith, Frank (1975). *Comprehension and learning: a conceptual framework for teachers.* New York: Holt, Rinehart and Winston.

Taiwo, Oladele (1975). Cultural relevance of reading materials. In Moyle, 1975, 261–6.

Taylor, H. J. S. (1971). Making the most of a textbook passage. *ELTJ,* **25**, 2, 156–60.

Torrey, Jane W. (1970). Illiteracy in the ghetto. *Harvard Ed. Review,* **40**, 2, 253–9, reprinted in Smith 1973.

Valette, Rebecca M. & Disick, Renee S. (1972). *Modern language performance objectives and individualization.* New York: Harcourt Brace Jovanovich.

Vernon, M. D. (1971). *Reading and its difficulties.* London: Cambridge University Press.

Walker, Christopher (1974). *Reading development and extension.* London: Ward Lock.

West, Michael (1950). 'Simplified and abridged'. *ELTJ,* **5**, 2, 48–52, reprinted in West 1955.

West, Michael (1953). *The teaching of English: a guide to the New Method Series.* London: Longman.

West, Michael (1955). *Learning to read a foreign language.* London: Longman. (First published in 1926, but reprinted along with six new articles.)

West, Michael (1964). Criteria in the selection of simplified reading books. *ELTJ,* **18**, 4, 146–51.

Widdowson, H. G. (1973). Directions in the teaching of discourse. In S. P. Corder & E. Roulet (eds.), *Theoretical linguistic models in applied linguistics.* Brussels: AIMAV, and Paris: Didier, 65–76.

Yorkey, R. C. (1970). *Study skills for students of English as a second language.* New York: McGraw-Hill.

SPECIAL-PURPOSE LANGUAGE LEARNING: A PERSPECTIVE

Peter Strevens

Wolfson College, Cambridge, and Bell Educational Trust

1. *Introduction*

Among current developments in the learning and teaching of languages, the change which appears to be moving at the fastest rate and which brings in its train the greatest consequences for learners and teachers alike, is the trend towards the learning of languages for specific rather than for general purposes. Increasingly, learners are seeking to learn, for example, Russian, specifically in order to read scientific papers on the aerodynamics of supersonic flight; German, specifically in order to act as an importing agent for German domestic electrical appliances; French, specifically in order to work as an international aid expert on tropical agriculture in Senegal; English, specifically in order to study textile engineering at Leeds University; Portuguese, specifically in order to extend local contacts in the port wine industry; and so forth.

These examples are only a tiny fraction of the very wide range of special purposes currently being pursued. In a later section we shall consider a bigger sample of such courses and indicate major subdivisions within special-purpose language teaching. But what do such courses contrast with? They represent, in fact, a reaction against conventional foreign-language instruction as part of the humanistic segment of a general school education, in which the unspoken assumption is made by both learner and teacher that the target for achievement is 'the whole of' the foreign language.

The face validity, as it were, of special-purpose language teaching rests upon the specification of the learner's particular purposes, a process which self-evidently delimits and restricts the learner's agenda, by implication makes all the learning relevant and therefore secures good motivation, and by popular repute leads to relatively high rates of achievement and of learner-satisfaction.

A serious study of special-purpose language teaching must search beyond and beneath apparent face validity, yet this serves as a useful point of introduction since it accounts in large measure for the popularity of this kind of course and especially for its attraction to the young learner, his general school education behind him, who suddenly finds the language-learning needs of his chosen career exposed before him and who seeks the maximum relevance and specificity for his language study, with the minimum of lost effort and time.

In this paper we shall first consider how to define special-purpose language teaching and look at the particular place of English for special purposes (ESP) within the general category; next we shall look briefly at the history of the development, relating it to a major, world-wide educational tide of change; we shall consider the relation between 'special purposes' and 'scientific purposes', including an outline of what constitutes scientific discourse; we shall analyse different kinds of SP–LT; we shall relate the development of SP–LT to current trends in syllabus design and especially to 'communicative' language teaching; and we shall refer to special needs in teacher training and the preparation of materials.

2. *Definitions: SP–LT and ESP*

Special-purpose language teaching (SP–LT) occurs whenever the content and aims of the teaching are determined by the requirements of the learner rather than by external factors such as general educational criteria. As we shall see below, this is insufficient as a definition, but it provides a base-line criterion without which special-purpose language teaching could barely be conceived.

In principle, any language that can be taught and learned may be demanded, and offered, in the form of SP–LT: in practice, the main pressure of demand is for the chief international languages, and overwhelmingly for English. Within the teaching of English as a foreign language, English for Special Purposes (ESP) is the most rapidly-growing subdivision. Many of our illustrations will be taken from ESP, but the point needs to be made that ESP, important though it is, is simply a special case of SP–LT.

Three practical difficulties impede our attempts to produce a definition of SP–LT. These are: (i) the difficulty of drawing the line between 'general' and 'special' purposes; (ii) the effect upon this problem of the great extension of the range of courses to which the label has in recent years been applied; (iii) the element of fashion, which tempts course organisers or textbook writers to attach the label of 'special purposes' to courses with little or no justification for doing so.

(i) *Definition: the difficulty of drawing the line*

This first difficulty is not easy to overcome. One expression of it is the defence, by upholders of conventional 'general' teaching of languages against what they feel to be a threat to humanistic and literary values, that 'general' language courses are themselves really 'special-purpose' courses: they could be re-titled (it is claimed in this defence) 'French for the special purposes of general education'; at a higher level, 'French for literary criticism', and similarly for other languages incorporated in general school education. Beneath the surface of this claim can be discerned the massive issues that currently preoccupy the modern language profession: the need to provide a fresh, modern and publicly-acceptable justification for school language courses; reaction to the unexpected difficulties encountered in changing from being a subject taught only to academic-stream pupils to a subject taught across the full range of abilities; in Britain at least, confusion over the mixed results – some highly successful, some disastrous – of introducing French in the primary school; dismay at the trend among adolescents towards the view that 'modern languages are for girls'; a feeling of betrayal at the diminution of public belief that the study of foreign literature provides even an obvious and desirable goal for the young, let alone a satisfying career; perhaps envy of their colleagues in the teaching of English as a foreign language, partly because of the sheer popularity of, and demand for, English at a time when demand for French, Russian, Spanish, etc., has diminished, perhaps even more because of the rapid growth of 'professionalisation' in TEFL (in the sense of more rigorous and specialised initial training and the greater expectation of further, in-service, training to higher degree level); and other concerns.

The notion of special-purpose teaching frequently arouses these anxieties, and some teachers of modern languages at school level focus their emotional response to these issues into a denunciation of SP–LT for not being a continuation of the great humanistic educational tradition, for whose maintenance they were originally trained. Within the modern languages profession the current reappraisal of its role and discussion of its basic problems will doubtless resolve these difficulties, given the fundamental intellectual strength that lies behind it; in so doing it may perhaps lead to the development of a wide range of special-purpose courses in French, German, etc., instead of leaving English as the only language to have made serious strides in this direction.

Leaving aside the casuistic view that 'general' courses are really special-purpose courses after all, a difficulty nevertheless remains in knowing where to draw the defining line between the two types of instruction. Suppose that an author has written a beginners' course for teaching English, say, or French, that is used with reasonable success by adolescents at school and young adults in colleges and universities as part of the subject 'English' or 'French'. This is clearly a 'general' course. Now suppose that the same author produces a fresh course with a view to its adoption for teaching adults in business and commerce, and that in doing so he retains the same selection of teaching items in grammar and vocabulary, but makes changes in his story-line and in the fictional background of his stock characters, and adds some vocabulary from office routine which did not figure in the earlier, 'general' course. Is this now a special-purpose course? Or take the case, of which many examples exist, of courses freshly designed for engineers, chemists, etc., whose syllabus closely resembles conventional

linguistic syllabuses for general courses in most pedagogical respects except for
(*a*) the addition of some technical vocabulary, and (*b*) structural changes such
as that from *Mr Smith is a teacher* to *Mr Smith is a chemist*, or from *This is a
book* to *This is a spring balance*. Is this a special-purpose course?

The difficulty recedes (though it does not disappear) (*a*) once the language
course can be shown to possess major characteristics not shared by general
courses, or (*b*) when a course deliberately restricts what it sets out to teach (e.g.
eliminating one or more of the 'basic skills') in order to conform to obvious
features of the purposes for which it is designed, or (*c*) when a course is
designed round a set of communicative needs having little or no affinity with
conventional general courses. Examples of each of these categories are: (*a*)
courses in which all the practice texts are taken from a particular subject or
occupation, such as German for polymer chemists, Spanish for social scientists,
English for jet engine maintenance engineers; (*b*) reading-only courses in
scientific English, or oral-only courses to teach immigrant doctors solely how
to understand vernacular spoken English ways in which British patients
describe their medical symptoms to a doctor (e.g. *I've a shockin' guts-ache*); (*c*)
language courses for air traffic controllers, in which the vocabulary and range
of grammatical structures is limited by international agreement, but where it
is essential to achieve accurate comprehension of spoken radio messages, quick
and comprehensible spoken replies, and the simultaneous use of written notes
and visual displays as operational techniques.

In short, defining SP–LT entails drawing a line between what is 'general'
and what is not. And there are always border-line cases which require arbitrary
decisions.

(ii) *Definition: the growing range of SP–LT courses*

As the fame of special-purpose language teaching has spread, more and more
applications of the idea have been attempted. Some new applications have been
for beginners in the foreign language whose language requirements are solely
for use in their job, who have little time to give to language learning, and whose
teachers lack specialised training in language. This is the case with many of the
trades – carpentry, plumbing, welding, house-building, electrical fitting, motor
vehicle maintenance, etc. – in developing countries where foreign aid programmes result not simply in an influx of money and equipment but also in the
temporary provision of foreign foremen, supervisors, instructors, inspectors.
Thus the recipients of technical aid frequently face, for a period of years, a
low-level, specialised language-learning requirement among a non-academic
sector of the working population whose vocational training lacks the help of
properly qualified language teachers. Russian for Syrian bulldozer drivers;
Hungarian for Egyptian locomotive engineers; English for oil tanker berthing-
masters at the ports of the Arabian Gulf; Czech for Libyan armourers; English

for Indonesian oil drilling-rig teams: these are some examples of SP–LT requirements. The actual language teaching provided seems to vary from one extreme, where high-level experts in applied linguistics are brought in to produce tailor-made solutions and to re-train local teachers, to the other extreme, where a few lists of dictionary equivalents and technical terms represent the only attempt at language teaching. In these latter cases, the problem for the definition of SP–LT is not whether the purposes are special – they clearly are – but whether it can be said that any serious language teaching is being offered.

(iii) *Definition: fashion and the bandwagon effect*

More than most subjects, the teaching and learning of languages are influenced by waves of opinion among teachers, administrators and the public which amount to fashions. Sometimes the fashions are for a particular approach or methodology (e.g. the audio-lingual method), sometimes for a technique (e.g. programmed workbooks) or a type of equipment (e.g. language laboratories). The essence of a fashion is that it is deliberately embraced at least as much because others are doing it as because of its own inherent merits: sometimes more so. Fashions also tend to become ends in themselves, leading people to seek the next fashion for its own sake rather than to keep their eyes on more fundamental issues. SP–LT shows signs of becoming fashionable. Courses are being labelled as 'special-purpose' language courses chiefly because that is what the course organisers believe will attract learners, rather than because there has been a professional reappraisal of the teaching to be offered in those cases, leading to a reasoned change from general to special-purpose teaching. Educational administrators, seeking to remain up-to-date in their programmes, are inclined to jump on the bandwagon of SP–LT and to require teachers to do the same, without realising the extent and novelty of the professional effort that they are saddling their teachers with. Of course, it is all too easy to be arrogant and hypocritical in our views of fashion in education. All conscientious teachers and teacher trainers regard it as essential to be aware of new ideas, to try out new techniques in their own particular circumstances, to adopt and adapt to new trends where these seem to offer advantages. In so doing, all teachers are likely to embrace at least a part of current fashions – and the present author is no exception. Indeed, part of the total assessment which must be made of every situation before the optimum teaching course for that situation can be decided upon, includes the expectations of the learners, the teachers and the public. To ignore fashion totally is to run the risk of being out of step with those we serve: to follow fashion blindly is to abdicate a major section of the teacher's responsibilities.

Special-purpose language teaching is becoming fashionable. Nevertheless it can confer major benefits upon learners. It is because of the benefits, not simply because it is fashionable, that SP–LT deserves the attention of teachers.

Peter Strevens

Definition: main criteria

The definition of special-purpose language teaching, then, will sometimes be obvious, sometimes arbitrary. The following general criteria apply in defining SP–LT:

(1) In SP–LT the language-using purposes of the learner are paramount.

(2) The content of SP–LT language courses are thereby determined, in some or all of the following ways: (i) *restriction*: only those 'basic skills' (understanding speech, speaking, reading, writing) are included which are required by the learner's purposes; (ii) *selection*: only those items of vocabulary, patterns of grammar, functions of language, are included which are required by the learner's purposes; (iii) *themes and topics*: only those themes, topics, situations, universes of discourse, etc. are included which are required by the learner's purposes; (iv) *communicative needs*: only those communicative needs (i.e. the means of interacting appropriately through language with other human beings, singly or in groups) are included which are required by the learner's purposes.

(3) The methodology employed in SP–LT may be any that is appropriate to the learning/teaching situation (i.e. SP–LT is not itself a methodology and does not impose the choice of any specific methods upon those who learn and teach).

3. History of SP–LT

It is sometimes assumed that special-purpose language teaching is a recent innovation. In fact it has historical roots going back at least half a century. It is undoubtedly true that the massive and spectacular expansion of SP–LT, particularly in English, is of recent date, but equally it is true not only that special purposes have been admitted in earlier times but also that current SP–LT constitutes the contemporary manifestation of a world-wide historical trend in education generally, in all subjects. Two kinds of SP–LT are particularly well known for their long history. One is the 'traveller's language course'; the other is of the type, 'German for science students'. The travel course is the perennial offering to those who propose to visit a foreign country and who wish to obtain the merest smattering of the language as a form of protection against the worst rigours of travel, together with a small, handy reference book of everyday phrases and vocabulary – but who do not propose to devote much learning time to the task. Teaching materials (particularly self-study courses) for these special purposes have abounded for more than half a century: in their simplest form, namely the bilingual phrase-book, they go back even further. Archibald Lyall, in the first edition (1932) of his *Guide to the languages of Europe: a practical phrase-book*, quotes from '*Colloques ou dialogues avec un dictionnaire en six langues* of my earliest predecessor, Henry Heyndricx, Antwerp, 1576'.

Language courses of the type 'German for science students' can more properly be regarded as the earliest form of SP–LT. Typically in the past, they presupposed the intermediary of a teacher who would teach the formal grammar points as required, while the practice texts were taken from a relevant field of science. Such courses, in English, French, Russian or German, were usually expected to enable the student to translate, with the aid of a dictionary, limited texts in the foreign language. Their status was generally low, in the sense that failure in the foreign-language translation test almost never led to failure overall if the student had passed in his science subjects. Under these conditions motivation was low (for teachers and learners alike) and it was impossible to arrive at a realistic assessment of the effectiveness of the learning and teaching.

The Second World War engendered massive programmes of SP–LT in the armed forces of Britain, the United States and other nations. It suddenly became necessary, at short notice, to produce large numbers of people with sufficient and appropriate command of a particular language to enable them to do a specific job; this requirement existed in a wide range of languages not normally taught in the public educational system. The degree of specialisation aimed at (and frequently achieved) may be illustrated by the example of the Royal Air Force personnel who learned Japanese solely for the purposes of (*a*) listening, in the Burmese jungle, to Japanese fighter aircraft talking to their ground control stations, (*b*) identifying their targets, and (*c*) using this information to alert RAF interceptor fighters. These students of Japanese never learned to read or write the language, but they achieved the requisite listening-only command of this restricted form of language in a matter of a few weeks of intensive learning. Other special-purpose courses in German, Russian, Arabic, Turkish, Burmese, Thai, Chinese and several other languages, embraced a great range of specialisation and of restricted aims.

More recently, the growth of international trade, the rise of multi-national agencies and the 'internationalisation' of business have led to a strong demand for 'business' language courses, in which the object of learning the language is to be able to conduct negotiations, discuss contracts, promote sales and resolve commercial difficulties, in the foreign language. The first lesson that has been learned as a result of a decade of such courses is that the objects summarised above represent a very tall order. To be able to conduct negotiations in a foreign language means, in its normal manifestations, being able to handle the language in both spoken and written forms, with a command of social niceties, over most of the range of styles and varieties required by a native speaker in the conduct of his business life. It is certainly the case that business negotiations and commercial correspondence possess a rhetoric and style of their own, and that this can be taught more quickly than it can be picked up, but the degree of linguistic sophistication involved, above all in the give-and-take of negotiation, requires also a command of the language in general. To teach and learn the register of business alone is quite insufficient. As a result of learning this lesson, commercial and business courses are tending to fall into two distinct classes: those which teach the language to beginners and which do not claim to provide the full range of language abilities; and those which cater for students already possessing a reasonable 'general' command of the language and aim to provide them in addition with the specialised language of business and commerce.

We have briefly considered types of special-purpose language teaching which have a history earlier than the past decade. But there is one other way in which the historical dimension is of importance in SP–LT, and that is in demonstrating the existence of a major 'tide' in educational thought, in all countries and affecting all subjects. The movement referred to is the global trend towards 'learner-centred education'. After several decades in which education has centred its effort upon the teacher and upon ways of improving his effectiveness by refining techniques and methods of teaching, the present trend is to focus attention rather upon the learner and upon ways of optimising his learning. Within the context of this development, SP–LT can be seen as responding to the new educational requirement to study the learner, to analyse his needs and aims, to define his contribution to the learning/teaching situation (e.g. by accepting that he is already a trained electronics engineer, or by starting from the position that the learner's wish to learn the language is totally contingent upon his prior decision to study economics, not vice versa) and to devise means of helping him to learn that which he wishes to learn, not just that which has been defined by some externally-imposed 'general' syllabus. SP–LT is a parallel development with the emergence of individualisation, in conformity with this global trend towards learner-centred education.

4. *Special-purpose language teaching and scientific discourse*

A great deal of SP–LT is concerned with the purposes of science. But not all: a major subdivision within SP–LT is between those purposes which relate to science and those which do not. Within the confines of English teaching it is customary to distinguish between ESP (all special purposes) and EST ('English for Science and Technology', which are some special purposes). However, scientific discourse as the branch of a given foreign language being taught brings with it at least two special kinds of difficulty for the teacher of SP–LT. Both these difficulties stem from the fact that teachers of foreign languages are educated and trained within the framework of the humanities and have almost never received any serious scientific education in their adult lives. Consequently teachers are faced (*a*) by the task of meeting the needs of scientists without themselves understanding or having experience of what these needs actually are, and (*b*) by the task of teaching the language used in a particular subject (electronics, computer programming, tropical agriculture, jet engine maintenance, navigation, textile engineering, etc.) with which they are totally unfamiliar, to the extent that the very teaching texts they will need to use are meaningless, incomprehensible and daunting to them. We shall return later to the question of the teacher's lack of background in his students' speciality, whether this speciality is scientific or not. Here we are concerned with the question of whether scientific discourse inherently constitutes an extra burden of teaching and learning.

What is the nature of scientific discourse? The answer to this question is complex, but one essential component of the answer is that science is international in a peculiar linguistic way. Not only are the numerals of mathematics, the written names of chemical elements, the symbols of logic, and a few other sets of operators, largely inter-comprehensible by scientists everywhere irrespective of the language used by the individual scientist, but in addition there is a stock of Latin or Greek roots and affixes which combine to form an extremely large number of words whose meaning is 'science-specific', as it were, rather than language-specific. Examples of these roots are: *aqua-*, *cyto-*, *hydro-*, *plasma-*, *pyro-*, etc.; prefixes include: *ante-*, *anti-*, *poly-*, *post-*, *pre-*, *sub-*, etc.; suffixes include: *-fer*, *ite*, *-logy*, *-valent*, etc. A central core of this scientific vocabulary makes up a normal part of the training of all scientists. The teacher of SP–LT courses has to be aware of this central area, to know and be able to teach the particularities of how this core is verbalised in the language being learned, and especially to know how it is spoken. To take a trivial example, he needs to know that the translation-equivalent of English 3·5 ('three point five') is 3,5 ('three comma five') in French, German and several other languages.

But there is of course a good deal more to scientific discourse than simply quantification and the Greco-Latin forms of the international scientific vocabulary. Even on the strictly linguistic plane (i.e. in terms of describing what the language of science consists of) a study of scientific language shows that it is 'normal' language, in the deepest sense that (i) a scientist does not use a different accent or pronunciation when he is being a scientist compared with his accent when he is being a husband, a brother, a son; (ii) the rules of grammar he uses for speaking or writing about science are the rules for the language as a whole – there are no tenses, for example, peculiar to science; (iii) the rules of spelling and orthography are not suspended for the scientist; (iv) even the vocabulary he uses, although it may include the special items we have discussed above and a large number of specialised terms other than the Greco-Latin items, can also make use of any and every lexical item in the whole language.

What, then, is different about scientific discourse? The answer is similar to the answer which has to be given when one asks how the style of one author differs from the style of another. It is not the basic components of his language that differ, it is the statistical properties of the mixture in which they occur, and the intention, the purpose, behind their selection and use. Thus, in English scientific prose one can point to, among other features, a higher frequency of occurrence compared with non-scientific prose of: (i) *rather long sentences* containing many clauses, often in complex degrees of dependency and with much embedding; (ii) *long nominal groups* containing strings of adjectives or nouns acting as adjectives, each providing the greater specificity that comes from modification upon modification, and (iii) *frequent passives* which have the effect of putting important ideas in initial position where in English they carry salience of meaning.

Examples:

(i) 'If one accelerometer is sited in the nose of the craft and a second accelerometer in the stern, each measuring accelerations at right angles to the line of the craft, the difference between the signals from the two pick-offs will be a measure of the angular acceleration of the craft; this signal will therefore have phase advance compared to the rate gyroscope.' (From a theoretical work on aerial navigation.)

(ii) '*One or more portable athwartship angle-stiffened web-plates, carrying up the fore-and-afters,* divide the length of the hatch-cover.' (From a treatise on naval architecture.)

(iii) 'Once an oil field *has been proved* using mobile drilling rigs, a production platform *must be built up* to serve the field for its productive life of up to 25 years. To date this *has invariably been achieved* by a steel platform and supporting structure or jacket permanently piled on the sea floor.' (From a technical article on oil-field exploitation.)

The purposes of the scientist on any given occasion, whether speaking or writing, determine the particular selection of items, the precise stylistic mixture of language, which he will employ. These purposes are extremely diverse but can be roughly categorised as being those of *description, analysis, classification, generalisation, hypothesis, theory-building, argument*, etc. And the most frequently used vocabulary is influenced accordingly.

One further comment needs to be made: within 'scientific discourse' one can distinguish different kinds of language, roughly corresponding to the divisions *scientific, technological* and *technical* (Strevens, 1973) and each of these possesses its own characteristic range of style.

The foregoing brief outline of the nature of scientific discourse is important in the context of special-purpose language teaching because any SP–LT course either does or does not embody scientific discourse. If it does, then the teacher has a specific additional learning/teaching task – it may well be a task for the *teacher* to learn, if the students are already trained in the branch of science concerned. At all events, all SP–LT courses may be characterised as '+/− scientific'.

5. *An analysis of SP–LT*

All SP–LT courses are either *occupational* or *educational* in nature. That is, they are undertaken by the learner because of language requirements in his job, or in his studies.

Figure 1

This distinction becomes important in practice, since job-oriented learners are usually more pragmatic, intolerant of what they feel to be irrelevant, critical of unauthentic materials, keen to achieve effective communication but contemptuous of aesthetic niceties such as elegance of style, native-like pronunciation, etc. In addition, students of occupational SP–LT tend to be less academic, to have less previous language-learning experience, to have fixed ideas (often in conflict with their teachers) about how they should be taught, and to be self-conscious about returning to the classroom from a settled career. However, they usually welcome role-playing or role-simulation techniques (Currie, Sturtridge & Allwright, 1972).

Both educational and occupational SP–LT courses require to be subdivided according to whether the language training precedes, follows or is simultaneous with their studies or occupational training. Thus, teaching the English of seafaring to a sea-school cadet is a different task from teaching the same language content to an experienced master mariner. Similarly, the most appropriate German course for the person who wishes to work in dye chemistry in Germany will be different according to whether the aspirant (*a*) has not yet begun his studies, (*b*) starts them at the same time as his German, so that his understanding of the chemistry is dependent on the progress he is making with his German, or (*c*) has previously studied and worked as a dye chemist and now wishes to work in a German factory. These distinctions are summarised in figures 2 and 3.

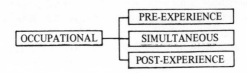

Figure 2

195

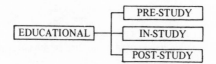

Figure 3

These distinctions can be conflated into a single diagram (Fig. 4). But SP–LT contains more internal distinctions than appear in this necessarily-simplified analysis. Quite apart from the scientific/non-scientific dimension referred to earlier, it is essential, in practice, to distinguish different frameworks of education (school, university, adult education, etc.), to allow for differences of quantity, intensity and duration of instruction, and to make appropriate changes according to the starting level of the learner's proficiency (beginner, 'false beginner', intermediate, advanced). For a more detailed discussion of these variables as they apply in ESP, see Strevens (1977 c).

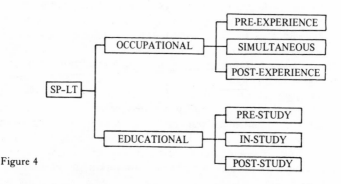

Figure 4

6. *Syllabus design and 'communicative' teaching*

It will be clear that SP–LT is so diverse that any single syllabus or even type of syllabus is inconceivable as the norm for all cases. All types of syllabus are in use, and all types of methodology, not excluding grammar-translation. The choice of syllabus and method depends upon the professional background, training and preferences of those in charge of devising the course. Nevertheless it is significant that SP–LT, and perhaps especially ESP, is more closely linked than any other single branch of language teaching with developments in the principles of syllabus design. The relationship is clear if it is stated the other way round: it happens that virtually all the European specialists in syllabus design, and many of those in the United States, concern themselves in a practical way with the development of special-purpose language teaching and the devising of syllabuses and materials. In consequence SP–LT courses are widely distributed in which the long-standing principles of *linguistic* syllabuses (with vocabulary control, principled grading, and so forth) are tempered or superseded by *situational, notional, functional* and *communicative* syllabuses.

As a consequence of the requirement that SP–LT should analyse the needs of the learner, these needs are increasingly stated in communicative terms: in terms of what it is that people in those jobs normally *do* through language. Here, by way of example, is an extract from a syllabus devised by the present author for an English course intended for workers in a factory or workshop. It is stated in terms of communicative categories to which would be appended (in the full statement, not given here) illustrations of the actual spoken and written language which will be taught:

Communicative Categories (for this specific group of learners)

I. GENERAL

A. *Instructions*
receiving and comprehending instructions
giving instructions to others
relaying instructions
degrees of authority, formality, politeness... used with instructions
acceptance, agreement/disagreement with instructions
stating incomprehension

B. *Questions*
important types: verb-first Qs
                WH-word Qs
                HOW+adjective Qs, etc.
querying one's instructions
asking reasons why

C. *Seeking advice*
asking for further information, confirmation
asking someone to advise or help

D. *Stating difficulties or objections*
stating difficulties
inability or impossibility
unwillingness

E. *Suggesting alternatives*
alternative action
somebody else

F. *Measurements and quantities*
comprehending and expressing quantities
understanding and referring to diagrams
verbalising numbers, common symbols

G. *Dangers and emergencies; signals; safety rules*
public instructions, notices, tannoy announcements
types of danger
warning others
sound and visual signals

H. *Injury, health*
types of hazard
personal condition of health
types of injury
casualty states
parts of the body
emergency services and personnel

II. SOCIAL COMMUNICATION

A. *Face-to-face conversation and social writing*
personal identity; name, age, origin, job, family, home
greetings, polite chat; sport, TV, politics, pub
washroom details
working hours, breaks, meal-times, works transport
discussion of management, workers, unions
pay, conditions, documents
discussion of cultural differences

B. *Receiving and making telephone calls*
speaking phone numbers
telephone techniques

III. SPECIAL COMMUNICATIVE PURPOSES (for specific jobs)

A. Operating safety rules.
B. Protective clothing and equipment.
C. Particular hazards.
D. Tools, equipment, instruments, materials.
E. Individual tasks; separate stages or processes.
F. Special register features.
G. Local dialect, accent.

(Adapted from Strevens, 1977 *a*)

It is not intended to suggest that the foregoing constitutes a definitive list of communicative categories: indeed, in the present state of development of communicative syllabuses individual authors necessarily produce their own proposals, borrowing from others where appropriate and inventing where necessary. The purpose of the above inventory is to illustrate the point that SP–LT courses are increasingly devised around notional–functional–communicative categories whose exemplifications create the language content of the course, rather than around *a priori* vocabulary lists and inventories of graded structures.

7. *Teacher training*

The extremely rapid increase in the demand for SP–LT courses has outstripped the specialised training of teachers. Most teachers of SP–LT courses came to them from a conventional background of preparation for general-educational language teaching. They are almost invariably Arts-trained, with little knowledge of the social sciences and less of science or technology. There is therefore a gap between the teachers and the taught, in SP–LT, and this can reduce the effectiveness of learning and teaching.

Three different solutions are bringing about an improvement in the situation. (i) Existing teacher-training programmes, especially courses of further training and higher degree courses in applied linguistics, more and more often incorporate segments on SP–LT in their offering. (ii) Increasingly, language teachers concerned with special purposes are willing and able to gain the collaboration of subject specialists in analysing needs, devising syllabuses, writing materials. There is even a trickle of subject specialists entering the language-teaching profession. (iii) Language teachers are coming to terms with their difficulties. These include, first, the unfamiliarity to them of the language of the various specialities; second, the fear that through ignorance of the subject speciality they may make elementary mistakes which would diminish their confidence, reputation and credibility; and third, the lack of teaching materials, which means that teachers often have to make their own.

Experience in the teaching of English suggests that the extent of difficulty experienced depends on the teacher's professional competence and morale. Teachers with inadequate training and little experience can be genuinely terrified at the prospect of having to teach ESP courses. Teachers with high-level professional qualifications and with long and wide experience, on the other hand, are often cheerfully willing to regard ESP as a welcome challenge. There seems little doubt that a school or institution which specialises in SP–LT and engages teachers of high calibre can soon develop a corporate spirit that ensures lively, relevant teaching and good relations with special-purpose students (Webb, 1975).

8. *Teaching materials*

As with syllabus design, so too with materials writing, there is no received dogma. The biggest problem is the shortage of usable textbooks, readers, etc., for any given speciality. The major publishers are aware of the need and some of them are already embarked upon large-scale publishing programmes in SP–LT, particularly in those areas which seem to be the most obvious and immediate target: some areas of medicine; general science; business; the social sciences; chemistry.

Peter Strevens

The approaches used by textbook and course writers vary from the highly conventional (not to say the barely-specialised, as mentioned in Section 1) to the totally innovative. If any trends can be seen which distinguish SP–LT materials from general materials, perhaps they are these: (i) more concentration on reading and less on speaking and writing; (ii) the use of edited authentic texts from the special fields, usually glossed, as comprehension practice; (iii) collaborative authorship between language teacher and subject specialist; (iv) inclusion of notional, functional and communicative criteria for the selection of material and the organisation of practical learning/teaching tasks. But these are no more than trends: many of the materials being published embody few, if any, of these features. There is no doubt that the coming decade will see the preparation of large numbers of new and different materials for SP–LT.

9. Conclusion

The growth of SP–LT continues undiminished and seems likely to go on for some years. Where it is taken seriously, where competent professional teachers are given the encouragement and opportunity to analyse special purposes and to devise appropriate courses, rates of success tend to be higher than for conventional teaching, as also do levels of satisfaction among teachers and learners alike. There are problems, of course, in the lack of materials, the shortage of suitably trained teachers, and the obtuseness of some organisers who seek to gain the rewards of advanced professional skill without investing in the necessary effort or training, and who simply re-label existing courses as 'SP' courses. Nevertheless there has been solid progress and improvement in recent years. SP–LT has helped teachers to understand better the whole process of learning and teaching languages, and has thereby contributed to the slow but continuous rise in the effectiveness of language learning.   *July 1977*

References

N.B. A detailed and annotated bibliography, which is virtually comprehensive and includes teaching materials, is to be found in British Council (1975) *English for Special Purposes: Information Guide No. 2*, London.

Allen, J. P. B. (1975). English, science and language teaching: the FOCUS approach. *EDUTEC*, **9**. Mexico City.

Allen, J. P. B. & Widdowson, H. (1974). Teaching the Communicative Use of English. *IRAL*, **12**, 1. Heidelberg.

Barber, C. (1962). Some measurable characteristics of modern scientific prose. In *Contributions to English syntax and philology*. Stockholm.

Bates, M. & Dudley-Evans, A. (1974). Notes on the Introductory English Course for Students of Science and Technology at the University of Tabriz. In *ELT Documents*, 74/4. London: British Council.

British Council (1975). *English for Special Purposes: information guide no. 2*. London.

Butler, C. S. (1974). German for chemists. In G. Perren (ed.), *Teaching languages to adults for special purposes*. CILT Reports and Papers No. 11. London.

Candlin, C. (ed.) (1975). *The communicative teaching of English*. London: Longman.

Candlin, C., Kirkwood, J. M. & Moore, H. M. (1975). Developing study skills in English. In *English for Academic Purposes*. London: British Council.

Candlin, C. & Murphy, D. (1976). *Engineering discourse and listening comprehension*. University of Lancaster, mimeo.

Corder, S. P. (1973). *Introducing applied linguistics*. London: Penguin.

Corder, S. P. & Roulet, E. (eds.) (1974). *Linguistic insights in applied linguistics*. Brussels: AIMAV, and Paris: Didier.

Coveney, J. (1974). French for engineers. In G. Perren (ed.), *Teaching languages to adults for special purposes*. CILT Reports and Papers No. 11. London.

Cowie, A. P. & Heaton, J. B. (eds.) (1977). *English for Academic Purposes*. BAAL/SELMOUS. Reading.

Currie, W. B., Sturtridge, G. & Allwright, J. (1972). A technique of teaching medical English. In *International Congress of Applied Linguistics, Proceedings, 3*. Heidelberg: Groos.

Douglas, D. (1976). What is scientific vocabulary? *ESPMENA, 5*, autumn 1976. University of Khartoum.

Edwards, P. J. (1974). Teaching specialist English, with special reference to English for nurses and midwives in Nigeria. *English Language Teaching Journal, 28*, 3. London.

van Ek, J. (1975). *The threshold level*. Strasbourg: Council of Europe.

ELTDU (1975). *English Language Stages of Attainment Scale*. London. Oxford University Press.

ELTDU (1976). *Stages of attainment scale and test battery: general information*. London: Oxford University Press.

Ewer, J. R. (1975). Teaching English for Science and Technology: the specialised training of teachers and programme organisers. In *English for Academic Purposes*. London: British Council.

Ewer, J. R. & Hughes-Davies, E. (1974). Instructional English. In *ELT Documents*, 74/4. London: British Council.

Ewer, J. & Latorre, G. (1969). *A course in basic scientific English*. London: Longman.

Gardner, P. L. (1974). Language difficulties of science students. *Australian Science Teachers Journal, 20*, 1.

Harper, D. P. L. (1974). English for foreign doctors and civil servants. In G. Perren (ed.), *Teaching languages to adults for special purposes*. CILT Reports and Papers No. 11. London.

Hesketh, P. M. (1974). An R.A.F. view of language learning. In G. Perren (ed.), *Teaching languages to adults for special purposes*. CILT Reports and Papers No. 11. London.

Huddleston, R. D. (1971). *Sentence and clause in English*. London.

Jones, K. & Roe, P. (1975). Designing English for Science and Technology. In *English for Academic Purposes*. London: British Council.

Jupp, T. C. & Hedlin, S. (1975). *Industrial English*. London: Heinemann.

Kachru, Braj B. (1976). Models of English for the Third World: white man's linguistic burden or language pragmatics? *TESOL Quarterly, 10*, 2, June 1976.

Lackstrom, J. E., Selinker, L. & Trimble, L. (1970). Grammar and Technical English. In R. Lugton (ed.), *English as a second language: current issues*. Philadelphia: Chilton Press.

Lackstrom, J. E., Selinker, L. & Trimble, L. (1973). Technical rhetorical principles and grammatical choice. *FORUM, 11*, 3. Washington D.C.

Morris, Robert W. (ed.) (1974). *Interactions between linguistics and mathematical education.* Report of a symposium by UNESCO–CEDO–ICMI. Nairobi.

Munby, J. (1977). Designing a processing model for specifying communicative competence in a foreign language: a study of the relationship between communicative needs and the English required for specific purposes. Thesis submitted for Ph.D., University of Essex.

Newberry, R. C. (1974). English language support for the teaching of mathematics and science in Singaporean primary schools. *ELT Documents, 74/4.* London: British Council.

Perren, G. (ed.) (1969). *Languages for special purposes.* CILT Reports and Papers No. 1. London.

Perren, G. (ed.) (1971). *Science and technology in a second language.* CILT Reports and Papers No. 7. London.

Perren, G. (ed.) (1974). *Teaching languages to adults for special purposes.* CILT Reports and Papers No. 11. London.

Pritchard, N. A. & Chamberlain, R. G. D. (1974). Special purpose English: changing approaches to English language teaching. *RELC Journal,* **5**, 2. Singapore.

Selinker, L. & Trimble, L. (1976). Scientific and technical writing: choice of tense. *FORUM,* **14**, 4. Washington D.C.

Selinker, L., Trimble, L. & Vroman, R. (1972). *Working papers in English for Science and Technology.* Seattle: University of Washington.

Shaw, A. M. (1976). Approaches to a communicative syllabus in foreign language curriculum development. Unpublished Ph.D. thesis, University of Essex, Colchester.

Sinclair, J. McN. & Coulthard, R. M. (1975). *Towards an analysis of discourse: the English used by teachers and pupils.* London: Oxford University Press.

Strevens, P. (1971). The language of instruction and the formation of scientific concepts. In *Scientific education in developing states.* New York: Praeger.

Strevens, P. (1973). Technical, technological, and scientific English. *English Language Teaching,* **27**, 3. London.

Strevens, P. (1976). Problems of learning and teaching science through a foreign language. *Studies in Science Education,* **3**. Leeds.

Strevens, P. (1977 a). *New orientations in the teaching of English.* London: Oxford University Press (forthcoming).

Strevens, P. (1977 b). English as an international language: when is a local form of English a suitable model for ELT purposes? *ELT Documents* (forthcoming). London: British Council.

Strevens, P. (1977 c). English for special purposes: an analysis and a survey. *Studies in Language Learning* (forthcoming).

Swales, J. (1974 a). *Notes on the function of attributive-EN particles in scientific discourse.* University of Khartoum.

Swales, J. (1974 b). *Writing scientific English.* London: Nelson.

Swales, J. (1976). Verb frequencies in scientific English. *ESPMENA Bulletin,* **4**, spring 1976. University of Khartoum.

Trim, J. L. (1973). Draft outline for a European unit/credit system for modern language learning by adults. Strasbourg: Council of Europe.

Trim, J. L. (1974). A unit/credit scheme for adult language learning. In G. Perren (ed.), *Teaching languages to adults for special purposes.* CILT Reports and Papers No. 11. London.

Webb, J. (1975). Reflections of practical experience in designing and mounting ESP courses at the Colchester English Study Centre. *ARELS Journal,* **2**, 1, winter 1975.

White, R. V. (1975). The language, the learner and the syllabus. *RELC Journal,* **6**, 1, June 1975.

Widdowson, H. (1974). An approach to the teaching of scientific English discourse. *RELC Journal*, **5**, 1. Singapore.

Widdowson, H. (1975). EST in theory and practice. In *English for Academic Purposes*. London: British Council.

Wilkins, D. A. (1973). The linguistic and situational content of the common core in a unit/credit system. In *Systems development in adult language learning*. Strasbourg: Council of Europe.

Wilkins, D. A. (1976). *Notional syllabuses*. London: Oxford University Press.

PUBLISHER'S NOTE

The eleven articles which make up this book are taken from the quarterly journal, *Language Teaching and Linguistics: Abstracts*, published by Cambridge University Press and compiled by the English Teaching Information Centre of the British Council and the Centre for Information on Language Teaching and Research. The journal aims to keep teachers and others fully informed of the latest research and developments in the study and teaching of modern languages, including English as a second language. It provides objective summaries in English of selected articles taken from nearly 400 journals. These cover relevant work in psychology, linguistics, language studies, teaching methodology and technology, and experimental teaching. In addition, each issue contains a section annotating new books in the field, and information about current research in Europe relevant to language teaching. An original and authoritative survey article, like the ones which make up this book, also appears in each issue.